Sexualities

Personal Lives and Social Policy

Personal Lives and Social Policy
Series Editor: Janet Fink

This book forms part of a series published by The Policy Press in association with The Open University. The complete list of books in the series is as follows:

Sexualities: Personal Lives and Social Policy, edited by Jean Carabine
Care: Personal Lives and Social Policy, edited by Janet Fink
Work: Personal Lives and Social Policy, edited by Gerry Mooney
Citizenship: Personal Lives and Social Policy, edited by Gail Lewis

Notes on contributors to *Sexualities: Personal Lives and Social Policy*

Jean Carabine is a Lecturer in Social Policy in the Faculty of Social Sciences at The Open University. Her current ESRC-funded research (with Davina Cooper and Surya Monro) is on 'The Changing Politics of Lesbian and Gay Equality in Local Government 1990–2001'. She is also an editor of the journal, *Critical Social Policy*. She has written extensively on sexuality and social policy.

Megan Doolittle is a Lecturer in Social Policy in the Faculty of Social Sciences at The Open University. Her research interests include the history of the family, fatherhood and masculinity, contemporary families and their alternatives, and relationships between law, social policy and the family. Her publications include *The Family Story: Blood, Contract and Intimacy in Modern England, 1840–1960* with Leonore Davidoff, Janet Fink and Katherine Holden (Longman, 1999); 'Close relations? Bringing together gender and family in English history', *Gender & History* (1999).

Rachel Thomson is a Lecturer in Children and Young People in the School of Health and Social Welfare at The Open University. Previously she has been involved in research with young people as well as policy and practice development in the area of sex education. Her research interests focus on intimacy, identity and social change and she has published widely in these areas. She is currently involved in an ESRC-funded longitudinal study documenting young people's changing lives over a 10-year period.

Margrit Shildrick lectures in bioethics and socio-cultural studies, with particular regard to issues of gender. Her research centres on the body, and especially on the concept of vulnerability. She has published extensively and is the author of *Leaky Bodies and Boundaries* (Routledge, 1997) and *Embodying the Monster* (Sage, 2002), as well as the co-editor of two collections of essays, and a Reader entitled *Feminist Theory and the Body* (Edinburgh, 1999). She is currently working on a further book which will focus on disability.

Sexualities

Personal Lives and Social Policy

Edited by Jean Carabine

This publication forms part of the Open University course DD305 *Personal Lives and Social Policy*. Details of this and other Open University courses can be obtained from the Course Information and Advice Centre, PO Box 724, The Open University, Milton Keynes MK7 6ZS, United Kingdom: tel. +44 (0)1908 653231; e-mail general-enquiries@open.ac.uk. Alternatively, you may visit the Open University website at http://www.open.ac.uk where you can learn more about the wide range of courses and packs offered at all levels by The Open University.

To purchase a selection of Open University course materials visit the webshop at www.ouw.co.uk, or contact Open University Worldwide, Michael Young Building, Walton Hall, Milton Keynes MK7 6AA, United Kingdom, for a brochure: tel. +44 (0)1908 858785; fax +44 (0)1908 858787; e-mail ouwenq@open.ac.uk

First published 2004 by The Policy Press in association with The Open University

The Open University
Walton Hall
Milton Keynes
MK7 6AA
United Kingdom
www.open.ac.uk

The Policy Press
Fourth Floor, Beacon House
Clifton
Bristol
BS8 1QU
United Kingdom
www.policypress.org.uk

The opinions expressed are not necessarily those of the Course Team or of The Open University.

British Library Cataloguing-in-Publication Data
A catalogue record for this book is available from the British Library.

Library of Congress Cataloguing-in-Publication Data
A catalogue record for this book has been requested.

Edited, designed and typeset by The Open University.

Printed and bound in Great Britain by The Bath Press, CPI Group.

ISBN 1 86134 518 6

1.1

Contents

Preface

Sexualities: Personal Lives and Social Policy is the first of four books in a new series published by The Policy Press in association with The Open University. The series takes an interdisciplinary and theoretically informed approach to the study of social policy in order to examine the ways in which the two domains of *personal lives* and *social policy and welfare practice* are each partially shaped and given meaning by the other. This process of mutual constitution is explored in the books through core practices of the everyday. Such an approach is both exciting and innovative. It is also indicative of a growing recognition within the social sciences that 'the personal' is a valuable lens of analysis. More generally, the series is concerned not only with debates and questions that are highly visible in social policy, but also with those that tend to be marginalized or silenced and how these might be interpreted through the use of different theoretical perspectives, conceptual tools and research evidence. Overall, therefore, the books move beyond what are usually considered to be the parameters of social policy and its study.

The four books make up the core texts of an Open University course entitled *Personal Lives and Social Policy*. This first book, *Sexualities: Personal Lives and Social Policy*, considers why questions of sex and sexuality matter for the study of social policy and, in turn, illustrates how such questions provide important insights into the relationship between personal lives and social policy. Its concerns with the normative and taken-for-granted assumptions about sexuality, that inform social policy and welfare practices, establish the central interest of the series – the dynamics by which social policy and personal lives intersect and become entangled.

The second book, *Care: Personal Lives and Social Policy*, focuses on the meanings and definitions attributed to care and examines the norms and values associated with care relationships that are embedded in welfare policy and practice. The book illustrates the highly charged and often contradictory nature of care relations by exploring issues of power, conflict and control and considering the different spaces and places where questions about care have been lived out, debated and struggled over.

The third book, *Work: Personal Lives and Social Policy*, traces the central place that work has been afforded, historically, in policy-making and the extent to which it has remained an unproblematic category not only for policy-makers but also in the study of social policy. The book foregrounds the contingent relationship between work and welfare in order to examine the ways in which this arena of policy practices and discourses has developed around particular constructions of personal lives.

The fourth and final book, *Citizenship: Personal Lives and Social Policy*, looks at ideas and meanings associated with citizenship in order to broaden and problematize the term. In particular, it emphasizes the importance of moving away from associating citizenship with rights and obligations within nation-states towards recognizing how a consideration of multiple belongings and practices of the everyday opens up the study of social policy to new and challenging questions.

Although these books are edited volumes, each chapter has been specially written to contribute not only to the exploration of the mutual constitution of personal lives and social policy, but also to the process of student learning. The books have, therefore, been constructed as interactive teaching texts which encourage engagement with and further reflection on the themes, issues and arguments presented in the chapters. The process of interaction is organized around:

- *activities* – variously made up of exercises, tasks and questions, highlighted in colour, which have been designed to extend or consolidate understanding of particular aspects of the chapters;

- *comments* – interpretations and discussions of the activities, which provide opportunities for readers to compare their own responses with those of the author(s);

- *in-text questions* – short questions, again in colour, that build into the chapter opportunities for consideration of core points or arguments;

- *key words* – terms and concepts, highlighted in colour in the text and in the margins, which are central to the arguments, theoretical perspectives and research questions being used and interrogated by the author(s).

In addition, the opening chapter of each book has been written to provide a critical introduction to key issues, ideas, theories and concepts associated with the book's field of interest. The individual books are self-contained but there are references to other chapters and other books in the series. Such references help readers not only to make connections between the books, but also to understand and reflect on the themes and debates that run across the series overall.

The series has been shaped and informed by discussions within the Open University Course Team. Each member of the Team brought to these discussions their own interests, enthusiasms and fields of expertise, but never lost sight of the overall aims of the series and their commitment to those aims. The series is, therefore, the product of a genuinely interdisciplinary and collaborative process. This also means that contributions have been made to all the chapters of the books within this series by people who are not explicitly named as authors. The process of collaboration extends further, however, than the production of materials by academics. In writing chapters, the Course Team and consultant authors have been advised and guided by an external assessor, a tutor panel and a developmental testing panel. The wide-ranging involvement and assistance from the editors, designers and picture researchers have been invaluable in the production of these accessible and attractive texts. Course managers have used their knowledge and skills to resolve the many questions and difficulties that arose during the course's development. Secretaries brought their expertise to the styling and organization of seemingly endless manuscript drafts – and did so with admirable good humour. We thank them all for their work and support which are reflected throughout this book, the series and the course as a whole.

Janet Fink

CHAPTER I

Sexualities, Personal Lives and Social Policy

by Jean Carabine

Contents

1 Introduction

Images of sex and sexuality are regularly used to sell us products and lifestyles such as cars, houses, holidays, cosmetics, music, magazines, books, films and alcohol. Such images convey messages that 'normal' sex and sexuality are heterosexual. Lifestyle magazines and television programmes give the impression that sexual activity and the pursuit of better and more frequent sex are the norm, as well as reinforcing the idea that sex is a central part of who we are. Through the use of advice and personal sex ratings such programmes and magazines simultaneously invoke and define the boundaries of normal sex. At the same time, the media present us with a diversity of sexual desires, experiences, practices and relationships which simultaneously reinforce and challenge sexual norms.

At a personal level, sex and sexuality may invoke differing sets of ideas and feelings in us to do with intimacy, privacy, pleasure, excitement, desire, embarrassment, attraction, age, fear, pain, abuse, control, freedom, fulfilment, danger, constraint, disease, well-being, our bodies, love and emotion. For many, particularly in the West, sexual attraction has become an important means of organizing personal lives and forming social relations, and people often describe their sexual relationships as the most 'important' (Jamieson, 1998, p.1).

By contrast in policy and welfare, sexuality tends to make an appearance when it is perceived as a problem – as in the case of homosexuality, lone motherhood, teenage pregnancy, under-age sex, prostitution, divorce, sexually transmitted infections (STIs) and sexual offences. Legal and social policies dealing specifically with sexuality focus in the main on protecting vulnerable individuals and the public from undesirable and unwanted sexualities and sexual behaviours, as in sexual offences legislation, teenage pregnancy and sex education policies, and age of sexual consent legislation. The effect of such policies is to prescribe, and sometimes legally enforce, at what age, with whom, when and where we can have legal and acceptable sexual relationships.

Sexuality has the capacity to invoke fierce political and public debate. Debates surrounding same-sex adoption, sex and relationship education, and proposals to equalize the age of sexual consent for homosexuals illustrate that sexuality, and particularly what constitutes 'normal' sexuality, is highly contested and contradictory terrain. As, too, are the meanings – personal, public, expert and policy – assigned to particular sexual acts, relationships, practices and identities. Frequently, debates about sexuality are attempts to fix what sexuality is. Since the nineteenth century, sexuality has been the focus of political campaigns and activism seeking either greater regulation of sex or sexual liberation. That sexuality is so open to contestation creates possibilities for defining and redefining, as well as regulating, what it comprises.

Significantly, social policy does not have to be specifically concerned with sexuality for it to 'speak' of sexuality and for it to regulate sexual relations and behaviour. Social policies about, for example, housing, health, education, social exclusion, income support or parenting can also contain assumptions and convey messages about acceptable and normal sexual relations and practices as taking place within a two-parent, married family. As the chapters in this book show, what we 'do' sexually, our sexual relationships and how we experience our sexuality can be affected by policy and welfare interventions which at first glance have little to do with sexuality. In policy, welfare analyses and practice, sexuality is usually taken as given, as something that 'just is', and welfare subjects are assumed to be universally heterosexual. The idea of heterosexuality is left unproblematized and unquestioned.

This book illustrates, then, how personal lives and sexualities are *constructed* in and through social policy and practice. At the core of this is an analysis of the effects of normative assumptions about sexuality – about what are 'normal' sexual practices and relationships, and assumptions that, typically, people will be heterosexual, marry and have children – in constituting social policy subjects, discourses, provisions, practices and theories. Discourses are ways of speaking about a topic such as sexuality or social policy and can take the form of talk, text and images. Our concern here is not with discourse as a means of communication and as language, but with the *meanings* that discourses convey about a topic, and the effects of these (this is discussed further in section 6). Of particular interest is the way in which social policy implicitly and explicitly conveys messages about appropriate and acceptable sexualities: that is, the role of social policy in constituting sexual norms. Central to this is a concern with heterosexuality and with the ways in which sexualities are socially constructed, historically and culturally specific, highly contested and contingent, and influenced by the meanings attached to them. Although a range of analytical tools is used to interrogate and explain the personal lives, sexualities and social policy relationship – including the post-structuralist, feminist and historical – the idea of sexuality and social policy as socially constructed is central to the approach adopted throughout the book.

Aims   In this and the following chapters we consider how ideas about family, the body, parenting and marriage – which are central to understanding what constitutes normal sexuality and to the privileging of heterosexuality in social policy – intersect with discourses and practices of difference, especially those of gender, 'race', age and disability. We also illustrate that, although laden with immense social power, ideas about what constitutes 'normal' in relation to sexuality, personal lives and social policy are also highly contested.

The aims of this introductory chapter are to:

- illustrate the importance of sexuality for understanding personal lives, and as a category in social policy and for policy analyses;

- introduce you to some of the different ways of thinking about sexuality;

- explore constructions of sexuality as central to definitions of who we are, as well as the implications of this for the ways in which social policy differentially regulates, marginalizes or legitimates different sexualities;

- show, using a post-structuralist approach, some of the ways in which sexuality and social policy are mutually constitutive.

2　Personal lives

Before looking at the intersection of personal lives, sexuality and social policy, it is important to understand the place of sexuality in our personal lives and some of the very different social meanings it holds for us.

Read carefully through Extracts 1.1, 1.2 and 1.3 below. As you do so, think about the different ways in which sex and sexuality are talked about, and what they convey about the significance or place of sexuality in the speakers' lives. Consider the following questions:

■　What ideas about 'normal' sexuality are conveyed in the extracts?

■　Can you identify some of the ways in which ideas about sexuality are affected by ideas about 'race', age, gender and homosexuality?

Extract 1.1　Alix

Now I had reached the age of forty-nine without ever having been married ... and until my early forties had never once been short of prospective partners, had assumed that sex whenever I wanted it was my God-given right, earned as a battle-hardened survivor of the sexual revolution. So what had gone wrong? Why, now, was I alone?

...

Oestrogen is draining out of my body ... The collagen withers in my skin and I am deluding myself if I think that Joseph Shields, who could have a woman half my age, is going to want me.

There is a decent thing to do, according to some of my friends, which is to embrace celibacy. To end the pact I made at twenty, that I would reward myself with nothing less than my own pleasure, this is what they are proposing. How can they ask it of me?

...

'The whole business is overrated,' some of my friends said. Not to me. Sex was always sublime, I came easily and still do. I never went to an orgasm workshop, or bothered with junky books like *The Joy of Sex*. I knew exactly what sex was, it was natural right from the beginning ... But with a rent-boy? And a girl was out of the question. What draws me to men is my love of their cocks inside me. I am a very vaginal woman.

(Grant, 2002, pp.92, 106–7)

Extract 1.2   Charlotte

I was not the kind of girl that boys would have thought to take out. I knew they didn't see me as beautiful. I knew they couldn't see the white in me although I tried my best to show it. It wasn't only them either; *I'd* bought into a whole way of thinking about black people that didn't amount to anything very positive ... .

...

Then the questions began, like bullets from a gun ... he got more relaxed and confident in his long heritage of superiority, while I got more tense. ...

'Do your sisters get any boyfriends?'

'Do they do it – y'know, have it off?'

'Girls like you are supposed to be good at it aren't they?'

'Are you brown all over? Nipples as well?'

'Is the hair on your fanny tufty?'

The sexual nature of his questions added to the agony. Each bullet penetrated deeper than the one before. I was trapped and yet so misguidedly, so stupidly, grateful to be out on a date.

(Williams, 2002, pp.66, 69, 70)

Extract 1.3   Max

I had always known that I was attracted to men, but because gayness was outside what I had been taught to expect, I wasn't able to accept my sexuality for a long time. So I married very young and was keen to start a family – I always had quite strong parental impulses. After seven years I met a man, and when I eventually slept with him it felt so right that all the denial just melted away.

My marriage wasn't very happy so ending it came as no surprise to my wife. ... When we split up, we agreed that the children would live with me and she would have them for alternate weekends. It is still unusual for dads to be main carers ...

(Rice, 2002, p.27)

COMMENT

Each of these extracts illustrates how sexuality evokes a complex web of feelings and emotions integral to our notions of self and bodily image, desire and attractiveness, to how we share love and intimacy, relate to others and to our sense of well-being. They simultaneously invoke and disrupt normative assumptions about sexuality. By this, we mean that they generate a number of ideas about sexuality, some of which reflect the ways we commonly think about sex and sexuality while at the same time challenging taken-for-granted assumptions. At a common-sense level, sexuality in the twenty-first century is often understood as central to our sense of self and identity, as natural and as heterosexual. As Jeffrey Weeks, at the beginning of his book *Sexuality*, puts it:

> [It is usually assumed] that our sexuality is the most spontaneously natural thing about us. It is the basis for some of our most passionate feelings and commitments. Through it, we experience ourselves as real people; it gives us our identities, our sense of self, as men and women, as heterosexual and homosexual, 'normal' or 'abnormal', 'natural' or 'unnatural' [and as racial subjects].
>
> (Weeks, 1986, p.13)

In the extracts we can see too that sexuality is important to each speaker's sense of self. Our identity – and this includes our sexual identity – locates us in the society in which we live through a series of belongings and exclusions which we experience as same or 'other' by being heterosexual, gay or lesbian, a pregnant teenager, a wife or a husband, and so forth. In this way, sexuality can be said to be marked by difference operationalized through a system of binary classifications centred on a heterosexuality/homosexuality coupling in which we are either heterosexual or homosexual.

---

essentialism　　Dominant explanations or knowledges of sexuality have sought to classify or categorize types of person on the basis of specific sexual acts, desires and relationships as natural/unnatural, good/bad or normal/deviant. **Essentialism** defines sexuality in terms of nature, determined mainly by biology, and, from the latter part of the nineteenth century, an essence central to self and identity. Within this perspective sex and sexuality are intricately tied to reproduction. Fundamental to this position is a model of oppositional sex grounded in a gendered difference which positions male sexuality as active and female sexuality as more passive and emotional. Women's sexuality is linked to reproduction and motherhood. The association with reproduction has meant that heterosexuality, the family and marriage became the privileged sites of sexuality and childrearing (this is explored further in Chapter 2). Essentialist explanations of sexuality have a long history and have taken, and continue to take, different forms – but the idea of sex as nature or biology has endured.

The possibilities for how we live our sexuality/sexual identity are mediated by cultural understandings about sexuality, such as the essentialist, and through dominant systems of representation – literature, television, film and newspapers, for example – as well as through social policies and welfare practices. As a result, we commonly think about our sexuality as grounded in the biological, and as such we often understand and talk about it in terms of nature, genes and hormones and therefore as something that 'just is' and as fixed. For example, in Extract 1.1 Alix 'knew exactly what sex was, it was natural right from the beginning'. She refers to sex in ways that suggest that, for her, it is something that just happened naturally, and not something that she had to learn about from sex manuals. This idea of sexuality as something which 'just is' and as fixed is also evident in Max's account in Extract 1.3. He had always known he was attracted to men. In Extract 1.2, too, a naturalized discourse – in this instance of racialized sexual ability – is evident in the boy's questioning of Charlotte.

It is commonly assumed that most people will be heterosexual and we take for granted as natural and normal that people will be attracted to someone of the opposite sex. Because of the taken-for-grantedness of heterosexuality it is likewise considered 'natural' for men and women to get married or to live together in a monogamous heterosexual relationship, and for most women to become mothers. By the same token, it is taken for granted as 'natural' that children should have a male and a female parent – a father and a mother. By contrast, lesbian and gay sexuality, relationships and particularly parenting, although more acceptable than in previous decades, are popularly conceived of as less 'normal' and even as unnatural and as dangerous to children.

Alix is very clear that she is sexually attracted to men and to heterosexual sex. And even though Max has always been attracted to men, the dominance of ideas about heterosexuality as normal meant that he thought he should be attracted to women, marry and have children. However, as both Charlotte's and Alix's narratives illustrate, ideas about heterosexuality are also mediated by other discourses such as those of 'race' and age. Implicit in the questioning of Charlotte are a number of racialized assumptions about black female sexuality, particularly the idea of black women as highly sexed, promiscuous and mysterious, different and 'other' to white sexuality (Saraga, 1998). For Charlotte this requires that she reconcile her experiences of racism with her longing to be out on a date and to be thought desirable. In addition, ideas about black sexuality also intersect with fears about interracial sex.

In Alix's case, stereotypes about older women as unattractive, sexless and incapable of sexual activity come into play. In her narrative, her own sexual feelings and desires are played out against her friends' ideas about appropriate sex (celibacy) for a woman of 49 years of age and her own fears about being unattractive. Max's account challenges the idea of heterosexuality and opposite-sex attraction as something that is natural or fixed. His narrative illustrates that ideas about heterosexuality can be very powerful – he married because 'gayness was outside what I'd been taught to expect'. In all the accounts there is a strong sense that heterosexuality is assumed to be inevitable for all of us, and in Extracts 1.1 and 1.3 marriage is spoken of as the norm. For Alix, not being married at the age of 49 years is experienced as a failing or a loss. Max married because that had been the expectation with which he had grown up.

Ideas about what is 'normal' sexuality are also intricately interwoven with ideas about what it means to be a 'man' or a 'woman' and about acceptable masculinity and femininity. We learn from a wide variety of sources – including our parents, friends, society, our culture, films, novels and other media – the appropriate ways for men and women to be sexually: that is, acceptable behaviours and appropriate relationships. Yet, as the extracts show, although we may learn what is considered to be normal and acceptable sexuality, we also play a part in constituting our own sexuality, albeit within the confines of existing knowledges of sexuality. We learn that male and female sexualities are different and that **gendered concept** sexuality is a fundamentally **gendered concept**. Popularly, sexuality is also understood primarily in terms of a male sex drive. Men, therefore, are commonly believed to be more highly sexed than women, and to be active sexual agents. Women are conventionally thought of as being more emotional and as wanting sex less often, and for different reasons, than men. Such ideas are supported by essentialist explanations of sexuality which emphasize the natural basis of sexuality and gender differences. Essentialism, at its most extreme, would have us believe that male and female sexuality are fixed across time and culture and that an idealized notion of heterosexuality is universal. Essentialist-informed discourses of sexuality also interact with, and are mediated by, discourses of 'race', disability and class to produce differentiating effects. For example, racialized ideas about black and Asian women and men have constituted them, albeit in different ways, as closer to 'nature', sexually voracious, lascivious, hyper-sexed, lacking sexual control, decadent, erotic, exotic, passive and even as animalistic (Stoller, 1985). Disabled men and women are simultaneously seen as incapable of sex, without sexuality and/or as sexually vulnerable and so requiring supervision and control (we explore this further in Chapter 4).

While the three accounts resonate with hegemonic views of sexuality as heterosexual, gendered, biological and natural, and as central to who we are, they also point to an experience of sexuality which is more fluid, dynamic and social and less driven by biology than essentialist or some commonplace accounts suggest. Max's account suggests that we learn that heterosexuality is the normal set of relations, thereby introducing us to the idea of sexuality as socially constructed.

social constructionism **Social constructionism** rejects transhistorical and transcultural universal definitions of sexuality. Physically identical sexual acts may have different social and cultural meanings, force and consequences attached to them, depending on how they are categorized and interpreted in different cultures and at different times. The social constructionist perspective can be summarized as follows. First, it rejects and challenges essentialist views of sexuality as a natural, biologically determined force. Second, social constructionism concerns itself with the development of individual sexual identity rather than with sexual activity. Sexual identity is understood as the negotiation of a complex process of social labelling and self-identification. Third, in social constructionist works on sexuality there is an emphasis on the social meanings which an individual attaches to specific sexual acts, behaviours, feelings, desires and relationships. Individuals not only attach meaning to these which make them sexual, but sexuality itself is deeply embedded in systems of meaning which are themselves shaped by social institutions. Meanings derive from the particular social, cultural and historical contexts in which an individual exists. Put simply, social constructionist approaches focus on what it is that makes one thing sexual and another non-sexual.

Linked to this the notion of context is important. What is sexual in one context may not be experienced or thought sexual in another context. Social constructionist perspectives differ, however, in the role attributed to biology and the body. There are those who would argue that sexual drives, desires and impulses do not exist but are socially constructed, while others accept the existence of an inherent sexual impulse which is constructed in terms of acts, desires, community and object choice. Humans are embodied subjects: that is, the physical body becomes the site where sexualities (and also 'race', ethnicity, gender, disability and class) are constituted and made apparent. Sexuality (and also femininity, masculinity, homosexuality and heterosexuality) is interpreted as being historically and culturally specific and socially constructed. Sexual identity is not assumed to be a fixed aspect of an individual's life, nor is it perceived as something which has an innate or inborn quality, although as the extracts above demonstrate, individuals may explain, and even experience, their sexual identity in this way.

Alix's account of herself as a survivor of the sexual revolution tells us that women's sexual freedom was something which had to be contested and fought for. Her account contradicts essentialist constructions of female sexuality as passive. Instead, we are presented with an image of active female sexuality where 'sex whenever I'd wanted it was my God-given right, earned as a battle-hardened survivor of the sexual revolution'. What these extracts show is that 'Sexuality is not given, it is a product of negotiation, struggle and human agency' (Weeks, 1986, p.25) and that our lived personal experiences of sexuality may be different from public and expert accounts or the constructions of sexuality which inform social policy.

3   Defining sexuality

As we have already seen, sexuality and sex can mean different things to different people and in different contexts. The term 'sex' can refer to biological sex, as in male and female, as well as to the act of 'having sex' (Saraga, 1998). Similarly, as we will see in Chapter 3, differences are often evident between everyday and academic or expert definitions and policy representations of sex. The term
sexuality   **sexuality** can be used to refer to a category of person and an identity, as with heterosexual, homosexual, lesbian, queer, celibate, bi-sexual, and so on. Who, and sometimes even what, we desire is also key to our sexuality. What we 'do' sexually and how we practise our sexuality and sexual relationships (through marriage, cohabitation, celibacy, reproduction, parenting, partnering or otherwise) is another aspect of sexuality. However, sexuality is not simply about what people 'do', it is also about the cultural meanings attached to sexual acts and practices. As Plummer (1975) suggests, nothing is sexual but naming it makes it so.

What we 'do' sexually does not always lead to the claiming of a sexual identity. For example, a man who has sex with other men may reject attempts to identify him as gay or homosexual for a variety of reasons (Dunphy, 2000, p.47). Similarly, a person can be married and identify as lesbian or gay, or be celibate and still claim a sexual identity as heterosexual or homosexual. Sexual identity can be assumed, attributed, chosen and claimed or actively rejected. There is, then, no direct 'cause and effect' relationship between sexual acts, practices and identities. In Chapter 4, on disability and sexuality, we see that it should not be assumed that, because a person is unable to experience genital feelings, 'have' sex or communicate their needs and desire, they do not identify as sexual or that their sexuality has no importance for them. Similarly, the notion of sexuality as central to who we are and as important in our lives and to our personal well-being is a relatively recent idea. This idea of sexuality is historically and socially specific. In other places and times, different notions of where and how sexuality fits into people's lives have existed (as Chapter 2 shows).

In this book, sexuality is understood to include identities, practices and relationships. Our particular interest is with the way in which personal lives, through sexuality, both constitute and are constituted through social policies. We also use the term 'sexuality' to refer to a system of knowledge encompassing what we know as sexuality, what dominates as the 'truth' of sexuality at any moment in time, and the power effects and relations (generally those of heterosexuality) which result. Central to this definition is the idea of sexuality as historically and socially constructed.

4   From personal lives to public policies

4.1   Institutionalized heterosexuality

As we saw in the extracts in section 2 above, sexuality is an important means of organizing personal life and social relations. Decisions about sexual attraction and relationships are clearly very personal decisions. But are they really a matter of individual choice and personal control? In many countries such decisions are usually subject to some form of legal and socio-cultural regulation and acceptance. In the UK, as in most countries, it is heterosexual relationships which are legally and socio-culturally sanctioned through the institution of marriage and the family. According to Kath O'Donnell:

> Throughout the history of family law, marriage has been seen as fundamental to any claim of family status. ... Wherever the nature of marriage has been questioned, courts have reaffirmed its essential nature as a heterosexual relationship.
>
> ... The sanctified relationship of marriage was seen as the appropriate controlling structure for intercourse and hence for procreation. Legal discussion of the concept of marriage still seems to preserve many of these ideals ...
>
> (O'Donnell, 1999, pp.79, 80)

O'Donnell is arguing that heterosexuality is about much more than individual practices and personal relationships. It is legally sanctioned and informs and structures everyday life through the social institutions and social practices of marriage, reproduction and parenting. In this way, heterosexuality can be said to

institutionalized   be **institutionalized**

In Chapter 2, Megan Doolittle explores in more detail the historical legacy of heterosexual marriage, family and parenting in British social policies during the years from 1860 to 1930.

ACTIVITY 1.2

Read through Extracts 1.4 to 1.7 on policy. As you do so, think about the following questions:

- Can you identify the different ways in which heterosexuality is assumed and institutionalized in them?
- What messages do they convey about marriage, family and homosexuality?
- What is the role of the state?

Extract 1.4 Women, marriage and social security

108. Most married women have worked at some gainful occupation before marriage; most who have done so give up that occupation on marriage or soon after; all women by marriage acquire a new economic and social status ... On marriage a woman gains a legal right to maintenance by her husband as a first line of defence against risks which fall directly on the solitary woman; she undertakes at the same time to perform vital unpaid service ... At the last census in 1931, more than seven out of eight of all housewives, that is to say married women of working age, made marriage their sole occupation... .

...

110. The principle adopted here is that on marriage every woman begins a new life in relation to social insurance.

...

117. Taken as a whole, the Plan for Social Security puts a premium on marriage, in place of penalising it.

(Beveridge, 1942, pp.49, 50, 52)

Extract 1.5 Carers

If you or your partner get income-based Jobseeker's Allowance, Income Support on its own or with any of the benefits in the list on page 9, you should claim Carer's Allowance.

By *partner* we mean someone you are married to and living with or a person you live with as if you are married to them.

(Department for Work and Pensions, 2003, p.6)

Figure 1.1   Cover from Carer's Allowance Claim pack, Department for Work and Pensions, Disability and Carers Service

> ### Extract 1.6   On sex and relationships
>
> As part of sex and relationship education, pupils should be taught about the nature and importance of marriage for family life and bringing up children. But the Government recognises ... that there are strong and mutually supportive relationships outside marriage. Therefore pupils should learn the significance of marriage and stable relationships as key building blocks of community and society.
>
> ...
>
> It [sex and relationship education] is not about the promotion of sexual orientation or sexual activity – this would be inappropriate teaching.
>
> (DfEE, 2000, pp.4, 5)

> ### Extract 1.7   Promoting homosexuality
>
> (1) A local authority shall not
> (a) intentionally promote homosexuality or publish material with the intention of promoting homosexuality;
> (b) promote the teaching in any maintained school of the acceptability of homosexuality as a pretended family relationship ...
>
> (Section 28 Part 1 of the Local Government Act 1988)

One effect of the institutionalizing of heterosexuality, and with it marriage and family as the preferred social arrangement for partnering and parenting, is to privilege it over and above other arrangements such as same-sex and cohabiting heterosexual partnerships. For over a decade, the promotion of homosexuality as a legitimate form of sexuality and family relationship was characterized by Section 28 of the Local Government Act 1988 as illegal, inappropriate or 'pretend'. Although no-one has been prosecuted under the Section, its effect has reached far beyond the actual remit of the law, which was restricted to the activities of local authorities. In 2001, Section 28 was abolished in Scotland. In an attempt to prevent the Scottish Parliament from repealing it, Brian Souter, owner of Stagecoach (an international transport provider), funded a £1 million poll opposing the change. The Section was repealed in England and Wales in November 2003.

The institutionalizing of heterosexuality as acceptable sexuality and as the norm has meant that those not conforming are marginalized or discriminated against. Through its institutionalization in a range of legal and social policies – but particularly through marriage – married heterosexual couples and parents are assigned sets of rights in relation to inheritance, tax and pensions. Legal recognition of marriage is significant here because, at the time of writing, cohabiting heterosexual and same-sex partners do not enjoy the same legal rights as married people. This is illustrated in Extract 1.8 below, which is taken from a booklet entitled *Is It Legal? A Parents' Guide to the Law*, produced by the National Family and Parenting Institute (NFPI). The front cover of this booklet is shown in Figure 1.2.

Figure 1.2   Front cover of the National Family and Parenting Institute booklet, *Is It Legal?*
              A Parents' Guide to the Law

Extract 1.8   Parents and the law: marriage and cohabitation

This section is a brief overview of some of the issues for couples in their role as parents, or future parents. It does not go into great detail about the specific legal processes. ...

What are the legal differences between marriage and cohabitation?

Cohabiting means living together without getting married. If parents are not married, the law can treat them differently from married parents. Even if you have lived a long time with your partner and had children with them, you will not necessarily acquire the same rights. There is no such thing in law as 'common law wife/husband'.

Here are a few of the differences:

Property: It is important for people who live together to record, on a formal basis, the way in which they own any property, and what they intend to do if the relationship breaks up or one partner dies. A jointly owned property can be held in one of two ways: as joint tenants or as tenants in common.

Most jointly owned properties are held as joint tenants. This means that if one legal owner dies, their share passes automatically to the survivor.

If the property is owned as tenants in common, each owns the stated share and each may leave their share of the property in their will to whoever they wish.

It is very important that cohabiting parents discuss the two methods of ownership with their solicitor when they buy the property.

Tax: If you cohabit, you and your partner are taxed as separate individuals. Married couples can transfer assets between themselves without having to pay Capital Gains Tax, and can inherit assets from each other without having to pay Inheritance Tax.

Illness: If one partner becomes ill, or mentally incapable of dealing with their financial affairs, the cohabiting partner may find it difficult to arrange things for them. In hospital, there can often be a problem deciding who is next of kin, particularly if there are any family disputes. There is no legal term next of kin; however cohabiting couples could sign a Health Care Proxy and Living Will Form, also known as a 'Next of Kin Declaration', available from hospitals.

Death: If you are married, your estate on death goes to a surviving spouse, where there are no children, parents, brothers or sisters. If there is a surviving spouse and children, the spouse will get the personal possessions, and a fixed sum (currently £125,000). In addition, the spouse will have the right to use one half of the remaining estate for the rest of their life. On their death, it will go to the children. The remaining half goes directly to the children.

If you are not married, the estate will not pass automatically to the person you are living with, so it is important to make a will. Get advice from a solicitor.

What about children?

A parent never loses parental responsibility, unless a child is adopted.

There are differences between a married and unmarried couples' legal responsibilities for their children. The law uses the term parental responsibility to describe the rights, duties, powers, responsibilities and authority parents have for their child. ...

...

Who has 'parental responsibility'?

You have it automatically if you are:

- The biological mother of a child
- The biological father of the child and you were married to the mother at the time of conception or birth, or you married the mother after the birth of the child.
- You are adoptive parents once an adoption order is made.

You can get it by agreement (or through a court order) if:

- You are the biological father but not married to the child's mother.

Fathers who are cohabiting do not automatically get parental responsibility by putting their name on the birth certificate. You can get a form to apply for parental responsibility from a solicitor or your local County Court.

(National Family and Parenting Institute, 2001, pp.22–4)

What the cohabitation example illustrates is that it is not heterosexuality *per se* that is privileged – afforded rights and protections – but an ideal type or norm, the married heterosexual couple/family. Institutionalized heterosexuality, therefore, can be understood as a site of power, regulation, contestation and inequality. At the time of writing, the rights of cohabiting and same-sex partners to have their relationships legally recognized and to adopt were being reviewed by the UK Parliament following challenges by, for example, lesbian and gay rights organizations such as Stonewall.

ACTIVITY 1.3

See if you can identify one or two examples of policy, laws or welfare practices which take for granted that all individuals are heterosexual or will live as part of a heterosexual couple. After you have made your own short list, read through Richard Dunphy's definition of institutional heterosexuality, given in Extract 1.9 below, which begins to identify the boundaries of institutional heterosexuality, and compare your examples with his and with those of the NFPI given in Extract 1.8 above.

Extract 1.9   Institutionalized heterosexuality

We almost all grow up in families where heterosexuality is assumed. We are educated in schools where it is universalised; work in environments where it is taken for granted; are affected by marriage laws, tax laws, inheritance laws, residency laws and laws governing how we behave in public, which afford privilege to heterosexuality as the only recognised form of being. Most people take this so much for granted that the very use of the word 'privilege' may cause surprise. Yet that which is granted to one group of persons and denied to others can indeed be described as privilege. We inhale heterosexuality with the air we breathe. This is really what is meant by institutionalised heterosexuality or heterosexuality as a site of power.

(Dunphy, 2000, p.68)

COMMENT

Absent from Extract 1.9 is the idea of heterosexuality as socially constructed or of the changing ways in which heterosexuality has been constituted over time. Further, the heterosexuality spoken of in Dunphy's definition is an undifferentiated heterosexuality with effects which are similar not only across time but also in different contexts and cultures. It makes no allowance, for example, for how heterosexuality differentiates between married and cohabiting couples. If we take the example of lone motherhood in the UK in previous centuries, we can see that responses to unmarried motherhood have varied. From the mid 1830s lone mothers, particularly poor working-class women, were constructed as sexually immoral and therefore as undeserving welfare subjects. At the turn of the twentieth century until about the 1940s unmarried mothers were likely to be regarded in terms of mental deficiency – as being inherently 'feeble-minded'; they were likewise seen to produce 'feeble-minded' offspring and thus as a threat to the 'purity' of the 'British race'. For their, and society's, 'good', many were confined in institutions and remained there until as late as the 1980s and 1990s.

In the 1950s, women who had children outside marriage were often pathologized (that is, seen as diseased) and their unmarried motherhood explained in terms of some psychological illness or problem. (For more detailed information and discussion of constructions of unmarried/lone motherhood, see Keirnan et al., 1998.) Certain themes – the unacceptability of unmarried motherhood; lone motherhood as a moral, social and/or economic issue, as a threat (to family, nation, society) – reappear albeit in different forms at different times. At the time of writing, lone motherhood is accepted to a greater degree than in previous centuries, but it is not awarded the same status as the heterosexual married couple family. It is subjected not only to the norm of heterosexuality, but also to a norm of lone motherhood, for not all circumstances of lone motherhood are considered acceptable – some lone mothers are more acceptable than others. In the UK under the New Deal for Lone Parents (**Fergusson, 2004**), the lone mothers regarded as unacceptable are those not engaged in paid labour and teenage mothers.

Gender differences are at the heart of most definitions of heterosexuality, as we have already seen, though this is not made explicit in Extract 1.9. Feminists have identified and successfully challenged the way in which heterosexuality is constructed on the basis of assumed gender differences that privilege men and their sexuality over women (Chapter 3 discusses this further). However, and just as importantly, there is no indication of the ways in which ideas or discourses of heterosexuality intersect with discourses of 'race', disability, age and class, as the chapters in this book show. The following quotation illustrates just one way in which racialized ideas about sexuality intersect and are operationalized in one area of social policy – immigration (see also Brah, 1996, pp.74–5):

> To gain entry permission [to Britain] ... They [Asian women] have had to undergo the ordeal of answering absurd and very intimate questions about themselves, their husbands and their families. Questions such as 'How long did you spend with your husband on the wedding night?' are common, and if either partner makes the slightest misjudgement then entry permission is refused. In 1978, there was an exposé of the vaginal examinations carried out on Asian women to determine whether they were married or not, and to determine they were fiancées of men already settled in England.
>
> ... This 'testing' is based on the racist and sexist assumption that Asian women from the subcontinent are always virgins before they get married and that it is 'not in their culture for women to engage in sexual activity before marriage'.
>
> (Parmar, 1982, p.245)

We will be looking at examples of how this process operates in relation to age and disability in Chapters 3 and 4.

Pause for a moment and think about what might be the implications for social policy planning and welfare provision of policy researchers taking heterosexuality as given and assuming that most individuals will live as couples, marry and have children.
Reflect on how normative assumptions about sexuality and relationships might influence how samples for social policy research are put together.

It is only very recently that UK government statistics have begun to collect information about lesbian and gay relationships, and not until 2001 that same-sex relationships were included in the UK Census. In August 2002 the Office for National Statistics announced that it would begin to ask questions about sexuality and different types of relationships so as to take account of these in future plans for benefits and pensions (*The Guardian*, 8 August 2002). The chapters which follow illustrate that, if social policy is to reflect more accurately the variety of ways in which individuals negotiate and live their sexual lives, then policy research has to challenge normative and taken-for-granted assumptions about sexuality.

4.2   Heteronormativity

heteronormativity   We use the term **heteronormativity** here in recognition, first, that, in constituting the heterosexual and heterosexuality as natural, normal and universal, a whole set of other universalizing processes are called upon about able-bodiedness, whiteness and gender. Each of these is organized around a series of binary oppositions such as able/disabled, white/black, same/other, heterosexual/ homosexual, male/female, adult/child, and so on. Second, we use the term in recognition that heterosexuality has come to be differently constituted and can therefore mean different things at any given time. Although heterosexual relations predominate, and heterosexuality is generally socially, culturally and politically privileged and institutionally valorized in both social and legal policies, it is also a differentiated heterosexuality: that is, not all heterosexual relationships are treated equally, but, rather, it is the ideal of heterosexual married family life that is valorized, as the cohabitation and lone motherhood examples above illustrate.

Now (as in the past) alternative forms of intimate and sexual relations, family, parenting and partnering demand legal and social recognition and achieve wider social acceptance. At the beginning of the twenty-first century, for example, there have been considerable shifts in the way people live as families and in what counts as a 'family', as well as in the meaning of 'family' to individuals. There is also a greater social acceptance of diverse family forms and intimate relationships – be they same sex, cohabiting or lone parent. A popular critique of modern life is that we are living in a period of rapid social change which is affecting the ways in which we live and organize our most intimate and sexual relationships, as well as what counts as family and the significance of friendship both for heterosexuals and for lesbians and gays. Commentators, such as Beck (1992) and Giddens (1991), acknowledging the influence of feminist and lesbian and gay activism, have characterized these changes as part of a more reflexive modernity coupled with greater individualism in which the traditional certainties of family, gender and sexuality – the security of life-long marriage, gender and sexual roles and relationships – are being eroded and renegotiated. The idea of reflexive modernity refers to how individuals, freed from the constraints of reproduction and tradition, 'are forced to negotiate lifestyle choices among a diversity of choices' (Giddens, 1991, p.5), providing greater opportunities for them to choose how to live their sexual lives and form relationships.

Within this reconstituted heterosexuality, however, other norms come into operation. Cohabitation may now be tolerated and even widely accepted, but it is not awarded quite the same status as the heterosexual married couple family. It too is subjected to, and judged against, the heteronormative ideal. This process, where the heteronormative ideal is the norm against which all sexualities, relationships, partnerships and parenting are evaluated, can be

normalizing strategy understood as a **normalizing strategy** (see section 6.2). Sexuality, therefore, is never simply a private issue nor just a matter of personal choice.

4.3   Privatization of sexuality: the personal as private or public?

Despite the social and legal regulation of sexuality, the notion of it as private is commonplace and influential. At an everyday level this is evoked through statements such as: 'what people do in the privacy of their own homes or bedrooms is their own affair provided this doesn't harm or affect anyone else'. Indeed, this association with the private was institutionalized in British legal and social policy in the 1957 Wolfenden Report. This Report was concerned with a number of areas of sexuality and led to the liberalization of laws on prostitution (in 1959) and of homosexuality (in 1967). It defined the role of law in these matters in the following way:

> The function of criminal law ... in this field ... is to preserve public order and decency, to protect the citizen from what is offensive or injurious, and to provide sufficient safeguards against exploitation and corruption of others ... It is not ... the function of the law to interfere in the private lives of citizens or to seek to enforce any particular pattern of behaviour.
>
> (Wolfenden, 1957, paras 13, 14)

However, some sexualities, such as homosexuality, are more privatized than others. The implications of the Wolfenden Report for homosexuality were that, as long as it remained in the private sphere and did not offend public decency or threaten public safety, then these were matters for the individual rather than matters of policy-making or legislation. This ruling, which was enacted in the Sexual Offences Act 1967, decriminalized homosexuality in private while making it illegal in places described as 'public', which included hotel rooms and instances when more than two adults are present.

One effect of the Wolfenden Report was to criminalize public demonstrations of male homosexuality while reaffirming the legality of (most) heterosexual demonstrations of sexuality in public spaces. In so doing, it reinforced the idea that public expressions of homosexuality were offensive to public decency while heterosexual ones were not.

Privatization is one way in which heteronormative processes operate. The Wolfenden ruling demonstrates that meanings of private or public, how we distinguish between them, and the boundaries of tolerance and intolerance, are dependent on whether they are being used in a heterosexual or homosexual context. As Richardson (1996, p.15) has stated: 'For lesbians and gays the private has been institutionalised as the border of social intolerance, as the place where you are "allowed" to live relatively safely as long as one does not attempt to occupy the public'. At the centre of the privatizing of homosexuality is a discourse which constitutes 'private' homosexuality as a 'self-regulating, harmless, assimilable and accidental difference and "public" homosexuality as a flaunting, dangerous, unassimilable and supplementary difference' (Smith, 1994, p.207).

We can also understand the criminalizing of homosexuality in public spaces as part of a legitimizing of sets of processes which control people's use of and access to space. According to Hubbard (2001, pp.54–5), 'assumptions about the right of different groups to occupy space serve to reinforce hegemonic heterosexuality ... [through public] displays of heterosexual affection, friendship and desire which are regarded as acceptable or "normal" in most [everyday urban] spaces' – such as shops, streets, cafés and bars, as well as in various sites of welfare, including hospital wards, residential homes and day centres, schools and colleges. At the time of writing, if two men kiss in public not only can this result in physical violence against them, but their kissing can be considered an act of gross indecency under Section 13 of the Sexual Offences Act, 1956.

Carol Johnson (2002), working with the notion of the 'good homosexual' and ideas about public space as heterosexual, argues that 'injunctions against public same-sex touching reflect a broader emphasis on private homosexuality and public passing' (Johnson, 2002, p.321). What this means is that the regulatory effects of the privatizing discourse are such that homosexuals are expected to police their public expressions of affection by restricting these to the home and bedroom, effectively making aspects of homosexual sexuality invisible. Johnson summarizes this as 'It's O.K. to be gay as long as you pass as heterosexual in public' (Johnson, 2002, p.321).

Research has highlighted that many homosexuals deny or disguise their sexuality when in public because of fears of abuse or intolerance (Hubbard, 2001). For Bell and Binnie (2000), constructions of space as private or public are significant because of their capacity to affect an individual's ability to exercise their citizenship rights. In a welfare context a similar process takes place with lesbians and gays reporting a reluctance to disclose their sexuality to welfare professionals. For lesbians and gay men it is often easier to let health and welfare professionals assume that they are heterosexual (Brown, 1998; Saulinier, 2002). But it is not only lesbian and gay welfare users who are required to pass as heterosexual. Many lesbian and gay welfare professionals may feel vulnerable about being 'out' at work, particularly when their job involves working with children (as in the case of youth and social workers and teachers) or the provision of intimate care (as with carers, nurses and doctors) (Brown, 1998; Langley, 2001). Lesbian and gay activists have challenged the privatization of homosexuality and constructions of the public as heterosexual by seeking legislative changes as well as by mass celebrations of gay sexuality through Lesbian and Gay Pride marches. What counts as public, as well as the limits of the personal, can be contested, and public space, although regulated, can provide possibilities for mobilizing recognition and rights claims (Bell and Binnie, 2000).

Those in relationships which are closer to the norm of heterosexuality, such as marriage, are more likely to have their privacy protected and are less likely to be subjected to state intervention and public scrutiny. The sexualities of, for example, pregnant teenagers, lone mothers, unmarried couples, lesbians, gay men and disabled people, on the other hand, as the chapters in this book show, are more likely to become the focus of public scrutiny. What is interesting about looking at the public/private relationship in the context of sexuality is that constructions of what each constitutes and the relationship of one to the other differ. What all this shows is that both the private and the public are social constructions and, as such, they are open to contestation, transformation and redefinition. Under proposals outlined in *Protecting the Public: Strengthening Protection Against Sex Offenders and Reforming the Law on Sexual Offences* (Home Office, 2002), a generic law which will probably be introduced in 2004 will criminalize all heterosexual as well as homosexual public acts of sex. Thus the distinction between private and public sex will be maintained, although less explicitly in terms of a heterosexual/homosexual binary (this is discussed further in section 6.1).

ACTIVITY 1.4

Read Extracts 1.10 to 1.12 below and consider on what basis the state legitimates policy intervention into personal sexualities. Can you think of other examples where what we do sexually might be a matter of public concern and/or regulated by social or legal policies?

Extract 1.10   Mixed marriages

There is nothing like a marriage for turning private affairs into public issues. After all, that's what a wedding is; a public declaration of a union – for better or for worse. But there are marriages and there are mixed marriages and the latter inevitably signal a whole lot more to their public than the mere fact of two people promising to live out their days together.

Early in the last century, Cardiff, like Liverpool, had been identified as an area of Britain where there was a need to tackle the fast growing 'colour' problem. And so in 1929 the Chief Constable of Cardiff proposed a legal ban on miscegenation, the fancy word for racial intermixing.

(Williams, 2002, p.56)

Extract 1.11   Supporting marriage

Supporting marriage does not mean trying to compel people to marry, nor criticising nor penalising those who choose not to do so. More couples cohabit before marriage and, increasingly, more of them have children without first marrying. In a free society, we must respect these choices, not condemn them, however we wish the choice had been for marriage.

(Lord Irvine of Laing, 1999)

Extract 1.12   Supporting families

... governments have to be wary about intervening in areas of private life and intimate emotion.

...

Many lone parents and unmarried couples raise their children every bit as successfully as married parents. But marriage is still the surest foundation for raising children and remains the choice of the majority of people in Britain. We want to strengthen the institution of marriage to help more marriages to succeed.

... There needs to be a clear understanding of the rights and responsibilities which fall to families and to government. Parents raise children and that is how

> things should remain. More direct intervention should only occur in extreme
> circumstances, for example in cases of domestic violence or where the welfare
> of children is at stake.
>
> (Home Office, 1998, p.4, paras 4, 8, 9)

The relationship of personal lives and sexuality to social policy is not solely a
regulatory one. It is also about recognition and the extent to which social policy
and welfare practice acknowledges the significance of sexuality – heterosexual
or otherwise – to individuals in their personal lives and to their well-being.
Research in the areas of social work and health suggests that professionals find
sexuality issues difficult to deal with in their practice (Brown, 1998; Neiman,
2002). Professionals often cite awkwardness, embarrassment and lack of
knowledge about sexuality as the key reasons for ignoring sexuality in their
practice (this is discussed again in Chapters 3 and 4 in relation to teachers and
personal care assistants). Further, the influence of ideas about sexuality as
personal and private can mean that welfare institutions, such as hospitals,
hospices and residential homes, deny the existence or importance of sexuality
and intimacy between patients and their partners. In the case of older residents
and patients, professional carers may assume that sexuality is an inevitable loss
of old age and, as a result, older people might be seen as asexual or their
sexuality regarded as unimportant to their well-being (Scrutton, 1992, pp.94–5).
The denial of sexuality by welfare organizations and professionals is further
exacerbated by a tendency to misinterpret sexuality as meaning a sexual act
rather than as also embracing relationships, intimacy, identity, self and body
image. Institutionalized heteronormativity can also mean that welfare
organizations and welfare professionals ignore or marginalize lesbian and gay
sexualities and same-sex and cohabiting relationships. For example, people
who can be classed as next of kin are defined as being either those married to a
person or close blood relatives. Same-sex or cohabiting partners are not
currently deemed to be next of kin. This can cause problems if one partner is ill
or dies – it is the next of kin who are consulted in hospital and who are entitled to
make funeral arrangements.

What the sections above and the personal narratives at the beginning of the
chapter illustrate is that sexuality plays a key role, not only in constituting the
subject, but also in connecting individuals to society – to the social. The
regulation of sexuality, and particularly the processes and techniques of
heteronormativity as they are played out through social policy, is one means by
which social order and the individual's place in the social is established and
maintained. They also illustrate that personal lives contribute in part to what
form social policy takes, its remit and its effects.

5   Sexuality and social policy

In policy analyses the distinction between the private and the public realms is also evident. The private realm has come to be associated with the domestic, family and sexuality. In the public realm the concern is with welfare institutions, formal welfare provision, markets and the state. In the 1970s and 1980s feminists challenged this distinction, arguing that sexuality, women's unpaid caring and domestic work and the family were central to the provision of welfare. Despite these challenges, sexuality continues to be ignored in most social policy accounts and theories (see Carabine, 1996a,b). This is despite more recent attempts to incorporate a theorizing of heterosexuality in social, political and legal theory (Richardson, 1996; Collier, 1999). This marginalizing of sexuality within the discipline has been due to a combination of factors – the influence of dominant discourses of (hetero)sexuality (resulting in a 'taken-for-granted' assumption of the universality of heterosexuality informing social policy analyses); a privatizing of sexuality and sexual relations; the historical development of the academic discipline of social policy, particularly the influence of Fabianism and the social administration legacy; and finally, an implicit consensus about what constitutes the 'real' concerns of social policy and welfare (see Carabine, 1996a, for a detailed discussion).

The origins of the discipline are well documented (Hill, 1993) and critiqued (see, for example, Taylor-Gooby and Dale, 1981; Williams, 1989; Bryson, 1992) and therefore will be discussed only briefly here. For our purposes in this book, it is sufficient to say that social policy grew out of a social administration tradition concerned more with the collection of empirical evidence than with its interpretation or the development of theories arising out of it. Of the various influences on social administration it was Fabianism which was to be the most influential, remaining until the 1970s as the bedrock of the mainstream. The Fabian Society was formed in 1884 and is still influential as a think tank in political ideas and public policy on the left of centre. Its early members included notable socialists Beatrice and Sydney Webb, H.G. Wells and George Bernard Shaw. At the heart of Fabianism were the values of equality, freedom and fellowship (Williams, 1989, p.30) sought through state-organized collectivism, rational administration, professionalization, and national and social efficiency. Fabianism embraced traditional ideas and assumptions about women, 'race' and sexuality. According to Williams:

> What is often overlooked is the extent to which it [Fabianism] *shared* with these groups [Liberals and anti-collectivists], as well as with sections of the growing labour movement, assumptions about the role of women, of racial superiority and the attempt to replace class solidarity with nationalist pride, which in turn found their expression in the developing welfare state.
>
> (Williams, 1989, p.5)

The role of women as mothers and wives was accepted as natural and normal along with the normality of the traditional heterosexual family. Assumptions about marriage, gender roles and the family were explicit in key welfare documents, such as the 1909 Poor Law Minority Report in which Beatrice Webb, a founder of the Fabian society, was a member, as well as in the Fabian submission on social security on the 1942 Beveridge Report.

An important influence on the early development of state-provided welfare in the UK was social imperialism. The Fabians were passionate social imperialists (see Jacobs, 1985). Social imperialism arose out of anxieties about the fitness, quality and superiority of the British population. Through the values of social imperialism the introduction of social reforms to achieve national efficiency and imperial expansion were championed, and social measures which favoured the strong but not the weak were promoted by the Fabians: 'The Socialist policy ... is a process of conscious social selection by which the industrial residuum is naturally sifted and made manageable for some kind of restorative, disciplinary, or may be, "surgical treatment"' (Ball, 1896, in Steadman-Jones, 1971, p.333). For some Fabians, such as George Bernard Shaw and H.G. Wells, this could only be achieved through sterilization (Steadman-Jones, 1971, p.333). The concern with national efficiency, 'race' and social reform meant that, for some commentators, the Fabians were clearly eugenicists (see Wilson, 1977; Jacobs, 1985). Eugenics was the preservation of the superiority of the 'British race' through planned reproduction, and state and biological intervention. For those Fabians who supported eugenicist aims, the control of sexuality was a necessary requirement and key to achieving social reform.

Other commentators, such as Weeks (1989), have tended to see the Fabian engagement with eugenics as a flirtation, the result of a pervasive vogue at its height in the early decades of the twentieth century. However, Sydney Webb, for example, argued for the introduction of social policies to encourage the 'right sort' of people to have children (Weeks, 1989, p.134). What the Fabians and eugenicists shared was a 'belief in planning and control of population' (Weeks, 1989, p.133). Issues of 'race', sexuality and social policy were intricately intertwined for Fabians. At the heart of Fabian interest with sexuality was its regulation in pursuit of national efficiency, purity and superiority of 'race'. The achievement of such aims required the state regulation of reproduction along with the endowment of appropriate motherhood and family. In the process of advocating social imperialism, Fabianism both invoked and constituted traditional notions of the family, motherhood, fatherhood, appropriate male and female sexuality, gender roles and sexual relations. In so doing, they contributed to discourses which constituted the norm for each of these aspects.

After the Second World War the popularity of eugenicist ideas declined considerably. However, concerns about the survival of the 'British race' did not completely disappear and were a significant concern of the post-war welfare settlement and the establishment of the welfare state (Weeks, 1989, p.232): 'At the heart of welfarism was a clear concern with the conditions of "reproduction" – both in its widest social sense, of producing a healthy workforce in the context of comprehensive social security and full employment; and its narrow biological sense, of improving the conditions of parenthood and childbirth' (Weeks, 1989, p.232). Again, central to this concern were normative assumptions about sexuality, the family, marriage and motherhood (Weeks, 1989, p.235).

Nor did the influence of the Fabians completely fade away after the war. Indeed, their legacy can be traced in the work of such eminent social policy commentators as Titmuss (1958) and Pinker (1971). This is not to suggest that these later advocates of Fabianism were eugenicists. Nor is it to suggest that eugenics directly influenced social policies but, rather, as Weeks (1989, p.31) suggests, that it was more influential in establishing the context for policy-making particularly in the first half of the twentieth century (we will explore this further in Chapter 2). However, traditional views about family, motherhood, 'race' and sexuality are evident, if to varying degrees, in the work of these later Fabians (Williams, 1989, pp.126–7). In the 1970s the value and ideological foundations of social policy began to be challenged – first, from a class perspective and, later, from gender, 'race' and disability perspectives. As we have seen, though, the assumption of universal heterosexuality prevails into the twenty-first century.

Another important influence which has shaped the discipline of social policy is politics and what is considered political or 'real' politics: 'Working class demands articulated principally through Labour party politics, had traditionally been seen as the principle engine behind the post-war expansion of the welfare state in Britain' (Taylor-Gooby, 1991, p.18). Coote and Pattullo (1990, p.181) comment that sexuality was 'not part of Labour's traditional agenda ... [and] ... had generally not been seen as [a] "political" issue'. This shaped the focus of the discipline despite a shift in the late 1980s away from class as the principal basis for individual identity. More complex understandings of the multiple nature of identities and of how these connect to welfare needs have only very recently begun to be reflected in mainstream social policy analyses. To some extent this is changing, particularly in approaches that recognize the influence of the new social movements on social policy (Williams, 1992; Cahill, 1994) and in work which adopts a post-structuralist or postmodern critique (O'Brien and Penna, 1998; Saraga, 1998). Under New Labour, sexuality issues have achieved greater legitimacy but they are not generally given priority except when they become a 'social problem', as with teenage pregnancy or child sexual abuse. This section on sexuality and social policy illustrates some of the ways in which discourses about what constitutes sexuality at any given moment have informed, and continue to inform, social policy analyses.

ACTIVITY 1.5

Extracts 1.13 and 1.14 illustrate two different approaches to the personal lives, sexuality and social policy relationship. The first is from *British Social Policy Since 1945* by Howard Glennerster (2000), a historian and theorist of social policy. The second is from *Sex, Politics and Society* (1989) by Jeffrey Weeks, a historian and theorist of sexuality. Both deal with the reform of laws in the 1960s (often referred to as the 'permissive moment'), such as the Abortion Act 1967, the Family Planning Act 1968, the Family Reform Act 1969 and the Sexual Offences Act 1967 – which partially decriminalized male homosexuality, introduced the notion of 'no-fault' divorce and made abortion and contraception more readily and legally available on the National Health Service (NHS). Read through Extracts 1.13 and 1.14 carefully. As you do so, think about and compare the ways in which they deal with personal lives, sexuality and social policy.

Extract 1.13   British social policy since 1945

Social policy ... is not only concerned with pieces of social legislation. ... One of the most difficult areas of all for governments to tread is the boundary line between the family and the state's legitimate functions.

...

But at the basis of Anglo-Saxon social policy has been the view that the family is a private world in which the state should have no role. Like the market, the state regulates its existence, the contractual basis of marriage, and indeed supports and encourages the institution, but should not actively intervene within it.

...

The 1960s marked an important phase. The state's right to intervene in sexual matters was questioned and modified. ...

Though it is commonplace to see the 1980s as the decade of individualism and rolling back state power, in the field of morals and personal life it was the 1960s that reduced the intrusiveness of the state and extended individual freedom ... Yet the legislation passed in that period was 'momentous' in that it has lasted and directly affected very large numbers of people, probably more deeply and personally than the changes to the structure of pension schemes or the National Health Service.

...

The faith of many intellectuals ... was that collective welfare, full employment and education would facilitate individual growth and autonomy, 'moral individualism'. In harmony with this goal the state should match its role of collective provision with a withdrawal from spheres that were not properly its province – regulating sexual behaviour, for example.

...

What we had, then, were some very important moves to reduce the intrusiveness of the state in sexual matters in the 1960s. It was limited and did not give free licence to abortions, or to sexual relations for young men. Marriage was still carefully constructed in a traditional mould.

(Glennerster, 2000, pp.139, 140, 141, 147)

Extract 1.14   Sex, politics and society

The creation of a Welfare State in the 1940s, based, however tenuously, on an ideology of social (and even sexual) reconciliation, inevitably involved a major reassessment of the whole field of sexuality. For at the heart of welfarism was a clear concern with the conditions of 'reproduction' – both in its widest social sense, of producing a healthy workforce in the context of comprehensive social security and full employment; and in its narrow, biological sense, of improving the conditions of parenthood and childbirth. This ensured that the major sexual controversies over the next four decades were to be around the balance between social intervention and individual freedom, and this was reflected in the three major areas of debate – population policies, family life and sexual unorthodoxy.

...

... the Report of the Wolfenden Committee on Homosexual Offences and Prostitution published in 1957 ... acknowledged and regretted, like many other contemporary documents, the 'general loosening of former moral standards', the disruptive effects of the war and 'the emotional insecurity, community instability and weakening of the family' inherent in modern society. It deplored any potential damage to 'what we regard as the basic unit of society', the family.

...

The real change in the 1950s was the growth of official concern and public anxiety to which police zeal was a response. This cannot be divorced from the heightened post-war stress on the importance of monogamous heterosexual love, which threw into greater relief ... the 'deviant' nature of both prostitution and homosexuality.

...

The key point is that privatisation did not necessarily involve a diminution of control.

...

The separation of law and morality developed in Wolfenden becomes the hallmark of 'permissive' legislation and marks a crucial stage in shifting the balance of decision making from the public to the private sphere. But this often had a double thrust, for as the [Sexual] Offences Act underscored, reform could sustain and strengthen social control as easily as remove it. ... what was taking place in the 1960s was not a simple reform of outdated laws, but a major legislative restructuring, marking an historic shift in the mode of regulation of civil society.

(Weeks, 1989, pp.232, 239, 240, 244, 252)

COMMENT

In your reading of these two extracts you might have come up with some of the ideas given in Table 1.1.

Table 1.1   Extracts 1.13 and 1.14 compared

Extract 1.13: Glennerster	Extract 1.14: Weeks
In Extract 1.13 the impact of the 1960 policy reforms on personal lives is acknowledged.	In Extract 1.14 sexuality is perceived as social/cultural as well as individual. Sexuality is central to the social. A link between sexuality, society and social stability is identified.
The notion of sexuality as a private, individual matter, outside the boundaries of state intervention, is reinforced. Individuals should be able to do what they want in the privacy of their homes provided this does no harm to others or does not offend public decency.	Sexuality is at the heart of welfare and social policy and is seen as a key part of state regulation and activity.
A very individualized notion of the relationship between sexuality and the state is presented. Sexuality is not seen as a legitimate sphere of intervention for government. The role of the state with regard to the family is similar to its role with regard to the market.	Sexuality is seen as much bigger than individual freedom or a personal matter – bigger than the family and population, and so on.
Sexuality is not perceived as part of the cultural/social.	The centrality of heterosexuality to understanding sexuality is highlighted.
Sexuality is treated as just another area of social policy rather than as something which might be central to the organization of welfare/social policy.	Governmentality is key – reforms are seen as part of a shift in the way society is regulated. Governmentality refers to 'all endeavours to shape, guide, direct the conduct of others, whether this be the crew of a ship, the members of a household, the employees of a boss, the children of a family or the inhabitants of a territory. It also embraces ways one might be urged and educated to bridle one's own passions, to control one's own instincts, to govern oneself' (Rose, 1999, p.3).
Although the author acknowledges that the reforms of the 1960s were 'momentous' and deeply affected people's personal lives, sexuality is not seen as an area of life to be looked at through the lens of social policy. The possible role of social policy in constructing, constituting, shaping and regulating the possibilities for personal lives and social organization is ignored.	For Weeks, the development of social policy/welfare is seen as part of the development of the history of sexuality. Whereas for Glennerster, sexuality (or, more accurately, morality) is seen as part of the history of the development of social policy in the UK.

Extract 1.13: Glennerster

Sexuality is perceived as a topic – morality – rather than as an analytical tool. That is, sexuality is seen to be about moral issues – particularly about individual morality (abortion, homosexuality, conception, etc.).

Power relations inherent in hetero-sexuality – particularly the ways in which heterosexuality is institutionalized in policies and welfare practices – are ignored.

6   Centring sexuality and personal lives in social policy analyses

Michel Foucault, a French philosopher, social constructionist and theorist (1926–1984) offered a particularly fruitful approach for understanding how personal lives are constituted in the sexuality discourses which inform social policy and practice. In this book we focus on his work on sexuality, discourse, power, knowledge and normalization (Foucault, 1990, 1991) as this offers valuable insights into the effects of heteronormativity in forming, regulating and constituting social policy subjects, discourses, provisions, practices and theories. These concepts are also useful in providing an appreciation of the role played by social policy in conveying messages about acceptable sexualities: that is, the role of social policy in constituting sexual norms.

6.1   Discourse, power and knowledge

discourse

We can think of **discourse** as consisting of groups of related statements – texts, speech and images, for example about sexuality as natural, and practices such as heterosexuality – which come together or cohere and which are *productive*. That is, discourses produce and convey meanings about a topic with material effects. When we say discourses are productive we mean that they produce the objects of which they speak – as with heterosexuality. In other words, discourses are *constitutive*. They construct a particular version of heterosexuality, family or

subjects

parenthood as 'real'. It is also through discourses that **subjects** – figures who embody the discourse – are constituted, as in the heterosexual, the homosexual, the married couple, the pregnant teenager or the sex offender. Discourses also

subject positions

generate **subject positions** – such as the responsible citizen, the underclass or the consumer – which are offered to us and which shape not only how we make sense of the world, but how we construct our identities, experience or subjectivity and thereby make sense of ourselves and others. Subject positions

Figure 1.3   Portrait of Michel Foucault

are neither fixed nor stable. Individuals choose or reject different subject positions at different points in their lives depending on the resources available to them. For example, we can understand heterosexuality as:

> a set of discursive constructs with which subjects interact, refusing certain elements and accepting others. ...
>
> Thus, individual subjects should not be seen simply to adopt roles which are mapped out for them by discourses; ... Individual subjects are constantly weighing up their own perception of their own position in relation to ... discursive norms.

(Mills, 1997, p.97)

Discourse generated around a topic can be different and even contradictory at one and the same time without disrupting its overall effect. Discourses are **power** productive in the sense that they have **power** outcomes or effects and embody power relations in society. Discourse 'governs the way a topic can be meaningfully talked about ... It also influences how ideas are put into practice and used to regulate the conduct of others' (Hall, 2001, p.72). In this sense discourses are powerful because of their productive and constitutive capacities. Further, when thinking about discourse that which is *not* said – the absences – is as important as that which *is* said, as Margrit Shildrick shows in Chapter 4. We can also think of discourses as fluid, and even as opportunistic, because not only do they utilize existing ways of speaking about a topic but they also hook into other dominant discourses. An example of this would be what happens when heterosexuality discourses intersect with discourses of, say, disability, childhood or health (as we will see in Chapters 3 and 4), or 'race', as Charlotte's account in

Extract 1.2 shows, to produce potent and new ways of evoking heterosexuality. Relatedly, discourses are not simply a series of unconnected statements, but are embedded within social contexts such as social policy.

Discourses also define and establish what is 'truth' at particular moments. Foucault describes the production of the 'truth' of sexuality in the following way:

> One hundred and fifty years have gone into a complete machinery for producing true discourses on sex ... It is this deployment that enables something called 'sex' to embody the truth of sex and its pleasures ... it put into operation an entire machinery for producing true discourses concerning it. Not only did it speak of sex and compel everyone to do so; it also set out to produce the uniform truth of sex.
>
> (Foucault, 1990, pp.68–9)

What do you think this might mean?

Foucault is suggesting that the acts that we call 'sex' are only so because of that name and that this name/discourse enters into the subject so that these acts are experienced as 'sex'. He is also suggesting something else: that during the last 150 years or so considerable energy has gone into explaining sexuality and towards establishing the 'truth' or knowledge of sexuality.

In *The History of Sexuality*, Foucault (1990) investigates the ways in which sexuality has come to be seen and spoken of – the development of knowledges about sex – as a means of understanding the operations of power. Key to understanding this is the idea that, without discourse, sexuality has no meaning, or, put differently, that sexuality only has meaning within the discourses which 'speak' of it. These knowledges or 'truths' about sexuality tell us what is 'normal' and 'natural' sexuality while establishing the boundaries of what is acceptable and appropriate sexuality. For Foucault not only is sexuality socially constructed and produced by effects of power, but bodies too are explicable only in terms of 'truths' which are themselves socially produced. In his unravelling of sexuality throughout history, Foucault reveals how sexuality has been produced differently at specific historical moments through the operation of discourse.

Also in *The History of Sexuality*, Foucault identifies a range of discourses – medical, moral, religious, political, educational, welfare and scientific – which contribute to definitions of what constitutes healthy, good, acceptable, normal and natural sexuality. A significant contribution emerged in the form of sexology. Epitomized in the late nineteenth and early twentieth centuries by sexologists such as Havelock Ellis, Hirschfeld, Carpenter, Freud and Krafft-Ebing, and in the latter part of the twentieth century by Masters and Johnson and Kinsey, sexology produced new scientific 'truths' of sexuality and a new, specialized body of **knowledge**. Central to this was the identification, categorization and classification of a whole range of sexual behaviours. Within these 'knowledges', categories or typologies of sexuality, such as homosexual, bisexual, invert and paedophile – which tended to focus on 'abnormal' sexual behaviours – were identified. It was through this process of focusing on what was considered 'abnormal' or 'perverse' sexuality that normal sexuality was constituted. For example, the 'homosexual' became a categorization for a type of

knowledge

person rather than simply an act (Saraga, 1998). Sexuality, Foucault argued, not only became the focus of 'experts', of scientific concern and of sexologists, who sought to categorize, define and explain it – in the process of doing so they generated knowledge itself (that is, how sexuality was to become understood, known and explained). A major criticism levelled at Foucault's account of discourse is that it risks neglecting the impact of material, economic and structural influences in the operation of power/knowledge (Hall, 2001, p.78).

Knowledge about sexuality permeates all aspects of society, including social policy; informs all aspects of policy, practice and institutional welfare cultures; and constitutes welfare subjects, as the chapters in this book illustrate. In social policy, discourses of sexuality and welfare intersect to produce 'deserving' and 'undeserving' welfare subjects constituted on the basis of their acceptable or unacceptable sexualities – as with, for example, the married couple, the 'good' mother, same-sex parents, the cohabiting couple, or disabled partners/parents.

Foucault's approach is sometimes criticized because it has a tendency to treat people as passive victims of discourse rather than as active agents. By suggesting that discourses influence how we think and behave, we do not mean to imply that discourses are all powerful or that individuals are ineffectual in their midst. Rather, discourses are constantly contested and challenged through activism and individuals' practice of their daily lives. The approach adopted in this book is not to view individuals as passive recipients of the identities and subject positions set out for them by discourses, but to view them instead as subjects actively engaging with discourses either to transform them or to produce new ones. As the extracts at the beginning of this chapter and as later chapters show, dominant discourses of heterosexuality or homosexuality never fully reflect how individuals live and experience their sexual lives: 'Discourse can be both an instrument and effect of power [and] also a hindrance, a stumbling block, a point of resistance and a starting point for opposing strategy' (Foucault, 1990, p.101).

Discourses of homosexuality provide an example of what Foucault means. Individuals respond to homosexuality discourses, and being labelled as homosexual, in different ways. Some lesbians and gay men protect themselves from the discrimination and persecution associated with homosexuality through denial or by passing or living as heterosexual. Others actively resist negative discourses and instead claim homosexuality as a positive identity and as natural and normal. The Wolfenden reforms and 1967 Sexual Offences Act led to the development, not only of new discourses and a new name for homosexuality and lesbianism – 'gay' (Saraga, 1998) – but also to new resistances through the launching of the Gay Liberation Front in 1970. Gay liberation rejected the ideas of heterosexual normality and of homosexuality as perversion and disease. Instead, it asserted that being gay was a positive identity. This was epitomized by the slogan 'Glad to be gay'.

When individuals and groups take on a categorization as a positive identity, and in the process of claiming it for themselves redefine it, they challenge or resist the dominant meanings expressed in that discourse. Dominant discourses can also be used as points of resistance. For example, some lesbian and gay activists have embraced rather than opposed dominant discourses about 'sex as nature', arguing instead that it is unfair to discriminate against lesbians and gays on the basis of the sexuality with which they are born and over which they have no control. Such approaches can be criticized because they leave dominant meanings of heterosexuality relatively unchallenged, thereby perpetuating a discourse they are seeking to oppose. This approach also reinforces an essentialist idea of sexuality as universal, fixed and biological.

Figure 1.4

Discourses are never fixed. Some themes or aspects of them may persist, albeit in slightly different forms, as with the idea of heterosexuality as natural and normal. But if we were to look back as far as the middle of the twentieth century we would see that ideas about heterosexual relationships, marriage and the family have all changed (see Figure 1.4). In this way, discourses can also be said to be historically specific ways of speaking about a topic. Discourses function as sets of socially and historically constructed rules designating 'what is' and 'what is not'.

Read Extract 1.15 below, which is taken from *Protecting the Public: Strengthening Protection Against Sex Offenders and Reforming the Law on Sexual Offences* (Home Office, 2002). As you do so, make notes on:

■   the ways in which sexuality is 'put into discourse' or 'spoken of' – how it is constituted – in the extract;

■   the subject positions that are constituted in the text.

Extract 1.15   Protecting the public

Public protection, particularly of children and the most vulnerable, is this Government's priority ... sexual crime, particularly against children, can tear apart the very fabric of our society. It destroys lives and communities and challenges our most basic values.

...

... we are dealing with highly complicated and sensitive issues which test the balance between the role of Government and of the individual, and of their rights to determine their own behaviour, responsibility and duty of care.

...

I know we cannot hope to provide 100% safeguards and protection. Nor must we intervene in the personal, private relationships of consenting adults. ...

[David Blunkett, UK Home Secretary, in the Foreword to the document, p.5]

[From the main part of the document]

The need to reform the law on sexual offences

8   The law on sex offences, as it stands ... does not reflect the changes in society and social attitudes that have taken place since the Act became law and it is widely considered to be inadequate and out of date.

9   ... The law on sex offences needs to set out what is unacceptable behaviour and must provide penalties that reflect the seriousness of the crimes committed.

      ...

14   It is the role of the criminal law to establish what is and what is not acceptable behaviour; yet it must also treat everyone in society fairly. Certain existing offences criminalise consensual sexual activity in private between men, which would not be illegal between heterosexuals or between women. In order to provide common sense and make policing the law fair and practicable, these offences will be replaced with generic offences. This will ensure that the criminal law protects everyone equally from non-consensual sexual activity, but does not criminalise sexual activity that takes place between consenting adults in private.

15   ... There is a clear difference between private and public sexual activity. No-one wishes to be an unwilling witness to the sexual behaviour of others and everyone is entitled to be protected from it by the law. Sexual activity in public that offends, irrespective of whether the people engaging in the activity are heterosexual or homosexual, will remain criminal and will be dealt with by a new public order offence dealing with sexual behaviour in a public place.

(Home Office, 2002, pp.5, 9, 10)

COMMENT

Sexuality is constituted in this extract in a variety of ways. First, it is constituted through a series of distinctions which are made between acceptable and unacceptable, consensual and non-consensual, and private and public sex. These distinctions operate to constitute legal and therefore acceptable sex as between adults, consensual, negotiated, safe and responsible, involving a duty of care and as taking place in private. Unlike in previous sexual offences legislation, it is not solely heterosexual. In the 2002 proposals the reconstituted model of acceptable sex embraces consensual sex between men. Unacceptable, and therefore criminal, sex is constituted as a threat, dangerous and damaging to individuals, communities and society. It is non-consensual, violent and voyeuristic, an abuse of power, irresponsible, uncaring and public. Second, sexuality is constituted as complex, affected by social influences, subject to social change and as requiring 'sensitivity'.

Different subject positions are also constituted in the text – the rational, responsible, negotiating and caring adult, and the vulnerable child and adult in need of protection. The legislation imposes on individuals a legal duty to act responsibly and consensually. In the text, government is constituted as responsive to social change, as respecting individual privacy, as a guardian of fairness and as responsible for protecting individuals, communities and society from the dangerous aspects of sexuality.

Let us look again at discourse, power and knowledge. Foucault (1990, 1991) argues that power is constituted through discourses. Power is important in the construction of knowledge and what counts as knowledge. Knowledge both constitutes and is constituted through discourses as an effect of power. Foucault argued that many social theorists continue to base their understandings of power solely on a model which conceptualizes power as emanating from a central source such as the monarch or the state or a group of people who possess that power and exercise it in a 'top-down' fashion. Such power, referred to by Foucault as sovereign power, is final and ultimate, operating through laws and rules which carry with them the threat or practice of violence, torture or physical punishment, even death. However, Foucault also demonstrates, in both *The History of Sexuality* (1990) and *Discipline and Punish* (1991), that not all power is exercised or enforced through the threat of death or physical force. He outlines an alternative mechanism of power – disciplinary power – that operates and circulates at all levels of society and he identifies 'normalization' as one way in which disciplinary power is deployed.

6.2 Normalization

normalization   Through **normalization** individuals are compared and differentiated according
to norms. Normalizing judgement is not simply about comparing individuals in a
binary way – as in heterosexual/homosexual, good/bad, mad/sane or healthy/
ill. It is also a 'norm' all individuals are expected to aim for, work towards and
seek to achieve, and against which all are evaluated – 'good' and 'bad', healthy
and sick, 'sane' and 'mad', heterosexual and homosexual. The processes of
heteronormativity discussed in section 4.2 operate through normalization.
Heterosexuality is continuously established as the norm for sexuality through
normalization techniques – that is, through discourses that convey messages not
only about what *is* the established norm but also about what is *not*. In effect,
these discourses construct the norm.

Social policy can be said to perform a normalizing role in relation to sexuality
when it contributes to the defining and reaffirming of heterosexuality as it is
constituted at any specific moment as acceptable and appropriate sexuality. In
his notion of 'norm' Foucault did not conceive of power as being imposed by
one section, class or group of people on another. In social policy, power
operates not only through the knowledges and values that inform social policy,
but also at the level of policy-making and through the work of policy-makers,
researchers, welfare practitioners, professionals, institutions and welfare users.
It is a dynamic or technique of knowledge, practised and learnt, and dispersed
through various centres of practice and expertise. Both social policy and
sexuality can be understood as being such centres.

In a social policy context we suggest that normalization operates in three main
ways:

1   Normalization constitutes what is considered appropriate and acceptable
     sexuality.

2   It operates in a regulatory capacity through which not only is
     heterosexuality established and secured, but bodies and sexualities are also
     disciplined and controlled. This regulatory function operates *explicitly*
     through legislation and statutes which prescribe the boundaries of legal and
     illegal sex – as with, for example, the Sexual Offences Act 1967, age of
     sexual consent legislation or 'Protecting the Public' proposals. It also
     operates *implicitly*: first, through the assumptions that are made about
     heterosexuality as normal and natural and which underpin and inform
     social policy (as we saw in section 5); and, second, by linking notions of
     eligibility for welfare to ideas about appropriate and acceptable sexuality.
     For example, under the UK Beveridgean post-war welfare state
     normalization established ideal gendered and sexual roles for men and
     women (look again at Extract 1.4 in section 4.1). Embedded at the heart of
     the Beveridgean welfare state was the notion of the heterosexual married
     couple: the father/breadwinner male and the housewife mother/carer.
     Women's inactivity in the labour market and their dependency on men was
     assumed and they were expected to earn their 'right' to welfare through
     their husbands' contributions. Natural, normal and acceptable sexuality was
     typified by this model of heterosexuality, and both social policy and welfare

provision reflected this. Accordingly, lone mothers, homosexuality, cohabitation and divorce were variously castigated and abhorred as immoral, abnormal and unacceptable, resulting in partial or marginal inclusion and conditional eligibility for welfare benefits and services.

3   The normalization process produces differentiating effects and fragmented impacts which are in turn variously regulatory, penalizing or affirmative in respect to different groups. The following passage from Section 13(1) of the Human Fertilisation and Embryology Act 1990 provides an example of what we mean by this: 'A woman shall not be provided with [fertility] treatment unless account has been taken of the welfare of the child who may be born as a result of the treatment, including the need of that child for a father' (Department of Health, 1990). By conveying that a child needs both a mother and a father the Act asserts the norm of the heterosexual family. Normalization is operationalized through the insistence on the child's need for a father, thereby reinforcing the unacceptability of lone motherhood (heterosexual or lesbian). By implication, 'acceptable' mothers are those who are married or in a long-term, stable heterosexual relationship (anecdotal evidence suggests that some clinicians are excluding single and lesbian women from access to fertility treatment – Stuart, 2002, p.8). The effect of this is to constitute single women seeking fertility treatments from the NHS as less eligible for such treatments on the basis of not having a male partner. In addition, NHS-provided treatments are usually restricted in practice to women who are under 40 years of age and who are not disabled (Ham, 1992). You will come across further examples of the differentiating effects of the normalization process in Activity 1.7 below.

Normalization processes sometimes appear uneven and contradictory. As Extracts 1.6 and 1.11 and 1.12 in sections 4.1 and 4.3 illustrate, the normalizing process asserts married family life as the preferred ideal while simultaneously respecting the right of people not to marry and recognizing that 'strong and mutually supportive relationships [exist] outside marriage' (DfEE, 2000, pp.4–5). This further illustrates that the personal lives we live play a part in the forms social policy takes. Significantly, our personal lives can reshape as well as reflect the remit of social policy. In the early twenty-first century the UK welfare regime reflects, albeit unevenly, a reconstituted heterosexuality in which men are not necessarily breadwinners, women are more independent, and families more likely to be dual-earning in a changing social landscape where increasing numbers of couples live together outside of marriage, or are divorced. The normalization process therefore needs to be understood as one which is in a continual state of evolution or reconstitution. At one and the same time, normalization consistently establishes and asserts heterosexuality as the norm, while – as we have seen throughout this chapter – that which constitutes heterosexuality is itself in a continual state of flux and subject to transformation and redefinition. Such is the shifting nature of heterosexuality that it now embraces that which was once castigated and tolerates that which was abhorred.

The increased acceptance of homosexuality and of lesbian and gay relationships has resulted in the emergence of a different normalizing strategy which can best be summed up as the 'good gay, bad gay' syndrome. 'Acceptable' gays do not flaunt their sexuality and are in long-term, stable, monogamous relationships.

They are not 'in your face' raging queens or queers, who engage in unsafe sexual practices and who have many sexual partners. Smith (1994, p.207) argues that British legal and social policies 'differentiate *homosexualities* and *promote* a homosexuality of a very specific type – that of the "good homosexual" subject'.

There is not simply one norm of heterosexuality, but rather, heteronormativity operates as a series of 'norms within norms'. This is not to suggest, however, that all norms are equally applied or have similar effects. Normalization works in hierarchically coded ways which variously include or exclude, centre or marginalize individuals, as the cohabitation, homosexuality and lone motherhood examples in this and the previous sections show. However, as we mentioned in section 6.1, although discourses – and therefore normalizing strategies – might have regulatory intentions, they can be contested and thus may not necessarily result in successful or complete regulatory outcomes.

ACTIVITY 1.7

Read through Extract 1.16, on unmarried motherhood in the early part of the nineteenth century, and Extracts 1.17 and 1.18, on cohabitation in the latter part of the twentieth century. As you do so, identify within each:

- normalizing processes;
- constitutive processes: that is, the ways in which social policy constitutes welfare subjects through sexuality to produce 'sexualized' welfare subjects.

Think about the effects of these processes.

The 1834 New Poor Law: To put Extract 1.16 into context, the Poor Law Commissioners were unhappy that illegitimacy was rising, leading to increased demands for poor relief. They believed that existing legislation was ineffectual in stopping illegitimacy and in ensuring that parents supported their illegitimate offspring. Furthermore, they believed that the bastardy laws and poor relief provision were significant in encouraging women to have illegitimate children.

Extract 1.16   The New Poor Law view

[It was argued that unmarried mothers were:]

defrauding of the relief of the impotent and aged, *true poor of the same parish*

...

continued illicit intercourse has, in almost all cases, originated with the females.

...

The allowance made to the mother for the support of her child, *and secured to her by the parish in the case of the putative father failing to pay the amount awarded,* is an encouragement to the offence; it places such women in a better situation than many married women.

...

the female in these cases is generally the party to blame; and that any remedy, to be effectual, must act chiefly with reference to her.

...

An unmarried mother has voluntarily put herself into the situation of a widow: she has voluntarily become a mother, without procuring for herself and her child the assistance of a husband and father. There can be no reason for giving to vice privileges which we deny to misfortune.

(Reports of His Majesty's Commissioners on the Administration and Practical Operation of the Poor Laws, 1834/1974, Main Report, vol.8, p.92, 94, 95, 97, 196, 198)

Extract 1.17   The Commission's view

The effect of these provisions ... [is that] a woman who is cohabiting cannot ... claim benefit in her own right and therefore is debarred from receiving benefit if the man is in full-time work.

...

It would not be right, and we believe public opinion would not accept, that the unmarried 'wife' should be able to claim benefit denied to a married woman because her husband was in full-time work. We express no opinion about whether this would be an encouragement to immorality. But it could certainly be attacked as a discouragement to marriage, as indeed in many cases it would be, since the couple would be better off on supplementary benefit than if they were married.

(Supplementary Benefits Commission, 1971, pp.2, 3)

Extract 1.18   The woman's view

The second major, and larger and more sensitive, problem of investigating means and establishing entitlement was the N.A.B.'s [National Assistance Board's] concern that the mother should not be cohabiting. An officer finding evidence of cohabitation or even strongly suspecting cohabitation could stop the mother's allowance, and, as the Board said, many women who were suspected of cohabiting voluntarily surrendered their allowances ...

...

That B – [NAB officer], he's a nasty sod he is. He's like a detective. He knocks at your door and he's looking at your line at the same time to see you're not doing any men's washing, and all the time he's in here looking under the sofas to see there's nothing there, no men's shoes or nothing.

...

They were really horrible. First one man came round, then another, saying, 'Do you sleep with Mr Barnes? Are you committing adultery with him?' And I

> told him it's my own private business, but the man says, 'You *can't* tell me that a man and a woman living in the same house don't go to bed together,' and I told him that's dirty talk and I don't like it at all.
>
> (Marsden, 1973, pp.252, 255–6)

COMMENT

In these, albeit very brief, extracts we can begin to identify the operation of a process of normalization in which individuals are contrasted, compared and differentiated between according to a desired norm. In the case of the New Poor Law, unmarried mothers are constituted as falling outside the norm of married motherhood. They were compared to other recipients of relief, such as widows and older people, and were found to be less deserving because they were unmarried. Widows and older people had, in the eyes of the Commissioners, an unquestioned and earned right to relief. Unmarried mothers, on the other hand, were described as 'defrauding of the relief of the impotent and aged, *true poor of the same parish*'. Not only did unmarried mothers receive benefits to which they had not earned the right (through marriage), they earned them though illicit intercourse. Widows earned their unquestionable right to relief by virtue of being married. After all, the 'unmarried mother has voluntarily put herself into the situation of a widow: she has voluntarily become a mother, without procuring for herself and her child the assistance of a husband and father'.

In the Poor Law Reports, whose stated aim is with the relief of poverty, unmarried mothers are discursively constituted as sexually immoral and to blame for illegitimacy. This normalization device of comparing unmarried mothers with others, judging them less eligible and as undeserving of poor relief due to immoral behaviour and the lack of a husband, had regulatory effects and was employed to stigmatize unmarried mothers as a group. Their eligibility for relief was in this way determined on the basis of their sexuality – 'There can be no reason to give to vice privileges which we deny misfortune.' In practice, after 1834 this meant that unmarried mothers were given poor relief but only through the workhouse where they were subjected to punitive practices and hard physical labour (Poor Law Commission, 1840–1851/1970; Webb and Webb, 1910, p.43). By constituting unmarried mothers as immoral and therefore as undeserving, a norm of acceptable moral sexuality and parenthood was simultaneously established and asserted. This illustrates the way in which ideas about acceptable sexuality as married sexuality can be seen to inform and influence access and eligibility to welfare. The 1834 New Poor Law – a policy introduced to deal with poverty and its relief – also spoke of sexuality. In the pages dealing with illegitimacy it was both influenced by and contributed to ideas about what constituted acceptable and appropriate sexuality at the beginning of the nineteenth century (see Carabine, 2001).

In Extracts 1.17 and 1.18 the process is similar. The ruling assumes (as do the benefit officials applying it) that, if a man and a woman live together in the same accommodation, they will be having a sexual relationship. It also assumes, drawing on a male breadwinner–dependent female carer norm of heterosexuality, that, if a man and woman are cohabiting, the man will be supporting the woman financially. In the *Report on Cohabitation* from which some of these extracts are taken (Supplementary Benefits Commission, 1971), the concern is not to provide benefits so as to reward the cohabiting couple in ways that would place them in a better situation than a married couple, or in ways that would act as a disincentive to marriage. Not only does the cohabitation rule reinforce women's economic dependency on men, it also reaffirms the centrality of heterosexuality and marriage as the norm. Further, in several of the accounts the women are constituted as attempting to 'cheat' the system by trying to get something for nothing. Implicit in this is a set of assumptions, prominent at the time the report was written, about single women and sex and sex within marriage, as the following quotation from Wilson illustrates: '[the cohabitation ruling] embodies in slightly more glaring form the innermost assumption of marriage which is still that a man should pay for the sexual and housekeeping services of his wife. We are so accustomed to this that it seems natural within marriage' (Wilson, 1977, p.81). In the extracts the single women are constituted as sexually active irrespective of whether they in fact are. Policy-makers often dismiss the decisions of welfare subjects about how they live their personal lives – their economic, moral and sexual rationalities – as inferior, flawed or as lacking moral integrity, preferring instead to impose their own set of moral values and practices. The ruling legitimated practices that entailed very detailed scrutiny of the women's personal and intimate lives. The women in the extracts were deemed less eligible for supplementary benefits on the basis of their assumed sexuality, even those suspected of cohabiting risked losing their benefit.

Foucault's proposition that discourses are 'practices which form the objects of which they speak' (Foucault, 1972, p.49) operates in the social policy/sexuality relationship in different but related ways. At one level, welfare and social policy – through the discourses and discursive practices they promulgate – can be said to play a constitutive role in producing welfare subjects, as in the universal heterosexual, the unmarried mother, the sexually active teenager, the homosexual, and disabled people. All of us – heterosexual or otherwise – are affected by assumptions about sexuality, sexual relations and practices that are contained in social policies and inform welfare practice. Social policies and practices convey messages about what is acceptable and appropriate (hetero) sexuality as well as what are considered inappropriate and unacceptable sexual practices and relationships – which materially affect our personal experiences of welfare.

7   Conclusion

In this chapter we have shown:

- the significance of sexuality to our personal lives and for how social policy is constituted, analysed and practised (sections 2, 5 and 6);

- that the various sites of welfare shape, constrain, inhibit personal autonomy and identity; and regulate/police or permit particular forms of sexual relations;

- that certain forms of heterosexuality have come to occupy a position of 'normal' through heteronormative processes (section 4);

- that what counts as sexual and sexuality is socially constructed (section 2);

- that normative constructions of sexuality as heterosexual are institutionalized through legal and social policies and social practices, and that assumptions about sexuality as heterosexual pervade social policy (section 4);

- that not only are sexuality and social policy mutually constitutive, but sexuality is itself a central feature in the mutual constitution of personal lives and social policy (sections 5 and 6).

In this chapter we have explored the place of sexuality both in our personal lives and in social policy, and the relationship between the two. Section 2 focused on how sexuality has come to be constructed through *essentialist* ideas as central to our sense of self and, more generally, that what counts as sexuality is itself a social, historical and cultural construction. We have seen, too, in section 4 that, although we may think of our sexuality as personal and private, it is anything but that and is instead subject to a range of social policy and welfare interventions and is regulated and legitimated in laws and social policies which stipulate both what is and is not acceptable and legal sexual practices and relationships. What counts as acceptable sexuality is influenced by dominant constructions of normal sex as heterosexual. The idea of *heterosexuality* as normal and universal is *institutionalized* and privileged in a range of social institutions and practices and permeates expert and professional knowledges and everyday beliefs. The institutionalizing of heterosexuality operates as part of a normalizing strategy through which we are all evaluated. It is our fit with the ideal of the married heterosexual couple and family that influences how we will be treated within social policy and by welfare practitioners and bureaucrats.

In the process of institutionalizing heterosexuality and in constituting it as natural and normal a whole set of universalizing discourses and practices are called upon about gender, whiteness and able-bodiedness: a process we have referred to as *heteronormativity*. We identified *difference* as central to this process. Difference, and particularly *gender* difference, is crucial to definitions of sexuality. Differences are constructed through a series of *oppositional binaries* in which one pole is usually constructed as the dominant one and the other as inferior – as with *heterosexual*/homosexual, *male*/female, *white*/black and *masculinity*/femininity. It is through heteronormativity that heterosexuality discourses intersect and interact with other discourses of difference to produce racialized, gendered, able or disabled and classed sexual subjects. These differences serve as the basis for determining rights and recognition, interventions and affirmations, exclusions and inclusions and entitlements and obligations as the chapters that follow demonstrate with their focus on gender and class (Chapter 2), gender and youth transitions (Chapter 3) and disability (Chapter 4).

It is not only sexuality that is socially constructed, but so too is the public and the private. Viewed through the lens of sexuality the *private/public divide* becomes more fluid and unstable. This idea that the relationship between the public and the private is reconfigured is developed further in the remaining chapters in the book, which demonstrate some of the ways in which the boundaries between the public and the private are blurred, breached, contested and transformed. Each points to some of the ways in which the public/private divide operates as a dynamic of power that regulates sexual relationships and practices.

In section 6 we sought to explain the personal lives, sexualities and social policy relationship through a Foucauldian post-structuralist perspective. Through the application of Foucault's concepts of *discourse, power* and *knowledge* we have argued that social policy, both as an academic discipline and as a practice, is influenced by normative discourses of sexuality with the effect that heterosexuality is assumed as the norm and welfare subjects are subjected to *normalization* processes and constituted as heterosexual which they may embrace, resist or adapt at different points in their lives. As the chapters that follow demonstrate, this is a mutually constitutive relationship in which normative ideas about sexuality constitute sexuality and whereby sexuality is itself also (in part) produced through the norms embedded in social policies and welfare practice.

Some of the chapters that follow also draw upon a post-structuralist perspective (Chapter 4 on disability) or use it in conjunction with a feminist theoretical approach (Chapter 3 on youth transitions). Chapter 2 utilizes a feminist historical theoretical perspective in its focus on fertility decline and birth control. What all the chapters have in common is a concern with taking a specific topic – fertility decline, youth transitions and disability – and exploring how normative assumptions about sexualities impact upon personal lives at the intersections of social policy discourses and practices, as well as assessing the extent to which individuals' sexual experiences and relationships are reflected in and represented by social policy.

Further resources

If you want to pursue some of the issues or topics discussed in this chapter in more detail or from a different perspective you could look at: Jeffrey Weeks's *Sex, Politics and Society* (1989) which provides a broad historical overview of the regulation of sexuality since 1800. In a related way, Frank Mort's *Dangerous Sexualities* (1987) applies a Foucauldian analysis to illustrate how ideas about health and disease are linked to notions of acceptable and unacceptable sexualities. For a clear introduction to the different theoretical approaches to studying sexuality and gender, together with an appraisal of the contemporary debates affecting sexuality and sexual politics, you could read Richard Dunphy's *Sexual Politics* (2000). Still on theories of sexuality see also Joseph Bristow's *Sexuality* (1997) for a more detailed introduction. For a more detailed critique of the relationship between sexuality and social policy see Jean Carabine's 'Heterosexuality and social policy' (1996b) and for a more detailed working of the normalizing and constitutive processes see 'Constituting sexuality through social policy: the case of lone motherhood 1834 and today' (2001), also by her. Sara Mills's *Discourse* (1997) provides an accessible analysis of Foucault's use of discourse.

References

Ball, S. (1896) 'The moral aspects of socialism', *Fabian Tract No. 69* in Steadman-Jones (1971).

Beck, U. (1992) *Risk Society: Towards a New Modernity*, London, Sage.

Bell, D. and Binnie, J. (2000) *The Sexual Citizen: Queer Politics and Beyond*, Cambridge, Polity Press.

Beveridge, W. (1942) *Social Insurance and Allied Services* (The Beveridge Report), Cmnd 6404, London, HMSO.

Brah, A. (1996) *Cartographies of Diaspora*, London, Routledge.

Bristow, J. (1997) *Sexuality*, London, Routledge

Brown, H.C. (1998) *Social Work and Sexuality*, London, Macmillan/British Association of Social Work.

Bryson, L. (1992) *Welfare and the State*, Basingstoke, Macmillan.

Cahill, M. (1994) *The New Social Policy*, Oxford, Blackwell.

Carabine, J. (1996a) 'A straight playing field or queering the pitch? Centring sexuality in social policy', *Feminist Review*, no.54, pp.31–64.

Carabine, J. (1996b) 'Heterosexuality and social policy' in Richardson, D. (ed.) *Theorising Heterosexuality*, Buckingham, Open University Press.

Carabine, J. (2001) 'Constituting sexuality through social policy: the case of lone motherhood 1834 and today', *Social and Legal Studies*, vol.10, no.3, pp.291–314.

Collier, R. (1999) 'Men, masculinity and the changing family: (re)constructing fatherhood in law and social policy', in Jagger, G. and Wright, C. (eds) *Changing Family Values*, London, Routledge.

Coote, A. and Pattullo, P. (1990) *Power and Prejudice: Women and Politics*, London, Weidenfeld and Nicolson.

Department for Work and Pensions (2003) *Carer's Allowance Claim Form* (DS700), http//www.dwp.gov.uk/lifeevent/benefits/carers_allowance (accessed 22 July 2003).

Department of Health (1990) *Human Fertilisation and Embryology Act 1990*, London, The Stationery Office.

Department of the Environment (1988) *The Local Government Act 1988*, London, HMSO.

DfEE (Department for Education and Employment) (2000) *Sex and Relationship Education Guidance*, DfEE Ref 0116/2000, Nottingham, DfEE Publications.

Dunphy, R. (2000) *Sexual Politics: An Introduction*, Edinburgh, Edinburgh University Press.

Fergusson, R. (2004) 'Connecting welfare and work' in Mooney, G. (ed.) *Work: Personal Lives and Social Policy*, Bristol, The Policy Press in association with The Open University.

Foucault, M. (1972) *Archaeology of Knowledge* (trans. A. Sheridan), London, Tavistock. (First published in 1969.)

Foucault, M. (1990) *The History of Sexuality, Volume 1: An Introduction* (trans. R. Hurley), New York, Vintage Books. (First published in 1976.)

Foucault, M. (1991) *Discipline and Punish: The Birth of the Prison* (trans. A. Sheridan), London, Penguin. (First published in 1977.)

Giddens, A. (1991) *Modernity and Self-Identity: Self and Society in the Late Modern Age*, Cambridge, Polity Press.

Glennerster, H. (2000) *British Social Policy Since 1945* (2nd edn), Oxford, Blackwell.

Grant, L. (2002) *Still Here*, London, Little, Brown.

Hall, S. (2001) 'Foucault: power, knowledge and discourse' in Wetherell, M., Taylor, S. and Yates, S.J. (eds) *Discourse Theory and Practice*, London, Sage.

Ham, C. (1992) *Health Policy in Britain* (3rd edn), Basingstoke, Macmillan.

Hill, M. (1993) *Understanding Social Policy* (4th edn), Oxford, Blackwell.

Home Office (1998) *Supporting Families: A Consultative Document* (10/98), London, Home Office.

Home Office (2002) *Protecting the Public: Strengthening Protection Against Sex Offenders and Reforming the Law on Sexual Offences*, Cm 5668, London, Home Office.

Hubbard, P. (2001) 'Sex zones: intimacy, citizenship and public space', *Sexualities*, vol.4, no.1, pp.51–64.

Jacobs, S. (1985) 'Race, empire and the welfare state: council housing and racism', *Critical Social Policy*, issue13, Summer, pp.6–28.

Jamieson, L. (1998) *Intimacy: Personal Relationships in Modern Societies*, Cambridge, Polity Press.

Johnson, C. (2002) 'Heteronormative citizenship and the politics of passing', *Sexualities*, vol.5, no.3, pp.317–36.

Keirnan, K., Land, H. and Lewis, J. (1998) *Lone Motherhood in Twentieth Century Britain*, Oxford, Clarendon Press.

Langley, J. (2001) 'Developing anti-oppressive empowering social work practice with older lesbian and gay women and men', *British Journal of Social Work*, vol.31, pp.917–32.

Lord Irvine of Laing, The Lord Chancellor (1999) Speech to UK Family Law Conference, London, Inner Temple, 25 June, www.open.gov.uk/led/speeches/1999/25-6-99.htm (accessed 24 February 2000).

Marsden, D. (1973) *Mothers Alone: Poverty and the Fatherless Family* (revised edn), Harmondsworth, Penguin.

Mills, S. (1997) *Discourse*, London, Routledge.

Mort, F. (1987) *Dangerous Sexualities: Medico-Moral Politics in England Since 1830*, London, Routledge, Kegan and Paul.

National Family and Parenting Institute (2001) *Is It Legal? A Parents' Guide to the Law*, London, National Family and Parenting Institute.

Neiman, S. (2002) *Sexuality, Cancer and Palliative Care: Researching Perceptions and Practice of Social Work Staff in a Central London Hospital*, Norwich, Social Work and Psychosocial Studies Monographs, University of East Anglia.

O'Brien, M. and Penna, S. (1998) *Theorising Welfare: Enlightenment and Modern Society*, London, Sage.

O'Donnell, K. (1999) 'Lesbian and gay families: legal perspectives' in Jagger, G. and Wright, C. (eds) *Changing Family Values*, London, Routledge.

Parmar, P. (1982) 'Gender, race and class: Asian women in resistance' in *The Empire Strikes Back*, London, Hutchinson/Centre for Contemporary Cultural Studies.

Pinker, R. (1971) *Social Theory and Social Policy*, London, Heinemann.

Plummer, K. (1975) *Sexual Stigma: An Interactionist Account*, London, Routledge and Kegan Paul.

Poor Law Commission (1840–1851/1970) *Official Circulars of Public Documents and Information,* Vols VII–X, New York, Kelley.

Reports of His Majesty's Commissioners on the Administration and Practical Operation of the Poor Laws with Appendices, Parts I, II, and III Reports from the Assistant Commissioners (1834/1974) Shannon, Irish University Press.

Rice, M. (2002) 'Happy families', *Observer Magazine*, 14 July.

Richardson, D. (1996) 'Heterosexuality and social theory' in Richardson, D. (ed.) *Theorising Heterosexuality*, Buckingham, Open University Press.

Rose, N. (1999) *Powers of Freedom: Reframing Political Thought*, Cambridge, Cambridge University Press.

Saraga, E. (ed.) (1998) *Embodying the Social: Constructions of Difference*, London, Routledge in association with The Open University.

Saulinier, F.C. (2002) 'Deciding who to see: lesbians discuss their preferences in health and mental health care providers', *Social Work*, vol.47, no.4, pp.355–65.

Scrutton, S. (1992) *Ageing, Healthy and in Control*, London, Chapman and Hall.

Smith, A.M. (1994) *New Right Discourse on Race and Sexuality,* Cambridge, Cambridge University Press.

Steadman-Jones, G. (1971) *Outcast London: A Study in the Relationship Between Classes in Victorian Society*, Oxford, Clarendon Press.

Stoller, R. (1985) *Observing the Erotic Imagination*, New Haven, CT, Yale University Press.

Stuart, J. (2002) 'Families: who needs a man?', *The Independent*, 23 September, pp.8–9.

Supplementary Benefits Commission (1971) *Cohabitation: The Administration of the Relevant Provisions of the Ministry of Social Security Act 1966*, London, HMSO.

Taylor-Gooby, P. (1991) *Social Change, Social Welfare and Social Science*, Hemel Hempstead, Harvester Wheatsheaf.

Taylor-Gooby, P. and Dale, J. (1981) *Social Theory and Social Welfare*, London, Edward Arnold.

Titmuss, R. (1958) *Essays on the Welfare State*, London, Allen and Unwin.

Webb, S. and Webb, B. (1910) *English Poor Law Policy*, London, Longmans, Green and Co.

Weeks, J. (1986) *Sexuality*, London, Routledge.

Weeks, J. (1989) *Sex, Politics and Society: The Regulation of Sexuality Since 1800* (2nd edn), London, Longman.

Williams, C. (2002) *Sugar & Slate*, Aberystwyth, Planet.

Williams, F. (1989) *Social Policy: A Critical Introduction*, Cambridge, Polity Press.

Williams, F. (1992) 'Somewhere over the rainbow: universality and diversity in social policy' in Manning, N. and Page, R. (eds) *Social Policy Review Vol. 4*, University of Kent at Canterbury, Social Policy Association.

Wilson, E. (1977) *Women and the Welfare State*, London, Longman.

Wolfenden, J. (1957) *Report of the Departmental Committee on Homosexual Offences and Prostitution* (The Wolfenden Report), Cmnd 247, London, HMSO.

CHAPTER 2

Sexuality, Parenthood and Population: Explaining Fertility Decline in Britain from the 1860s to 1920s

by Megan Doolittle

Contents

1   Introduction

Sexuality and parenthood encompass some of the most ordinary and yet most profound experiences that life has to offer. Until recently these two domains were intricately linked, and the idea that it is possible and desirable to have sex solely for pleasure without risk of pregnancy or having children is a relatively new one. This split between sexuality and parenthood has come about through a myriad of interlinking social changes, including shifting social relations and attitudes to sexuality, and widening access to reliable contraception and legal abortion.

In this chapter we look back at a time when sexual practices leading to conception were the norm, when the risk of pregnancy was an integral part of heterosexual sexualities, and when heterosexual sexuality and parenthood were inextricably connected. We will examine these interrelationships through the phenomenon known as the fertility decline, when couples in increasingly significant numbers deliberately began to limit the number of children in their families. In Britain, fertility decline occurred roughly between 1860 and 1930 – a span which includes the middle and end of the Victorian period (1860–1900), the Edwardian period (1900–1914), the First World War (1914–1918) and the 1920s. We will focus on the British experience, although a similar phenomenon has been noted in many other parts of the world. Fertility decline, also known as the demographic transition, is characterized by a shift from a 'traditional' norm of large families and high mortality rates to the 'modern' trend of small families and low mortality rates. While there were long-established continuities in patterns of sexuality and parenthood, evidence of declining fertility indicates that something fundamentally new was happening between 1860 and 1930. At the heart of this change lay millions of everyday negotiations (both spoken and silent) by couples concerning their sexual activities, the conception of children and parenthood.

In Britain today control over fertility is largely taken for granted and becoming a parent is seen as a decision that has little to do with sexuality. By looking at the demographic transition, we can trace the changes that led to this disconnection through the attempts of many people to determine the kind of parents they wanted to become through deliberate changes to their sexual practices and relationships. Because fertility decline gave rise to significant debates in social policy, it provides an opportunity to explore the relationships between social policy and personal lives through the lens of procreative sexuality and parenthood.

Very little is known about the history of sexuality within marriage. It was only with twentieth-century surveys such as The Kinsey Report, published under the title *Sexual Behaviour in the Human Male* (Kinsey et al., 1948), that sexual practices across broad spectrums of populations were investigated. For the nineteenth and early twentieth centuries, evidence about normative sexuality is very difficult to locate and interpret. However, the one indication that heterosexual sexual practices were undergoing significant changes at this time was that the average number of children being born in each family was declining.

Aims   In this chapter we will explore these themes and topics drawing upon a feminist
        theoretical perspective which places gender divisions and constructions of
        heterosexuality at the centre of its analysis. Class, ethnicity and other divisions
        are also integral to social policy and personal lives, sexuality and parenthood,
        and they will be explored to some extent. However, it is inequalities of gender
        that are highlighted and developed most fully. This chapter aims to:

fertility decline
- Use a feminist historical approach to critically examine theories about how
  and why **fertility decline** in Britain occurred and to explore the
  importance of gender and power in reshaping parenthood and sexuality in
  social policy and personal lives.

procreative
sexuality
- Use histories of marriage, sexuality, parenthood, birth control and
  population policy to illuminate the connections between **procreative
  sexuality**, personal lives and social policy in particular those relating to
  fertility decline in Britain between the 1860s and the 1920s.

- Focus on parenthood and sexuality within marriage as the unmarked
  category, the norm against which other sexualities and parenthoods are
  defined.

- Demonstrate the use of a historical approach to explore the specificities of a
  particular time and place in the past in order to illuminate processes of social
  change.

<hr>

ACTIVITY 2.1

Pause for a moment and imagine what being a parent might have been like in late
nineteenth and early twentieth-century Britain. Your images and ideas about families in
the past may come from television dramas, for example, or historical novels or films.
Perhaps you have researched your family tree or studied some history in school or
university.

- What do you think would be different from being a parent today?

- What do you think might be similar?

- What influences might social divisions have, such as class, ethnicity, age or gender?

Keep these questions in mind as you read the rest of the chapter to see if your ideas are
confirmed or contradicted by the historical evidence we will be examining.

<hr>

1.1   Defining parenthood

As a starting point, we need to distinguish parenthood from parenting.
parenthood   **Parenthood** is more about the role, social status and meanings associated with
being a parent, of bringing children into the world, and having children to look
parenting   after. **Parenting**, on the other hand, is associated with the activities of looking
after children and raising them to adulthood. Parenting can be undertaken by a
range of people; a man, a woman, a relative or an unrelated carer. It implies a
sustained *process* of care for children, but not necessarily a permanent
relationship. Parenthood is closely associated with responsibilities for offspring

with whom someone has what is often called a 'blood tie'. In defining parenthood in a legal context, Andrew Bainham (1999) identifies it as the *status* held by a child's genetic father and mother. There are important prefixes which can be attached to parenthood – step-parent, adopted parent, foster parent – indicating that these statuses and roles are not exactly equivalent to parenthood on its own and accordingly that there are significant differences between the meanings attached to social and genetic parenthood. Furthermore, the degree to which genetic parenthood is considered to be a fundamental element of parenting has varied according to class, ethnicity and other social differences (Ribbens McCarthy et al., 2000). Although parenthood and parenting are closely interrelated, in this chapter we will not be attempting to explore how people did their parenting or what it meant to them, but rather we look at how the role and status of parenthood were perceived and experienced.

Just as sexuality is a fundamentally gendered concept (see Chapter 1), parenthood is not gender neutral. If we think about the difference between the meanings of 'to mother' a child and 'to father' one, we can see that there are crucial gender differences between the meanings of motherhood and fatherhood (Holden, 1996). These differences can be hidden when 'parenthood' is invoked in an uncritical way. We will explore some of these gender differences in the following section.

1.2   Sexuality and parenthood

In this chapter sexuality is used to refer to heterosexual reproductive sex, relationships and relations, and the meanings and discursive constructions which are associated with these. Sexual practices resulting in conception and the experience of parenthood are among the few remaining areas that are considered a 'natural' part of human existence. Just as sexuality has been seen as a 'natural', elemental drive in human identity, parenthood has also been closely associated with the 'natural', even animal, instinct to reproduce. This is in sharp contrast to those sexualities that are seen as 'unnatural', 'deviant' or 'exceptional', which as we have seen in Chapter 1 have been the primary subjects of the 'science' of sexuality. In this chapter we focus instead on the 'unmarked category' of procreative sexuality and parenthood located within marriage. This is where the normative and usually unexamined performance of sexuality and parenthood took place, and against which 'deviant' or 'other' sexualities and parents were measured.

In the late nineteenth and early twentieth centuries, parenthood was the usual consequence of procreative sex and was an ever present possibility in the personal lives of sexually active, fertile heterosexual couples. As we shall see in section 2, parenthood was increasingly confined within a particular construction of marriage and family, which included assumptions based on **heterosexuality** and monogamous sexual practices of husbands and wives. According to Weeks, during the many centuries of Judaeo-Christian dominance, parenthood was the only justification for sexual relations (Weeks, 1986). Thus procreation, the generation or production of a child, was seen as a central purpose of both marriage and sexuality within it, and as such constituted as a key element of what we might refer to as **heteronormative relations** as they were constructed

heterosexuality

heteronormative
relations

at that time (see Chapter 1). Within this norm of procreative sexuality, there were debates about the role of sexual pleasure in marriage between those who argued that procreation was its sole purpose and those who held that sexual pleasure without a reproductive purpose was a legitimate part of married life. Consequently the meanings attached to sexuality within marriage were constructed around a narrow set of parameters with procreation at its heart.

Although historical evidence about heteronormative sexuality is sparse, it is clear that there were great diversities of experience despite the dominance of monogamous marriage between 1860 and 1930. Sexual relationships are never entirely contained within marriage, and neither is sexual activity within marriage always understood as procreative. Within marriage, procreative sex might be performed by a couple who are not solely heterosexual. After all Oscar Wilde, an iconic gay figure of our historical period, was married and fathered children. However, very few people, including policy-makers, would have used the word 'heterosexual' to describe themselves at the time. The terms 'heterosexual' and 'homosexual' were both first used in 1869 (Katz, 1990). The terms were subsequently taken up in medical and scientific discourses in the early twentieth century. Katz argues that the term 'heterosexual' was only coined to define the norm of a sexual partnership between a man and a woman against which 'homosexuality' could be distinguished. As such, heterosexuality remained largely unexamined in scientific discourse.

In the late nineteenth and early twentieth centuries, differences between masculine and feminine sexualities were considered to be particularly acute, closely associated with what were understood as biological differences in procreation. Men were portrayed as sexually and procreatively active, with women in an opposite, complementary, passive role. The biological processes of conception were not well understood at this time and the underlying assumption was that men provided the active element for new life contained within their sperm, while women were the passive nurturers of an embryo implanted by the man. This mirrored the common beliefs of the time of men as the active initiators of sex and male sexuality as a powerful, even destructive natural force, which had to be tamed by civilization and rationality, particularly through the responsibilities of parenthood. We can see these tensions expressed in Henri-Frederic Amiel's advice to men in 1850: 'in his relationship with the female sex, a man it seems to me, becomes a complete human being only when the angel and the animal blend into each other' (quoted in Gay, 1984, p.123).

It was widely believed that women did not normally experience sexual feelings at all. It was very different in the medieval (c.1100–1400) and early modern periods (c.1500–1800) when female sexuality was often shown as highly active, even predatory, and marriage was understood as a crucial means of controlling female sexual energies. Victorian and Edwardian women on the other hand were meant to be protected from what were seen to be the bestial and earthy aspects of life which included most matters of a sexual nature. Women were expected to experience their deepest personal satisfactions through motherhood, and to embody the higher (that is desexualized) feelings of a more civilized world.

1.3   Sexuality, parenthood and social policy

Just as procreative sexuality within marriage has rarely been the focus of historical research, as a social phenomenon it has also been viewed as inherently unproblematic in terms of social policy. Unlike today, there was very little explicit legislation or public policy that directly addressed the 'private' sphere of marriage and family during the fertility decline. However, there were a number of broad social policy formations that made assumptions and reinforced dominant messages about normative constructions of sexuality, procreation and parenthood (see Chapter 1). The reproduction of the population was a key focus for such policy formations; religious leaders, doctors, scientists, philanthropists and political movements constantly revisited this issue. The ability of the nation to produce an adequate population to provide labour for industry and the armed forces as the British Empire extended its influence became a matter of acute concern. The health of the population was also constantly evoked through fears about sexuality outside marriage (as we shall see in section 3.3), an important area of contestation in social policy. The policy frameworks of marriage and family that underpinned population questions were increasingly re-examined, both by policy-makers seeking to support heteronormativity, and radicals who were critical of normative sexualities and gender inequalities.

The dominant liberal conception of social policy which became largely (but never completely) hegemonic by the 1860s was based on the state acting as a regulator rather than a provider of services, not only in the area of welfare, but in a wide range of social and economic contexts. Family, sexuality and personal lives were seen as occupying an entirely different realm from the state, having little or no connection to policy. However, from the 1880's, there was an ideological shift and the state began to be seen as an appropriate vehicle for improving and regulating family life. A number of factors have been identified in this shift including the great social surveys of Charles Booth (1896–1902) and Joseph Rowntree (1899), which exposed that an alarmingly large proportion of the population – about thirty per cent – were living in poverty despite an overall rise in living standards. Local government was expanding, providing new services to families and households such as clean water, electricity and hospitals. The increasing involvement of women in local government, education authorities and the Poor Law brought more attention to the appalling domestic conditions suffered by many wives and mothers (for example, Llewelyn Davis, 1977). The poor physical condition of recruits during the Boer War (1899–1902) became a national scandal, drawing attention to widespread fears about the ability of the nation to produce a healthy working and fighting population. Finally, by the turn of the century there were more political figures who believed that the state (whether national or local) was not only an acceptable but also more efficient and equitable welfare provider. Within this expansion of what was deemed to be legitimate terrain for social policy, measures to regulate, ameliorate and reform the role of parents, particularly mothers, were increasingly proposed as solutions to population concerns.

1.4   The personal

The close relationship between parenthood and sexuality illustrates the importance of the personal in social policy in a number of ways. First, it shows that the growing interest in procreation, sexuality and parenthood by policy-makers was never a one-way process whereby policy was simply imposed on people. Rather, individuals who set new terms for their experience of parenthood through changes in procreative sexuality were also helping to shape the policy formations within which they found themselves. While people sometimes conformed to current conventions and regulations and thus reinforced definitions of what was normal and acceptable, at other times they subverted policy intentions or directly challenged existing policy parameters. We will explore this two-way process by which policy and personal lives intersected and constituted each other later in this chapter.

Second, parenthood and sexuality are both domains which can be seen as closely linked to the production of individual identity as the other chapters in this book show. Parenthood is a life-changing event for mothers and fathers, both now and during the historical period under review. However, the subsequent ways in which parenthood becomes part of one's identity and the roles and qualities with which it is associated are complex and diverse. As we see in section 3, forms of parenthood were being shaped by changes to sexual practices aimed at restricting family size. These changes were played out in the lives of individual parents and their children. By the 1920s being a caring parent came to mean one who focused on the needs of each individual child, enhancing each of their life chances, in contrast to parents of previous generations who saw themselves as producing as many children as possible to give the family as a whole the best chances for survival and prosperity. The arrival of children had also been seen as beyond human control, determined by fate or God's will. The biological processes of conception were not widely understood nor seen as particularly relevant. We can see these two views expressed by women who had children in the 1920s in two interviews by Diana Gittins (1982):

Q: Did you want to have lots of children?

1:   Oh we never even really thought about it. It just happened. I guess, and we loved them and that was it (p.148).

2:   Two was enough to – to bring them up as we'd like to. You know, in the ordinary way, so that they didn't go short of anything – and we'd do what we could for them ... I said, 'Two,' I said, 'and give 'em a good education if we can' (p.152).

Fears about the personal consequences of having large numbers of children combined with increasing knowledge about adapting sexual practices to restrict fertility, created opportunities for couples to have fewer children.

Third, both parenthood and sexual relationships can also be seen as constitutive of adulthood and a marker of adult identity for both men and women. For men the onset of fatherhood confirmed virility both sexually and reproductively, together with the arrival of adult responsibilities. For women it signified an entry into a desexualized and idealized maternal identity. A first pregnancy as the visible evidence of sexuality was, in Victorian and Edwardian times, often an uncomfortable transition for women, the subject of jokes, anxieties and concealment, foreshadowing an identity as mother, an ambiguous adult identity which could never be as fully independent as a man's.

Finally, we can also see the personal through the web of emotional connections between spouses, expressed through both sexuality and parenthood. It was sexual love for each other that was supposed to be the essence of creating a new life, transforming lovers into nurturers. Thus sexual feelings and acts were harnessed to emotions concerned with loving children and of caring for them. For women especially, love for children was often seen as superior, replacing baser sexual feelings. However, the realities of sexual experience and the arrival of children were rarely as elevated as this ideal and undercurrents of power and abuse were often played out in sexual relationships and in the role played by procreation within them.

Extract 2.1   Letter from Mrs SE

In this letter dated 1921 to Marie Stopes the birth control campaigner, the wife of a farmworker (Mrs SE) pleads for help in resolving the acute emotional and health difficulties she faced as a wife and mother.

On Dec. 3, 1920 we had a stillborn daughter, this was the worst confinement which I have ever had [she already had six living children] ... The third day after my confinement my husband came to my bedside and said it served me right that I was so bad [unwell], other women could prevent having children and so could I if I tried and he was so angry he never came into my room once more for 2 months ... since then he has been very cruel to me because that I will not submit to his embrace. He has often compelled me as he had done very very many times before to submit with my back to him. He says if you wont let me at the front, I will at the back. I don't care which way it is so long as I get satisfied. Well Madam this is very painful to me, also I have wondered if it might be injurious. I feel that I hate my husband and cannot submit for fear of having any more children and then again be accused of unfaithfulness but when all is said and done I am still his wife and although I do not like just to be used for his pleasure and then abused when I am pregnant, still unless I do submit, he declares he will ask other women. Can you please give me any advice ...

(Hall, 1981, p.15–16)

In this letter Mrs SE expresses some very complex and conflicting emotions that relate to her sexual experiences as a wife and mother. On the one hand she feels she is being forced to submit to her husband's demands, which she finds unreasonable and physically painful. She is particularly upset about being blamed for getting pregnant when she had been trying so hard to avoid it, and for his lack of sympathy for the loss of her baby and the considerable physical danger which she had very recently faced. On the other hand she feels she should submit to him because she is his wife, and also because if she does not her husband will turn to someone else for sexual satisfaction. In writing to Marie Stopes she hoped to take some control over her situation.

We can see the acute differences of power between husband and wife that have aroused feelings of both hatred and duty. Victorians might define this as a problem of masculine sexuality, that this husband should restrain his sexual demands in order to protect his wife's health and to prevent conception. He might even be described as a 'brute' for his failures. However, by the 1920s, this might be perceived differently as a failure of a wife to know about and use contraception which prevented the true expression of sexual activity in the marriage. Although husbands were urged to be considerate to their wives after childbirth, in the longer term she might be seen as unfairly denying her husband a fulfilling sexual relationship as well as being sexually repressed herself. This shows us how in the context of negotiations around sexuality and the experiences of procreation we can understand sexuality to be simultaneously personal and structured in historically specific ways.

1.5   Using a historical approach

By adopting a historical approach we gain some distance from the present and everyday, viewing more clearly our taken-for-granted assumptions. Today's formations of parenthood and sexualities did not suddenly appear fully formed, but are the results of centuries of change. By looking at a particular historical phenomenon, fertility decline in Britain, we can explore some of the tensions and contradictions between deeply embedded and newer ideas and practices emerging at that time. These struggles are still with us, embedded in constructions of parenthood and sexuality, and reflected in a whole range of debates about social policy today. As Weeks put it: 'The aim is to understand "the present" as a particular constellation of historical forces, to find out how our current political dilemmas have arisen, to see, in a word, the present as historical' (Weeks, 1991, p.159).

historiography   The starting-point for historical study is to look at the research evidence and the analysis produced by other historians. This is called the **historiography** of a subject or topic; the history of that topic's interpretations. The phenomenon of fertility decline is particularly rich in historical interpretations and we will draw upon this historiography to see what it can tell us about parenthood, sexuality, personal lives and social policy. History is constantly being rewritten as popular and academic interpretations about particular topics ebb and flow. Events in the past are often seen differently at different times and it is important to recognize that historical interpretations are never definitive but are always open to reinterpretation.

2   Explaining fertility decline from a feminist perspective

Feminist theory underpins one of the most influential historiographies of fertility decline and it allows us to foreground gender as a dominant feature in questions of heterosexuality and parenthood. This is not to suggest that divisions of class, 'race', (dis)ability and generation are unimportant in this historical phenomenon, and any full understanding of fertility decline would be incomplete without including them. But in this chapter the main focus will be on gender and these other social divisions will not be discussed at length.

Feminist explanations for fertility decline arose as a critique of a long-standing historiography dominated by the analysis and interpretation of demographic data (that is statistics about birth, death and fertility). This data gave rise to the theory of **demographic transition**, which suggested that fertility decline was inherent in the development of all modern societies. Indeed low population growth has been interpreted as an essential marker of economic and social modernity. A three-stage transition was identified beginning with pre-industrial populations when high birth rates are balanced by high mortality, followed by an interim 'transition' stage of rapid industrial growth when death rates fall but birth rates remain high leading to a rapid population increase. Finally, in the third stage, fertility declines and populations reach a new, 'low-pressure' equilibrium. According to this theory rising living standards along with advances in medicine and technology improve mortality rates before influencing fertility. To support this hypothesis, demographic historians looked for evidence about the timing and extent of rising living standards, drawing on detailed quantitative information on historical wages and prices. Falling fertility was seen as a slower process, a result of cultural changes whereby the material benefits of smaller families, the triumph of rational choice and improvement in the condition/status of women gradually replaced 'traditional' and 'non-rational' beliefs about the value of fecundity. People were almost completely absent from this theory, which ignored individual agency, emotions and desires.

demographic transition

Demographic historians were particularly interested in the class-specific pattern of fertility decline in Britain, whereby the aristocracy and the professional middle classes were first to have smaller families, followed by the lower middle class, then the skilled manual class, and finally the unskilled. It was initially argued that it was the diffusion of knowledge about birth control from the middle to the working classes that determined this pattern (Beveridge, 1925). The catalytic point in Britain was identified as the 1877 trial for obscenity of Annie Besant and Charles Bradlaugh for publishing a US pamphlet about contraception in a cheap and accessible edition, which attracted enormous publicity, breaking through the silences about birth control.

But this event on its own is an unsatisfactory explanation for the profound cultural changes that led to fertility decline. Himes (1936) identified a number of wider cultural influences including secularism, feminism, hedonism and the rational pursuit of materialism as leading to a 'democratization' of birth control, making its use increasingly acceptable. Sociological explanations about the importance of household economies were also added, with growing restrictions on child labour and compulsory education (from 1870) seen as critical factors in fertility decisions (Charles, 1934). Banks (1954) developed this argument further by showing that bourgeois families required increasing material resources to maintain their prosperity and status, with children's education and upbringing representing an increasing financial burden. Smaller families were seen as the answer to these tensions.

Demographic transition theory has continued to be very influential particularly in policy relating to developing countries, but it has also attracted many critics. In Britain, early modern (c.1600–1800) fertility patterns were found to be highly variable and complex before 'the transition', and the transition itself was far from uniform when examined in detail. An overarching single dynamic of change was displaced by a much more complicated tangle of ideas and practices from which the norm of smaller families gradually emerged (Szreter, 1996).

Feminist historians questioned not only the unitary nature of transition theory, but also its very starting point in demography.

ACTIVITY 2.2

As you read through Extract 2.2 by Alison Mackinnon, try to identify her criticisms of transition theory. Which of these relate specifically to gender?

Extract 2.2   'Were women present at the demographic transition?'

The term [fertility decline] is strangely disembodied, indicating, as several feminist historians have pointed out, some type of transhistorical, elemental and natural force akin, perhaps, to the ebb and flow of the tide rather than the historically specific refusal or unwillingness of considerable numbers of women to continue to have large numbers of babies. ... The term 'fertility decline' operates to ground contemporary issues in a natural universe uncontaminated by social change.

How has it come to be a characteristic of populations, rather than of persons? How has it come to have an apparently unitary and seamless meaning? What meanings have collected around the term, and how has it come to be so central in explanations of social change, while at the same time masking the social and sexual relations of men and women, the changing social expressions of desire, the changing social positioning of those who conceive and bear generations of children? Finally, why are fertility concerns such a powerful element in the symbolic order of nations ...?

(Mackinnon, 1995, p.224)

COMMENT

Mackinnon argues that demographic explanations fail to engage with personal experiences, and it is only by exploring how men and women made changes in their personal lives that fertility decline can be understood. She also questions the dominance of demographic explanations, seeing their power as rooted in a political agenda which ignores the agency of those who produced this change. She highlights:

▪   the importance of women as active agents;

▪   the role of sexualities and desires in achieving change;

▪   the social conditions within which men and women found themselves; and

▪   the links between fertility and concepts of the nation.

All of the strands identified by Mackinnon have been developed in the work of feminist historians who have made their starting point the investigation of the connections between aspects of personal life and fertility decline. Sheila Johansson (1979), for example, has argued that the focus on families masks the different interests of husbands and wives in fertility control, reflecting a long-standing feminist emphasis on unpacking 'the family' to recognize the differences of power between genders and generations. Others such as Diana Gittins (1982), interested in looking at social and economic conditions for women, turned the historical focus onto women's patterns of work as well as family ideologies and the availability of birth control.

By investigating the role of birth control in personal lives, researchers could directly address sexuality by exploring the dynamics of negotiations about sexual practices between men and women, whether overt or silent, which reduced the chances of pregnancy (see section 4). Wally Seccombe (1993) examined conjugal relationships to argue that the most common methods of fertility control – abstinence and coitus interruptus – required male co-operation. It was the 'first wave' feminist movement of the late nineteenth century, he argues, that gave women new ways of negotiating their position as mothers. He points to the rising use of abortion from the beginning of the twentieth century, 'representing women's fierce determination to terminate pregnancies that their husbands had not been conscientious enough to prevent' (Seccombe, 1993, p.193) Other research indicates that women were not necessarily the key instigators in fertility decisions as it was more often husbands who were able to determine conjugal sexual practices. 'Many women revealed that taking a dominant role in contraceptive use was difficult because it meant playing a proactive sexual role they were unaccustomed to' (Fisher, 2000, p.311).

Such insights are useful in understanding a range of social policy concerns, but it has been the areas of population and constructions of the nation that have been most widely subjected to a feminist analysis which links parenthood and social policy. Anna Davin (1978) writing from a Marxist feminist perspective made connections between the growth of the infant welfare movement from the 1890s, concerns about fertility decline, and the requirements of nation and Empire for a healthy population. She pointed to the emergence of the idea that children were not just the concern of their parents, but of the imperial nation, as seen most strikingly in the movement to educate working-class women to be better mothers. The St Pancras School for Mothers was an influential model for the infant welfare movement, where mothers were seen as central to efforts to improve infant and child health. Figure 2.1 visually reflects the movement's idealization of working-class motherhood.

Figure 2.1   St Pancras School for Mothers (1907)

3   Social policy and its contexts during the fertility decline

From the selective feminist historiography of fertility decline covered in the previous section, we can see how a historical approach that focuses on gender can illuminate the relationships between sexuality, personal lives and social policy. A feminist theoretical perspective concerned with agency and power in gender relations has been particularly helpful in exploring the changes in sexual practices that resulted in fertility decline. It has also drawn attention to the connections between personal lives and the social policy contexts within which gender relations were being reshaped in the arena of sexuality over the period under review.

This historiography is built on a large body of evidence about fertility decline and social policy between the 1860s and the 1920s. We will explore this evidence in more detail in the key areas of marriage, parenthood, sexuality, birth control, and population policy. It is not necessary to remember all the details of particular policy or events discussed here, but rather to gain a general understanding of the social policy context in which to place explanations for fertility decline. We begin with some demographic evidence.

Figure 2.2 shows (a) estimates of mean (average) completed family size, and (b) survivorship of children, for England and Wales (but excluding Wales before the

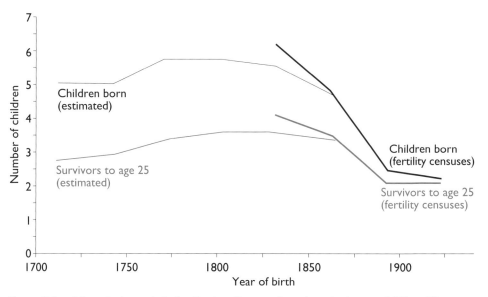

Figure 2.2   Historical trends in family size (Source: based on Anderson, 1993, p.38,
              Figure 1.7)

1831 birth cohort). In the upper pair of lines, the lighter line is derived from an
indirect estimating technique (Wrigley and Schofield, 1983, Table 12), and the
bold line gives the Registrar General's estimates. The lower pair of lines shows
estimates of the average number of children per family surviving to 25 years of
age. These are based on the average ages of survival for different birth cohorts (a
birth cohort consists of all those born in a particular year or group of years).
The results were corrected for illegitimacy rates and for the number of people
who never married (Anderson, 1993, pp.38–9 and n.92).

birth cohort

ACTIVITY 2.3

The graph in Figure 2.2 provides a dramatic, visual image of the change in the population
structure of England and Wales. Take a few minutes to look at what it is showing us.

■   What is meant by 'completed family size'?

■   What do the two downward lines represent?

COMMENT

Michael Anderson (1993) described the top lines of it thus:

> The patterns are clear, with a peak of between 5.7 and 6.2 children per married woman being
> reached for those born between 1771 and 1831 and a steady fall in fertility occurring from the
> 1870s. Those born in the 1880s had only half as many children to care for, entertain, clothe
> and feed as their parents had had; their own children had only two-thirds as many as they did.
> In two generations – and across almost the whole population – the average number of
> children born per married woman fell from around six to only a little over two.

>   (Anderson, 1993, p.39)

He goes on to point out that the improvements in mortality rates meant that average *completed* family size did not decline quite so rapidly as the average number of children *born* per family. Thus, there were conflicting pressures, births were declining, but more children were surviving into adulthood, however, the overall results were declines in both births *and* completed family size.

It is important to remember that these figures are averages, and that the number of children in any particular family has always varied. Thus while average completed family size was declining, there were many children who lived in large families long after the fertility decline began.

It is clear from these statistics that something very important was happening. To explain both how and why fertility decline occurred, we need to understand the social contexts within which it took place. In any historical account of social policy a range of evidence and a number of approaches are drawn upon, none of which are definitive or uncontested, just as social policy itself has constantly been challenged and redefined.

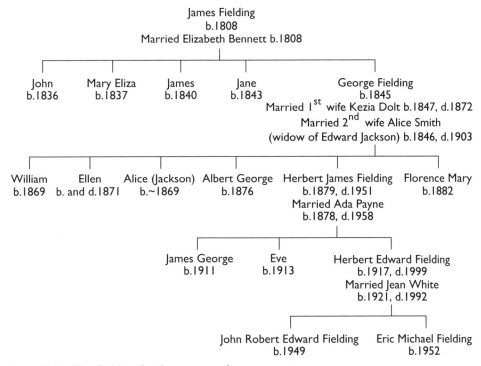

Figure 2.3   The Fielding family tree over four generations

The family tree in Figure 2.3 depicts the changes in family size over four generations by showing the composition of one family in each generation. The Fieldings started as a family of farm labourers and straw plaiters living in Hertfordshire in the nineteenth century. In George Fielding's family we can see how step-families were brought together through the death of spouses while their children were still young. Of the six children, two were from his first marriage to Kezia Dolt, a neighbour. His second wife, his sister-in-law's sister, brought a child to the family from her first marriage, and three children were born from this second marriage. They had moved from the countryside to the outskirts of London where George eventually became a brewery foreman. In the next generation, Herbert James worked as a delivery-man for a department store. In his marriage, we see a sharp reduction in family size to three children, all of whom lived to old age. His third child, Herbert Edward, became a milkman after serving in the Second World War and Jean, his wife, came to London from a mining town in Wales to work as a domestic servant before the war. They had only two children, one worked in the civil service, the other in higher education, showing the final stages of the process of fertility decline.

3.1   Marriage

Like other areas of personal life and sexuality in the late nineteenth and early twentieth centuries (see section 1.3), marriage was emerging as a more explicit area of social policy and state regulation, and parenthood and sexuality were being re-examined and reshaped within marriage. In this section we explore changes in the legal framework for marriage and the gender divisions within it. We will begin by looking at one person's story about married life just before these changes began to be felt.

ACTIVITY 2.4

Extract 2.3 is from *The Life of a Farm Worker*, an unfinished autobiography by James Bowd about his life in rural Cambridgeshire. Born in 1823, Bowd was married in 1849 and lived a generation before the fertility decline. In this extract he describes the early years of his marriage and his entry into parenthood. Look carefully at the language he uses and the ways he describes these experiences. What does he say, or imply, about sexuality, fertility and parenthood in his life?

Extract 2.3   'The life of a farm worker'

But hear his one thing I must not I cannot forbear to Mention and that is when this Mr Kimpton Came to Swavesey [where he lived] he Brought with him a very handsome present and do you know that present proved to be for me and I was very very Fond of it, and now as I had become a Man and what must I do now been about twenty four years of age, what did I do but followed the advice that is given to us in the Second Chapter of Genesis Verse twenty four Therefore shall a Man Leave his Father and Mother and Cleave unto His Wife and they shall be one flesh and now I Began to Make known Myself to this person and in Corse of time She became my Lawful wife. ... While we were Living with with them [his father and mother] Our Family Incresed and very fond of it we was for it was a Little Girl but my wife had a very hard time of it we had to Call the Docter in he said he would not give a farthing for her Life if it had Been an hour Later but by the Blessing of the Almighty she began to get Better and you may be sure that I was very pleased for I was as fond of my wife

> Has a Cat is of New Milk I felt as if I Dare not tell her how much I Loved her
> because I thought she Would be trespising on were I should be and that would
> be the Head of the house.
>
> (Bowd, 1955, p.297)

Bowd talks about his marriage using words from the Bible, which at the time
offered a rich language to express both personal feelings and social
expectations. The church was also central in the rituals of marriage and
christening of children. In the extract, he hints that sexual attraction was an
important element in his relationship with his wife, but he felt constrained in
expressing this both to her and in this written account. He shows us that his
marriage involved unequal power relations, which might have been more
precarious in his case because he had not yet managed to 'leave his father and
mother'. He tells us about becoming a parent in a rather impersonal way – 'our
family increased' – almost as if it happened by chance. This may just be a turn of
phrase, but we might speculate that he did not feel much sense of agency in the
arrival of parenthood. He also talks about the mixed feelings of love for his
daughter and concern for his wife's health, which parenthood engendered at a
time when many women died in childbirth and babies died in infancy. In fact
only two of James Bowd's four children survived beyond infancy.

In Extract 2.3 we can see some evidence of the norms of procreative sexuality
within marriage, the difficulties many people found in expressing sexual desire
and the profound effects of marriage and parenthood on shaping personal lives.
By the 1860s all of these were changing. The publication in 1859 of Darwin's
ideas about evolution began to undermine the deep-seated Christian idea that
life and death were determined by God's will, and that family structures were
bound by fixed religious and moral precepts. The place of the church in
regulating family and sexual life was also changing since both marriage and
divorce had been moved from canon law administered by the Church of England
to civil law through the civil registration of marriage in 1837 and the Divorce Act
of 1857. Marriage was increasingly becoming a concern of the state and civil
society and less a matter for God and individual conscience, and its role in British
society began to be debated as an explicit element of social policy.

From the early nineteenth century to the 1930s there was a continuing shift
towards legally recognized marriage as the institution within which 'normal'
parenthood was overwhelmingly located. Although 'living tally', or
cohabitation, did not disappear it became largely confined to the poorest or
remotest communities (Gillis, 1985). One result of this trend was that illegitimate
children were increasingly stigmatized. As charity and the Poor Law became
bureaucratized in more anonymous and mobile urban communities, it was
obligatory to show a marriage certificate to apply for poor relief and during
wartime, to claim military allowances. Both charitable and state support for the
poor was becoming tightly mapped onto the model of a family consisting of a
breadwinner husband and his dependent wife and children, suggesting that
social policies were increasingly becoming linked to the promotion and
regulation of certain kinds of sexual practices and relationships. However, such

formations were not simply imposed on working-class communities; they also reflected the growing importance of respectability in working-class identities. Respectability came to sum up a cluster of behaviours that included the curtailment of public excess especially drunkenness, saving resources for future contingencies, cleanliness as a mark of control over dirt and contamination, avoidance of public displays of sexuality, and disapproval of sexual relationships outside marriage.

At the beginning of the 1860s, husbands were invested with considerable authority and control over their wives, who in turn were expected to defer and to submit to the demands of their husbands (Shanley, 1989). A husband's authority over his wife was reinforced through marriage vows of obedience and by constant advice from clergy, doctors and popular literature directed at women. Under the common law doctrine of coverture dating back to medieval times, a husband controlled all property and legal contracts of the marriage. This included property a wife earned or brought with her, although various legal devices had been developed to protect the property of wealthy wives from the actions of irresponsible husbands. Husbands also had 'conjugal rights'; that is they could demand sexual access to their wives who could not legally refuse them. As we saw in Extract 2.1 by Mrs SE, wives were very clear that their duties included the sexual servicing of their husbands, whatever their own wishes may have been. Thus there was no recognition of rape within marriage, despite widespread feminist demands for change at the time and in the late twentieth century, when the law was finally changed.

However, there is a great deal of evidence that wives contested their subordination at both personal and political levels. For example, histories of the 'first wave' feminist movement of the late 1800s show how critiques of the inequalities within marriage led to key reforms such as the Married Women's Property Acts of 1872 and 1882, which allowed wives to retain their own earnings and property as if they were single (Holcombe, 1983). Such reforms were of most benefit to middle-class and wealthy women, enabling some to lead more independent lives. For working-class wives, the problem of unequal family resources was much more about how to pay the rent and put food on the table. Many wives managed at least some of their husband's and children's earnings but disputes were endemic, with wives resorting to a range of tactics to maximize household resources. This music hall song performed by James Fawn in the late 1880s sums up some of these sexual, marital and material exchanges:

> By who up the stairs are we carefully led
> And when we're asleep and our senses have fled
> Runs through our pockets, when we are in bed?
> Woman, lovely woman
>
> (Ross, 1993, p.76)

These lyrics point to the subversion of husbands' authority by wives who lead them on sexually and then take advantage of their weakest moments to steal their wages. Wives on the other hand often felt that husbands did not contribute enough towards the care of their children, and therefore that such means of redressing the balance were fully justified.

3.2   Parenthood

The deeply embedded inequalities of marriage were also prevalent in parenthood, reflecting the key role of gender in structuring the inequalities found in both. Under common law fathers were given complete control over their children, while mothers had no rights of custody, care or access if the marriage broke down, or even if the husband died. A man could be adulterous or fail to provide for his family without depriving him of his rights. The Poor Laws provided the only legal requirement on a man to support his family; if his wife or children applied for Poor Law support a man could be forced to provide for them if he could. This did not usually mean that the rights of fatherhood included responsibilities for parenting, as female relatives, servants or staff at boarding schools often undertook the day-to-day care of motherless children. Gradually over the nineteenth century mothers improved their situation through campaigning for legislative changes, but adultery on a wife's part continued to cut her off from caring for her children, at least among the upper and middle classes. The 1857 Divorce Act replicated this sexual double standard – women could be divorced for a single adulterous act, while men could only be divorced for adultery combined with another serious marital offence such as violent cruelty, bestiality, incest or bigamy. This double standard reflected long-standing concerns among the aristocracy about maintaining the legitimacy and blood ties between a husband and his children, which explicitly enforced monogamy for wives through the threat of losing their children. Without the material support of family networks, separated or divorced wives also faced the threat of descent into 'the abyss' of poverty and were vulnerable to sexual exploitation because of their loss of reputation, which debarred them from respectable occupations and social networks.

It has been argued that by the middle of the nineteenth century, motherhood was discursively placed at the centre of the ideal family as the core of morality, comfort and domesticity whose central purpose was to provide a protected site for childhood (Gillis, 1996). This vision also conflated the status of motherhood with the processes of mothering. Feminists at the time drew on such constructions to argue that wives were entitled to rights concerning their children and protection from predatory male sexual demands. Gradually the guiding factor in divorce and custody cases became the 'best interest of the child', although it was not until 1923 that the sexual double standard was removed from divorce and child custody decisions continued to be taken for many more decades on the basis of the sexual behaviour of parents (Holmes, 1997). Feminists within the socialist movement and the Labour Party (founded in 1901) also actively campaigned for better domestic conditions for wives and mothers (Thane, 1991). They sought to ease the physical demands of domestic work through, for example, municipal laundries and improved housing at a time when washing, cooking and cleaning were often undertaken without indoor water or basic domestic appliances. Improvements to maternal health and medical treatment in childbirth were also seen as priorities to reduce the risk of death or permanent injury, which was still very common in giving birth.

Fatherhood was also being reshaped. By the 1860s, middle-class fathers were expected to provide financial support for their dependent wives and children, although they were not always able to do so. Fathers were also expected to protect their wives and children from the moral and physical dangers of public spaces such as public entertainments, and the competitive world of commerce and employment, and to ensure that their children had the best start in adult life. The widening gulf between the home and the workplace meant that fathers spent less time with their families. At the same time, their financial responsibilities increased in order to maintain a home within which an ever-increasing consumer culture was featured through elaborate furnishings, indoor plumbing, gas lighting, and a greater reliance on servants. The increasing tensions between fathers' roles as providers and carers, as well as the challenges to their legal authority over their dependents, could be difficult for families to resolve. Gillis (1996) argues that one way that families expressed these tensions can be seen in the growing significance of rituals of welcoming fathers home from work each day and family occasions such as Christmas and birthday festivities. The cartoon in Figure 2.4 from *Punch* magazine shows Father Christmas as a symbolic father figure, generously providing gifts from the outside world, and being welcomed across the threshold as the central focus of the family's celebrations. There were also fears that men were increasingly opting out of marriage and parenthood altogether by working abroad in the Empire or resorting to gentlemen's clubs for their domestic and emotional needs. For working-class families the role of sole breadwinner was also gaining acceptance as an ideal and demands for a 'family wage' emerged as central to labour struggles throughout this period. The breadwinner/housewife model served to conceal the ways that many wives undertook casual or home work, taking in laundry or keeping lodgers to make ends meet (Davidoff et al., 1998).

However, there were few direct interventions through explicit social policy to ensure that men fulfilled their obligations as providers and protectors. It was only where fathers were absent or grossly negligent that policy emerged, for example with the founding of the National Society for the Protection of Children in 1889 a voluntary society invested with powers by the state to investigate and prosecute fathers and mothers for neglect or abuse of their children. Domestic violence was also the focus of public concern when it involved working-class men, resulting in legislation in 1895 which enabled wives to apply to local magistrates for separation and maintenance from violent husbands (Hammerton, 1992).

However, mothers and fathers were largely left to find their own solutions to the tensions and difficulties of parenthood. Repeated scandals erupted into public view throughout the period under review (Behlmer, 1982), these included baby farming (1870s), the sexual exploitation of girls (1880s) and street children (1890s), indicating that concerns about the failures of parenthood were endemic at this time. The difficulties in the personal lives of mothers and fathers in trying to fulfil these roles were played out in domestic tensions over the management of resources, decisions regarding children over education and work, and in sexual relationships between husbands and wives. In Figure 2.5 we see a portrayal of the 'Marriage debate', raging in the letters pages of the press in 1891, sparked by an article by the feminist Mona Caird.

Social policy concerning both motherhood and fatherhood was necessarily related to changing ideas about childhood. The participation of children in the

PUNCH, OR THE LONDON CHARIVARI.—December 25, 1880.

"HERE WE ARE AGAIN!!"

Figure 2.4   Father Christmas is welcomed into the domestic domain

labour market was increasingly restricted by various Factory Acts passed
between 1802 and 1895 as well as underlying changes in work practices.
Arguments to remove children from paid labour drew on a construction of
childhood as a period of innocence, separated from the corrupting knowledge
and responsibilities of adulthood. The Romantic Movement of the early
nineteenth century, which valorized emotion and the beauty of 'nature' in, for
example, the poetry of William Wordsworth and the philosophy of Jean-Jacques

Figure 2.5   'Is marriage a failure?', *The Police News*, 1891

Rousseau, was a key influence on this recasting of childhood, echoed in fictional and visual portrayals of children. Such portrayals were not universally accepted, as parents often relied on children's economic contributions, for example helping with the harvest or caring for younger siblings, and they were often prepared to defy authorities to keep their children in work.

In Extract 2.4 from *The Old Curiosity Shop* first published in 1841, Charles Dickens describes Little Nell, the quintessential example of childhood innocence.

Extract 2.4   Little Nell

... her small and delicate frame imparted a peculiar youthfulness to her appearance ... I love these little people; and it is not a slight thing when they, who are so fresh from God, love us ... I saw a little bed, that a fairy might have slept in: it looked so very small and was so prettily arranged ... It always grieves me to contemplate the initiation of children into the ways of life, when they are scarcely more than infants. It checks their confidence and simplicity – two of the best qualities that heaven gives them.

(Dickens, 1972, pp.45–8)

In this romantic vision each child is valued for his or her own qualities and character. And as child mortality began to decline, the chances of each child surviving into adulthood were improving, although infant mortality (death under one year old) remained stubbornly high until the 1920s. Schooling for all younger children became compulsory after 1870, indicating the extent to which childhood had become separated from the world of work (McCoy, 1998). Parenthood increasingly included obligations both to protect children from the

The beautiful child in her gentle slumber, smiling through her light and sunny dreams.

Figure 2.6   Little Nell from *The Old Curiosity Shop* (1841/1972), untainted by the old
curiosities of adult knowledge that surround her

adult world, and to prepare them for it. Thus children were less and less likely to
be contributors to family economies through paid or domestic labour, and were
increasingly likely to require greater individual care and the expense of an
education.

The discussion above illustrates some of the ways in which the personal lives of
men and women were in part the result of gendered practices and ideologies. It
also shows that changes in gendered practices were both cause and effect of
wider social change. We can also see that there was no single body of policy that
could be described as 'family policy'. Underpinning the diverse policies that did
emerge were particular constructions of marriage, motherhood, fatherhood and
childhood, which included the regulation and domestication of a certain kind of
heterosexuality. Legally sanctioned marriage, which was increasingly
compulsory, enshrined significant inequalities between husbands and wives
around both sexual relationships and parenthood, although these were always
contested, sometimes successfully. The roles and meanings of motherhood,
fatherhood and childhood were undergoing considerable changes, as the family
consisting of a provider breadwinner, a domestic housewife, and protected
children was becoming increasingly dominant, and although many families did
not easily fit this model, social policy was widely predicated on such
assumptions (see Chapter 1). Maintaining this model of a family involved heavy
material and emotional costs, as wives and children were increasingly less likely
to contribute financially to family economies and as parenthood demanded
greater attention and resources. One solution to the tensions that this model
engendered was for couples to attempt to restrict the number of children they

had, limiting the burdens of parenting and in the process redefining the role of parenthood.

3.3 Sexuality

Just as 'normal' parenthood was seen as outside the realm of social policy (although framed and supported by it), sexual practices within marriage were widely seen as an essentially private matter. Foucault (1984) argued that while sexualities were very actively shaped by the Victorians through a range of discourses, particularly those of professional, medical and scientific interests, within marriage it was increasingly an area of silence. Up to the eighteenth century matrimonial relations had formed the centre of sexual discourses, particularly through the church and civil law. But from the nineteenth century heterosexual monogamy was 'spoken of less and less, or in any case with growing moderation. Efforts to find out its secrets were abandoned; ... It tended to function as a norm, one that was stricter, perhaps, but quieter' (Foucault, 1984, p.38). Foucault is referring to sexuality in its broadest sense here, as a field of discourses concerning practices, roles, identities and relationships.

This quieting of discourses around heterosexual monogamy is reflected in the paucity of historical evidence about 'normal' sexual experiences, especially within marriage. Historians have sought to understand these silences in the evidence by looking closely at what could and could not be said, and thus recorded and retained for the future. It is widely argued that there was a narrowing of vocabularies that could be used in respectable society (Hall, 2000, p.24–5), particularly for women, for whom even knowing an explicit word for a sexual act was seen as having inappropriate sexual experience resulting in a loss of reputation. For example, D'Cruze's study of sexual violence against nineteenth century working-class women points out that 'simply by speaking out about sexual and physical assault women and girls put their character in jeopardy' (D'Cruze, 1998, p.160).

This silence around sexuality led to widespread ignorance on the part of both men and women, which was dramatically exposed in the letters written by readers of Marie Stopes's *Married Love* in the 1920s. Indeed, Marie Stopes's own first marriage was annulled when she realised (after some months) that she and her husband were not achieving 'full sexual union'. The fears associated with first sexual experiences were particularly acute and were not just confined to the middle classes, as we can see from Extract 2.5 by Robert Roberts who was born in 1905 and wrote about his childhood in Salford. His father was a carpenter and his mother ran a small shop from their home.

> ## Extract 2.5   'A ragged schooling'
>
> Eighteen years of age, already married, Barney lived with his wife's large family in an ally behind the shop. ... When familiarity had loosened his tongue Barney whispered to one or two of us of sex, and specifically of his own intimacies. The 'first night', we were given to understand, had been a considerable ordeal. 'Neither of us knowed nothink, really!' They had occupied a single bed in a room which held, besides, the wife's parents, a grandmother and two younger brothers.
>
> 'Now Lucy didn't want it, see, 'cos it hurt; but she kep' on whisperin', "Go on! It's me duty now! Never mind me cryin', make me have it!" It's their duty, see?' ... But I had to put my hand over her mouth to stop her cryin' out, else we'd 've got a real showin' up!'
>
> 'How many times?' asked Eddie, breathless.
>
> 'Three times. All in the dark, o' course – very quiet.'
>
> 'And was it all right?' I enquired my mind much disturbed. 'No,' said Barney, 'it wasn't. But it gets better later on.'
>
> 'And will you have a baby now?'
>
> 'She's four months gone already and her Old Pot-and-pan's dead mad, with me bein' out of collar [unemployed]. But what can yer do? It's natural, see?'
>
> (Roberts, 1976, p.91)

In Extract 2.5 it is interesting to note the paradox of sex being seen as natural, yet also evoking fears and anxiety. Here we see working-class boys able to talk about sex quite explicitly, if nervously, in ways which girls would probably have found much more difficult. Barney's position as an adult was a marginal one and this loosened his tongue with boys who were still in some ways his friends. Being unemployed and the lack of privacy for his sexual relationship, neither of which was uncommon for young men at this time, were both indications of the precariousness of his transition to adulthood. Roberts comments that once he had a job, Barney stopped talking to him (Roberts, 1976, p.87).

The effects of ignorance and inexperience on the emotional lives of newly-weds could be profound, sometimes leaving permanent scars on their relationship. The amplification of motherhood as the most important source of women's identity and emotional attachments had implications for sexual relationships as well: 'Victorian notions of motherhood were so deeply identified with purity that any identification of wife with mother was likely to make her a highly equivocal object of desire' (Tosh, 1999, p.68).

As well as tensions about personal experiences, wider perceptions that unchecked sexual activity presented dangers to both marriage and parenthood erupted into public view to influence social policy, emerging most strongly around the problem of venereal disease (VD). Syphilis in particular haunted marriage and parenthood until a reliable treatment was found in 1909. Although it was usually men who brought venereal disease into their homes, threatening the lives of their wives and children, it was prostitutes who became the target of policy. Concerns about the fitness of the armed forces led to a series of Contagious Diseases Acts in the 1860s that enabled doctors to detain, examine, confine and treat women suspected of working as prostitutes in towns with large military garrisons. The campaign to repeal these Acts was spearheaded by Josephine Butler and included feminists as well as more conservative social critics. They held that venereal disease was not only the fault of prostitutes, but of their clients as well. They successfully argued that criminalizing women for prostitution was unjust and ineffective, being based on an unequal and immoral sexual double standard (Walkowitz, 1980).

By the 1870s, critiques of male sexuality entered public discourse in the social purity movement, which argued that male chastity was the remedy for the social evils that resulted from the sexual double standard, and insisted that men should aspire to women's superior moral level. A network of organizations called the White Cross League was set up to enlist men to pledge to leave behind their 'animal' natures and exercise sexual continence. Calls for male chastity were evoked both by conservative moralists and by some feminists, including the suffragettes in their slogan: Votes for Women, Chastity for Men. In Figure 2.7 a suffragette in 1913 advertises an anti-VD pamphlet by Christobel Pankhurst, which lambasted the sexual double standard. It urged men to restrain their sexual activity and drew on the image of 'whiteness' from the social purity movement.

Figure 2.7   The Great Scourge

However by the 1880s, some feminist and radical socialist circles were questioning the purpose of sexual restraint. Cohabitation, or 'free love union', was debated and attempted by a few brave couples. The argument that sexuality was a natural and a necessary part of a healthy relationship appeared in the writings of the socialist and sexologist Edward Carpenter and the sexologist Havelock Ellis as a movement for 'sex reform' emerged. This movement covered a very wide range of views on sexuality, including demands for 'homosexual' law reform, but also social purity perspectives on issues such as prostitution. In 1912 *The Freewoman* journal, founded by suffragists, hosted a debate about female chastity and whether women suffered physically and mentally from the social constraints on their sexual expression. Such debates began to be heard in literary and political circles and included discussions of contraception as a means of facilitating sexual pleasure for women as well as limiting fertility.

From this ferment of sexual debates came the work of Marie Stopes. She declared that both men and women deserved sexual fulfilment in marriage but that many required practical help, which she offered in her runaway bestseller, *Married Love*, first published in 1918. Stopes took the radical step of naming the pleasures of sex for those who expected to be parents, and at the same time, offered a solution to the risk of repeated pregnancies.

> When two who are mated in every respect burn with the fire of the innumerable forces within them, which set their bodies longing towards each other with the desire to inter-penetrate and to encompass one another, the fusion of joy and rapture is not purely physical. ... From their mutual penetration into the realms of supreme joy the two lovers bring back with them a spark of that light which we call life. And unto them a child is born. This is the supreme purpose of nature in all her enticing weft of complex factors luring the two lovers into each other's arms.
>
> (Stopes, 1918, pp.77–8)

In this quotation we can see Stopes connecting together both conservative and radical ideas about sexuality. For her the highest purpose of sexual love is the generation of new life, an idea that was in keeping with long-standing religious teachings about sex within marriage. But she also saw sexuality as mystical, not animalistic, and as mutually pleasurable for both men and women. 'Stopes's vision of birth control was not about "preventative restraint", but a gateway into a new world of healthy wanted babies and erotic joy' (Hall, 2000, p.98).

Stopes's new ways of thinking about sex for respectable men and women were instrumental in eroding long-standing silences, although reticence about sexual matters had never been completely successful, as demonstrated by the rich language of euphemism and innuendo in popular culture especially in music hall acts. But here we have investigated the more direct challenges to the silence around sexual experience within marriage and in procreation. These began in the opposition to repressive laws that aimed to reduce venereal disease and through general critiques of male sexuality. However, critics of conventional marriage and the burdens of parenthood also began to articulate new possibilities for sexual relationships based on greater equality between men and women.

3.4 Birth control

The fertility decline in Britain was not the direct result of social policy aimed at reducing the birth rate. The deliberate use of birth control was widely condemned as unnatural and immoral by the medical profession, the church and a wide range of conventional opinion, even though doctors and vicars were the first to limit their own families. There was widespread ignorance about the mechanics of human reproduction and how to control it, but for those in the know there were many methods of contraception and abortion available. Most of these had been practised since ancient times, but they were all unreliable or dangerous by today's standards and over the period under review their use was closely associated with prostitution and 'vice'. Condoms in particular were associated with preventing venereal disease rather than conception, although the invention of vulcanised rubber in the 1870s led to some improvements in their usability and reduced their cost. Douches and sponges using various herbs and chemicals were also known and advertised, although in highly euphemistic

Free to Ladies.

A SAMPLE of the MOST RELIABLE REMEDY ever discovered for irregularities and suppressions, from any cause, can be had post free. Thousands of letters of thanks testifying to their speedy efficacy after all other things have been tried in vain. Each purchaser sends back testimonials, as they afford relief in every instance. Or write for our Extra Special Treatment at 4s. 6d., which we guarantee to cure every case, from any cause whatever (genuine). Guaranteed effective in a few hours. Impossible to fail. Delay is dangerous. Send at once to—

NURSE M. A. MANN,
49, Frith Str..., London, W.

An interesting guide, 48 pages, 60 illustrations. Sent post free.

'DAMAROIDS'
(Regd. No. 295152.)

FOR WEAK MEN.

are a Safe and Sure CURE of GENERAL WEAKNESS, SPINAL EXHAUSTION, PHYSICAL DECAY, LOSS OF NERVE POWER, VARICOCELE and SPERMATORRHŒA. They are a Unique & Wonderful Specific for men. **Effectually restore lost vitality and stamina**, counteract results of late hours, excesses, &c. They have cured thousands of cases.

2s. 9d. and 4s. 6d. per box. or the special Extra Strong, 11s. per box, which take effect in a few minutes. Call or Write.

95, Charing Cross Road, London, W.C.

Interesting Booklet and Sample Free.
TELEPHONE 13215 CENTRAL.

RUBBER GOODS.

Descriptive Booklet Catalogue, post free, or with one sample, 2 stamps, or with 12 Specials, including some of the most expensive sorts, 2s. 6d. Special Silk Finished, 4s , 5s , and 8s. per dozen. Post Free to any part of the world (call or write).

95, Charing Cross Road, London, W.C. Telephone 13215 Central.

LADIES.

SEND for DR. PATTERSON'S FAMOUS FEMALE PILLS, which remove Irregularities, etc., by simple means in a few hours. Recommended by eminent Physicians and thousands of ladies, being the only Genuine Remedy. Sample Packet, absolutely free. Or in boxes 2s. 9d. special extra strong, 4s. 6d. Secretly packed, guaranteed relief. Manageress—

95, Charing Cross Road, London, W.C. Established 60 Years. Telephone 13215 Central.

"SANTALGONS."

(REGISTERED NO. 308873.)

contain only the finest distilled ESSENCE of Santal Wood; this is admittedly the best remedy for the cure of Gonorrhœa, Gleet, etc., "Santalgons" are manufactured and filled with the greatest accuracy and skill. The quickest and most beneficial results will INEVITABLY ensue from their use, dissolving slowly and being especially prepared, they do not repeat nor cause nausea in the unpleasant way the soft Sandal Wood Oil Capsules, Santal Pearls, etc., etc. do.

2/6 per Bottle, or 3 Bottles for 6/- post free. Full Directions Enclosed.
CERTAIN CURE.

CAUTION—Santal Essence being somewhat expensive is very liable to adulteration. "Santalgons" are GUARANTEED to contain only absolutely PURE ESSENCE, distilled from selected East Indian Sandal Wood. "Santalgons" should be ASKED FOR and only obtained at the depot where these were purchased, they will be found to be ten times more efficacious than ordinary capsules containing CHEAPER and MIXED quality Sandal Oil.

SPECIAL NOTE—Several unscrupulous firms are copying these goods imitating the package and labels in a fraudulent manner; purchasers are WARNED against these imitations, which are frequently inferior and injurious drugs.

None Genuine unless bearing the Name "SANTALGONS" Regd.

And can only be obtained

From The Hygienic Stores, Ltd., Specialists,
95, Charing Cross Road, London, W.C.
Telephone 13215 Central.   Telegraphic Address, "Hygistor," London.

Figure 2.8   A group of advertisements from *The Popular Herbal* (1910)

terms. Women often knew that breast-feeding after the birth of a child would reduce the risk of becoming pregnant again. The reliance on restricting sex to the 'safe period' of the menstrual cycle was of very limited value at this time because most advice, including Marie Stopes's, located it in the most fertile time of the month. There is some evidence that abortion was also widely practised, although it was illegal and often dangerous. There were many popular advertisements for what appear to be abortifacient products, and also many home remedies were attempted; a scalding hot bath, a deliberate fall down the stairs or drinking a bottle of gin being widely believed to induce abortion. Figure 2.8 shows sex-related products including two for abortifaciants (to prevent 'irregularities'), one for condoms (rubber goods), one for a cure for masturbation (for 'weak men') and one for a medicine for venereal diseases ('certain cure').

But the most common birth control methods were likely to have been withdrawal (coitus interruptus) and long periods of abstinence. These were probably the most reliable, as well as the cheapest methods available although they carried emotional, psychological and physical costs.

ACTIVITY 2.5

In an interview by Elizabeth Roberts in the early 1980s, Mrs Pearce, who was born in 1899 and worked as a weaver in Preston, talked about her visit to the doctor when pregnant with her sixth and last child.

In the part of that interview given here in Extract 2.6, see if you can you pick out some of the issues raised about:

■ the constructions of parenthood and childhood;

■ marriage and women's place within it;

■ the links between sexuality and fertility; and

■ attitudes to birth control methods.

Extract 2.6 Mrs Pearce

There must have been tears in my eyes because I was thinking about keeping them. I loved children but it was the thought of keeping them. You want them to be as nice as others as well as feeding them. He said, 'It's no good crying now, it's too late!' I felt like saying that it wasn't the woman's fault all the time. You are married and you have got to abide by these things, you know. He [her husband] once said that if anybody had seen this squad in here, they would think that we had a wonderful time, but they don't know what I have gone through to try to avoid it, you know. We never would take anything in them days. God had sent them and they had to be there. I'm not a religious person, but that were my idea.

(Roberts, 1984, p.88)

COMMENT

We can see here the idea that each child should be valued and cared for, and therefore large families were seen as a drain on family resources. Even where women wanted to avoid pregnancy, they could not always rely on their husband's co-operation because men could insist on 'these things'. The wish to prevent pregnancy placed great strains on the marriage and sex within it partly because contraception was seen as immoral, against God and nature.

By the time that Marie Stopes and others began to champion the use of contraception in the 1920s it is clear that many couples had already managed to restrict the number of children they were having, despite considerable practical obstacles and opposition from many influential directions. It is difficult to pinpoint how this occurred, partly because experiences of reproductive sex and parenthood were very diverse and also because there is so little documented evidence in which married people explicitly discussed their sexual practices. On the one hand it could be argued that the critiques of male sexuality and feminist demands for women's control over their bodies (discussed in section 3 above) worked with the grain of sexual restraint which restricting family size often entailed before reliable contraception became available. It could also be argued that it was men who were more likely to determine sexual practices and thus played a more important part in achieving fertility decisions, pointing to a significant change in the constructions of fatherhood in which large families were no longer highly valued. Social policy formations concerning marriage, parenthood and sexuality therefore underpinned the ways birth control was used, but those who took up such practices were also actively shaping social policy in these domains.

3.5   Population policy

The period of fertility decline in Britain coincided with a time when anxieties about population control came to dominate a wide range of debates about social policy. These debates originated in two different theories of population: Malthusian ideas about overpopulation and **eugenics** – the 'science' of selective breeding.

eugenics

An Essay on the Principle of Population by Reverend Thomas Malthus, published in 1798, argued that populations would inevitably increase more rapidly than the production of food to sustain them. Malthus held that only the 'positive checks' of disease, war or starvation would keep the population at a sustainable level. To avoid such disasters, he called for 'preventative checks' of marital restraint and deferred marriage. He also argued that poverty was caused by overbreeding by the poor, as the social controls that had limited early marriage through apprenticeship and farm service were diminishing and young adults were having children 'improvidently' before they had the means to support them. Malthusian ideas underpinned much social policy of the nineteenth century; the most striking example was the establishment of workhouses by the New Poor Law of 1834. Families faced with poverty were no longer able to obtain financial assistance or 'outdoor relief', but were forced to move into a local workhouse where they were separated, with men, women and children living in strictly segregated quarters, a highly visible disincentive to those seen as financially and sexually profligate. The use of the workhouse to discipline the poor, although much amended, continued until the 1930s, despite constant demands for its abolition (**Widdowson, 2004**).

If Malthusians were concerned with overpopulation, eugenicists focused on the consequences of population decline. The term 'eugenics' was first used in 1883 by Francis Galton, Darwin's cousin, to describe a science of selective breeding to improve the qualities of the population, or 'the race' as it was popularly called at this time (see Chapter 1). It was based on the assumption that many physical, mental and moral characteristics were determined by heredity, although its physiological mechanisms were not known. By encouraging 'fit' members of the population to breed and discouraging or preventing the 'unfit', it was argued that the 'national stock' would be improved. By the end of the nineteenth century there was an increasing sense of national decline as other countries (particularly Germany after unification in 1870) began to challenge Britain's industrial and economic predominance. This feeling came to a head during the Boer War (1899–1902) when the poor physical condition of recruits became a national scandal. The eugenic movement called for social action to prevent any further decline of the national stock, evoking 'national efficiency' as a key weapon in a Darwinian struggle for survival and dominance in the world. Eugenic anxieties were heightened by emerging evidence that upper- and middle-class parents were having fewer children, while the poor and groups defined as 'racially' 'other', such as Irish Catholics and Jews arriving from Eastern Europe, continued to have large families (Hickman, 1998). Middle-class couples were accused of selfishly refusing to take on the burdens of parenthood. And in response to the increasing influence of feminism, women were blamed for refusing to marry, taking on careers or higher education instead, and avoiding their responsibilities to the 'race' (**Holden, 2004**). Eugenicists were divided about which social ills could be ameliorated by environmental improvements and which were subject to laws of heredity, with alcoholism, feeble-mindedness and having illegitimate children often seen as inherited characteristics.

At this time the term 'race' pointed to a language of differentiation between peoples on the basis of a few, selected physical characteristics and their categorization into distinct 'racial' types, hierarchically arranged with the white Anglo-Saxon 'race' at the pinnacle. Such constructions were deeply embedded in the language of population policy, articulated through an elision of national efficiency with 'racial' supremacy. Significantly, they were incorporated into the Liberal Party's policies of Social Imperialism between 1906–14, when unemployment and sickness benefits and old age pensions were introduced for the first time, when reform was justified in order to 'assist in breeding the Imperial Race in Britain to defend and maintain the Empire' (Williams, 1989, p.126). By 1914, eugenic discourses had become very influential across a wide range of social issues (Bland, 1995, pp.222–8). Particularly important was the Fabian Society. Formed in 1884, the Society favoured gradualist reform for socialist ends, believing that capitalism should be replaced by social ownership and the state should alleviate social deprivation. Many Fabians drew on the language of eugenics, particularly in arguing that the state should take responsibility for the health and wellbeing of the population (see Chapter 1).

It is difficult to overstate the influence of eugenic thinking, although in Britain it failed to significantly impact on particular policies. Unlike the USA, there were no measures for compulsory sterilization of the unfit, and unlike France, there was no financial support for mothers paid by the state. However some limited measures which addressed national efficiency were introduced, such as the provision of free school meals for the poor in 1906 and the growth of infant welfare services. The language of eugenics was also used by Marie Stopes to tie together feminist demands for motherhood to be more highly valued and for women to have control over fertility and sexuality, with a nationalist agenda for the renewal of the population. As such it became possible to present knowledge about birth control as respectable and socially responsible rather than obscene and immoral, linking together the personal with population policy.

4   Conclusion

In section 3 we have looked at marriage, parenthood, sexuality, birth control and population policy in the period of fertility decline in Britain between 1860 and 1930. We can trace the two-way processes by which on the one hand, people drew on formations of social policy when shaping the place that fertility played in their lives, and on the other how social policy reflected and was changed by practices at a personal level. The key role of silences and absences at every level has been emphasized, but we have also investigated some of the points where articulations of concern and anxiety about parenthood and sexuality emerged into public debate and explicit policy developments.

Historians have pointed us to many of the complexities and particularities of class, gender, and location that were at play in these processes. From the evidence and explanations we have investigated in this chapter, we can see the difficulties in developing a single, comprehensive explanation. Indeed, as historians, we would expect any such explanation to be immediately challenged and contested whenever new research questions are raised.

However, despite the contingencies of all historical explanations, there is enough evidence to draw together an argument using the theoretical perspective of feminism. During this period, many couples were questioning and renegotiating their sexual relationships in order to reshape their roles as parents. This process was highly uneven, as couples from different social groups in terms of class, ethnicity, location, religious belief and generation had very different starting points, but in this exploration we focused on gender inequalities as particularly significant in determining how and when fertility decline occurred. Central to these uneven processes were the breaking of silences and the articulation of many unspoken assumptions about the nature of marriage, parenthood and sexuality. The voicing of social policy concerns in all these areas was crucial in providing a language with which to name and delineate sexual experiences, and therefore a means to adapt and change them.

We can identify some areas of social policy of particular importance in these processes. First there were the feminist challenges to the sexual double standard within marriage. Second there were concerns about the population, where questions of the strength of the nation and its labour and military resources led to debates about the role of the state in improving the conditions of responsible parenthood and discouraging others from having children. Finally, debates about birth control began to bring into the open the deep tensions within marriage between the expression of sexuality and the responsibilities of parenthood.

Further resources

For an overview of demographic change, Michael Anderson's chapter in the *Cambridge Social History of Britain* (1983) provides a nuanced overview of what historical demography can offer. John Gillis's *A World of Their Own Making* (1996) is a fascinating account of the changes in family rituals and meanings in Western societies since the medieval period. Lesley Hall's *Sex, Gender and Social Change in Britain since 1880* (2000) provides a good introduction to histories of sexuality. A useful general social history of this period is Jose Harris's *Private Lives; Public Spirit: Britain 1870–1914* (1994) and Pat Thane's *Foundations of the Welfare State* (1996) provides a general history of social policy. For an important Foucaudian analysis of sexuality in this period see Frank Mort's *Dangerous Sexualities* (1987) and for feminist analyses of the issues raised in this chapter, see the collection edited by Carol Smart, *Regulating Womanhood* (1992).

Useful websites include the following (all were accessed on 29 August 2003):

History Online (http://ihr.sas.ac.uk/search/welcome.html)

A general history website with links to many other resources for historians.

The Workhouse (http://www.workhouses.org.uk/)

An extensive website about the Poor Law.

Lesley Hall's Web Pages (http://homepages.primex.co.uk/~lesleyah/)

A website that provides a wealth of ideas and links for feminist history and the history of sexuality.

References

Anderson, M. (1993) 'The social implications of demographic change' in Thompson, F.M.L. (ed.) *The Cambridge Social History of Britain Vol. 2*, Cambridge, Cambridge University Press.

Bainham, A. (1999) 'Defining parenthood: parentage, parenthood and parental responsibility – subtle, elusive yet important distinctions' in Bainham, A., Sclater, S.D. and Richards, M. (eds) *What is a Parent? A Socio-Legal Analysis*, Oxford, Hart.

Banks, J.A. (1954) *Prosperity and Parenthood: A Study of Family Planning Among the Victorian Middle Class*, London, Routledge and Kegan Paul.

Behlmer, G.K. (1982) *Child Abuse and Moral Reform in England, 1870–1908*, Standord, CA, Stanford University Press.

Beveridge, W.H. (1925) 'The fall of fertility among the European races', *Economica*, vol.5, pp.10–27.

Bland, L. (1995) *Banishing the Beast: English Feminism and Sexual Morality 1885–1914*, London, Penguin.

Bowd, J. (1955) 'The Life of a Farm Worker', *The Countryman*, vol.51, pp.293–300.

Charles, E. (1934) *The Twilight of Parenthood: A Biological Study of the Decline of Population Growth*, London, Watts.

Davidoff, L., Doolittle, M., Fink, J. and Holden, K. (1998) *The Family Story: Blood, Contract and Intimacy, 1830–1960*, London, Longman.

Davin, A. (1978) 'Imperialism and motherhood', *History Workshop*, no.5, pp.9–65.

D'Cruze, S. (1998) *Crimes of Outrage: Sex, Violence and Victorian Working Women*, London, UCL Press.

Dickens, C. (1972) *The Old Curiosity Shop*, Harmondsworth, Penguin.

Fisher, K. (2000) 'Uncertain aims and tacit negotiation: birth control practices in Britain, 1925–50', *Population and Development Review*, vol.26, no.2, pp.295–317.

Foucault, M. (1984) *The History of Sexuality*, London, Penguin.

Gay, P. (1984) *The Bourgeois Experience: Victoria to Freud*, Oxford, Oxford University Press.

Gillis, J.R. (1985) *For Better, For Worse: British Marriages, 1600 to the Present*, Oxford, Oxford University Press.

Gillis, J.R. (1996) *A World of Their Own Making: Myth, Ritual, and the Quest for Family Values*, New York, Basic Books.

Gittins, D. (1982) *Fair Sex: Family Size and Structure, 1900–39*, London, Hutchinson.

Hall, L.A. (2000) *Sex, Gender and Social Change in Britain since 1880*, London, Macmillan.

Hall, R. (ed.) (1981) *Dear Dr. Stopes: Sex in the 1920s*, Harmondsworth, Penguin.

Hammerton, A.J. (1992) *Cruelty and Companionship: Conflict in Nineteenth-Century Married Life*, London, Routledge.

Harris, J. (1994) *Private Lives, Public Spirit: Britain 1870–1914*, London, Penguin.

Hickman, M. (1998) 'Education for minorities: Irish Catholics in Britain' in Lewis (ed.) (1998).

Himes, N.E. (1936) *Medical History of Contraception*, London, Allen & Unwin.

Holcombe, L. (1983) *Wives and Property: Reform of the Married Women's Property Law in Nineteenth-Century England*, Toronto, University of Toronto Press.

Holden, K. (1996) *The Shadow of Marriage: Single Women in England 1919–1939*, Dissertation Thesis, University of Essex.

Holden, K. (2004) 'Personal costs and personal pleasures: care and the unmarried woman in inter-war England' in Fink, J. (ed.) *Care: Personal*

Lives and Social Policy, **Bristol, The Policy Press in association with The Open University.**

Holmes, A.S. (1997) '"Fallen mothers": Maternal adultery and child custody in England, 1886–1925' in Nelson, C. and Homes, A.S. (eds) *Maternal Instincts: Visions of Motherhood and Sexuality in Britain, 1875–1925*, London, Macmillan.

Johansson, S.R. (1979) 'Demographic contributions to the history of Victorian women' in Kanner, B. (ed.) *The Women of England: from Anglo-Saxon Times to the Present: Interpretive Bibliographical Essays*, Hamden, CT, Archon Books.

Katz, J. (1990) 'The invention of heterosexuality', *Socialist Review*, vol.20, pp.7–34.

Kinsey, A.C., Pomeroy, W.B. and Martin, C.E. (1948) *Sexual Behaviour in the Human Male*, Philadelphia, PA, W.B. Saunders.

Lewis, G. (ed.) (1998) *Forming Nation, Framing Welfare*, London, Routledge in association with The Open University.

Llewelyn Davis, M. (ed.) (1977) *Life as We Have Known It by Co-operative Working Women*, London, Virago.

Mackinnon, A. (1995) 'Were women present at the demographic transition? Questions from a feminist historian to historical demographers', *Gender and History*, vol.7, pp.222–240.

McCoy, L. (1998) 'Education for labour: social problems of nationhood' in Lewis (ed.) (1998).

Malthus, T.R. (1996) *An Essay on the Principle of Population* (facsimile of 1807, 5th edn, London, J.Johnson), London, Routledge.

Mort, F. (1987) *Dangerous Sexualities: Medico-Moral Politics in England Since 1830*, London, Routledge & Kegan Paul.

Ribbens McCarthy, J., Edwards, R. and Gillies, V. (2000) *Parenting and Step Parenting: Contemporary Moral Tales*, Occasional Paper 4, Centre for Family and Household Research, Oxford Brookes University.

Roberts, E. (1984) *A Woman's Place: An Oral History of Working-Class Women 1890–1940*, Oxford, Basil Blackwell.

Roberts, R. (1976) *A Ragged Schooling: Growing up in the Classic Slum*, London, Fontana.

Ross, E. (1993) *Love & Toil: Motherhood in Outcast London 1870–1918*, Oxford, Oxford University Press.

Seccombe, W. (1993) *Weathering the Storm: Working-Class Families from the Industrial Revolution to the Fertility Decline*, London, Verso.

Shanley, M.L. (1989) *Feminism, Marriage and the Law in Victorian England, 1850–1895*, Princeton, NJ, Princeton University Press.

Smart, C. (ed.) (1992) *Regulating Womanhood: Historical Essays on Marriage, Motherhood and Sexuality*, London, Routledge.

Stopes, M.C. (1918) *Married Love: A New Contribution to the Solution of Sex Difficulties*, London, A.C. Fifield.

Szreter, S. (1996) *Fertility, Class and Gender in Britain, 1860–1940*, Cambridge, Cambridge University Press.

Thane, P. (1991) 'Visions of gender in the making of the British welfare state: the case of women in the British Labour Party and social policy, 1906–1945' in Bock, G. and Thane, P. (eds) *Maternity and Gender Policies: Women and the Rise of the European Welfare States, 1880s–1950s*, London, Routledge.

Thane, P. (1996) *Foundations of the Welfare State* (2nd edn), London, Longman.

Tosh, J. (1999) *A Man's Place: Masculinity and the Middle-Class Home in Victorian England*, New Haven, CT, Yale University Press.

Walkowitz, J.R. (1980) *Prostitution and Victorian Society: Women, Class and the State*, Cambridge, Cambridge University Press.

Weeks, J. (1986) *Sexuality*, London, Routledge.

Weeks, J. (1991) *Against Nature: Essays on History, Sexuality and Identity*, London, Rivers Oram.

Widdowson, E. (ed.) (2004) 'Retiring lives: Old age, work and welfare' in Mooney, G. (ed.) *Work: Personal Lives and Social Policy*, Bristol, The Policy Press in association with The Open University.

Williams, F. (1989) *Social Policy: A Critical Introduction: Issues of Race, Gender and Class*, Cambridge, Polity Press.

Wrigley, E.A., Schofield. R.S. (1983) 'English population history from family reconstitution: summary results 1600–1799', *Population Studies*, vol.37. no.2, pp.157–184.

CHAPTER 3

Sexuality and Young People: Policies, Practices and Identities

by Rachel Thomson

Contents

1   Introduction

What we're doing isn't part of the timetable for lovemaking, it doesn't count. We're trying to get inside each other's skins, but without taking our clothes off, and the parts that touch are swaddled in stringy rucked-up shirts, jeans, pants. There are no leisurely caresses, no long looks, it's a bruising kind of bliss mostly made of aches ... We're dissolving, eyes half shut, holding each other's hands at arm's length, crucified on each other, butting and squirming. Our kisses are like mouth-to-mouth resuscitation – you'd think we were dying it's so urgent, this childish mathematics of two into one won't go ... One day Gail told me that Vic had told a friend who'd told his girlfriend, who'd told her, that we'd gone all the way and that he had a trophy, a smear or splatter of blood on his washed out jeans, to prove it. She was shocked that something so momentous had happened and I hadn't confided in her. But it hadn't, I protested, truly, or I would have – and he and I had an angry and reproachful conversation about loyalty, betrayal and boasting, because after all, we hadn't, had we? It was all so unthinkable that when I felt ill, bloated, headachy, nauseous and, oh yes, my period hadn't come, I stayed in bed and we called our new doctor. ... Could I be – um – pregnant? No I said, feeling hot suddenly, No ... He'd heard I was a clever girl, doing well at school, didn't we ever have biology lessons? I must have known what I was up to ... From his first words and his tone, which had weariness and contempt in it, I knew it was true, just as absolutely as until that moment I knew it couldn't be. I'd been caught out, I would have to pay. I was in trouble, I'd have no secrets any longer, I'd be exposed as a fraud, my fate wasn't my own, my treacherous body had somehow delivered me into other people's hands.

(Lorna Sage, 2000, pp.234–5, writing of herself aged 16)

There is nothing new about teenage sex. Yet the consequences of an unplanned teenage pregnancy firmly locate the intensely personal yet public experience in a historical and social location. Lorna Sage is writing about a time poised on the cusp of social change, a moment before popular feminism and of accessible abortion, yet also a moment of growing expectations for young women and of increasing social mobility through education. In this personal narrative Lorna marries Vic and has the baby, yet she also struggles through her education – making it to university and a new social world. For Lorna Sage, this pregnancy is a critical moment in her subsequent biography. Decisions that people do or do not make in relation to their sexuality can transform their personal and family relationships, their identities and the opportunities available to them. In any particular historical period, these experiences and choices will fall into patterns, framed by the constraints and potentials of their social locations (Thomson et al., 2002). In this way we can understand sexuality to be simultaneously personal, social, structural and historically and culturally specific.

Contemporary theorists such as Giddens (1992) and Beck and Beck-Gernsheim (1995) make a great deal of the impact of feminism and freely accessible birth control on the character of intimate relations (see Chapter 1, section 4.2). Sexuality, they argue, is increasingly detraditionalized, freed from the constraints of reproduction and tradition, becoming a medium of communication between increasingly equal partners engaged in 'pure relationships'. Yet this optimistic picture is complicated by empirical evidence of the continuing intransigence of physical bodies, of the lack of real negotiation in sexual partnerships and the enduring power of gendered understandings of appropriate feminine and masculine sexual behaviour (Jamieson, 1998). These constraints may be experienced acutely by young people who have little economic and personal freedom. While much has changed since the 1950s, the incongruities of bodily interaction, the gossip of friends and the intervention of medical authority, described so well by Lorna Sage, continue to characterize the sexual experiments of the young.

Aims   In this chapter we will explore the dynamic relationship between the ways in which sexuality is experienced by young people and how it is constructed through social policy. The chapter aims to:

- locate the meaning of teenage sexuality in time and space;

- identify significant moments when social policy categories have been redefined;

- explore how these categories in turn play a part in everyday sexual cultures;

- explore how notions of what is 'normal' are constructed, inhabited and resisted.

We begin the chapter by locating children and young people within wider discussions of social change, before sketching a picture of contemporary sexual cultures. The second part of the chapter employs a policy case study of the development of school-based sex education. Because of constraints of space, our focus is primarily on consensual heterosexual practice and on the UK. The approach we adopt is influenced by feminist and social constructionist perspectives on sex and gender, yet employs a range of conceptual tools. Understandings of teenage sexuality are contested and the perspectives presented here are unlikely to be consistent with the values and beliefs of all readers.

2   Situating young people within wider discussions of sexuality and social change

The boundaries between childhood and adulthood are fluid and under pressure from a range of social changes. Terms such as teenager, young person and young adult are used by many commentators (my own preferred term being young person), yet these intermediate states are rarely reflected in legal or policy documents where individuals are defined either as a child or as an adult in relation to legal ages of consent. In order to talk about sexuality and young people we must first consider the relationship between sexuality and children.

2.1   Childhood and sexuality

In the course of this chapter you will see that there are enduring tensions within social policy between competing imperatives to protect children *from* sexuality, and pragmatically to acknowledge and deal *with* the consequences of the sexuality of young people. These impulses inevitably become confused in the heat of controversy that surrounds attempts to create or reform policy initiatives. In seeking to make sense of the evolution of social policy in this area it is necessary to understand the symbolic role of childhood in the mediation of a wider process of social change.

From a social constructionist perspective, explanations of childhood sexuality cannot be accepted at face value; they need to be understood as shaped by prevailing forms of knowledge and institutional practices. Social historians have demonstrated the historical and cultural specificity of understandings of childhood, observing that the notion of childhood as a time of innocence and economic dependence is, in historical terms, relatively new. The figure of the innocent child has been central to the evolution of modern understandings of sexuality. Not only does sexual activity play a defining role in informal meanings of what it means to be 'grown up', but contestations over sexuality have been central to the definition and policing of more formal boundaries between childhood and adulthood.

The philosopher Michel Foucault has argued against the notion that there is a natural state of either childhood or sexuality. Instead he points to the 'pedagogization of children's sex' as one of a number of 'strategic unities which, beginning in the eighteenth century, formed specific mechanisms of knowledge and power centring on sex' (Foucault, 1990, p.103). Within this strategic unity children's sexual activity is understood as a potential, both 'natural' and 'contrary to nature', posing physical and moral danger to individuals and the collective. This potential demands that 'parents, families, educators, doctors, and eventually psychologists ... take charge, in a continuous way, of this precious and perilous, dangerous and endangered sexual potential' (Foucault, 1990, p.104). Foucault suggests that such activity was most evident in 'the war against onanism' (masturbation) which in the West lasted over two centuries.

This theme is developed by Wendy and Rex Stainton Rogers (1999) in a discussion of 'what is good and bad sex for children'. In the nineteenth century, masturbation in children was a central social policy concern, considered to be a source of social and individual harm, with a proliferation of techniques developed in order to identify and treat the self-abusing child (see Figure 3.1). By the early twentieth century there had been a shift in medical opinion towards a psychosexual perspective, influenced in part by the theories of Sigmund Freud, in which childhood sexuality was considered to be 'natural'. Childhood sexuality was comparatively silent within social policy and new 'liberatory' views of sex characterized the advice dispensed to parents by experts such as the famous Dr Spock. What was formerly understood in terms of self-abuse was now understood as a natural childish exploration of the body.

Freudian ideas were slow to influence British sexology. Yet the language of Freudianism increasingly found its way into newly emerging psychological

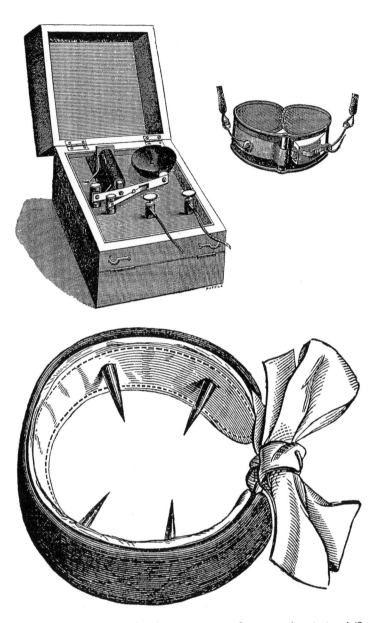

Figure 3.1   'Devices ... for the prevention of nocturnal emissions' (Source: Porter and Hall,
          1995, pp.146–7, Figures 12 and 13)

theories of child and adolescent development. For Freud, human development
and behaviour was driven by sexual energy – the libido. Childhood sexuality
was understood as structured into progressive psychosexual stages: the oral,
anal and phallic, culminating in the Oedipus and Electra complexes at about the
age of seven, in which male and female children respectively experience
attraction to the parent of the opposite sex and resentment for the parent of the
same sex. In 'normal' development these conflicts are repressed in the
unconscious and resolved through identification with the same sex parent and
the taking up of a heterosexual gender role. From this perspective pathology

occurs when, through excessive frustration or gratification, individuals become stuck or 'fixated' at particular stages. Subsequent developments in psychology, such as Eric Erikson's influential theories of adolescent development, built on these foundations, extending the developmental process to include the newly emerging cultural category of the 'teenager' (Erikson, 1968). Erikson sought to integrate adolescent sexuality within a wider model of identity formation, warning that the early relationships of young people should not be subject to social pressures but rather should be understood, if not encouraged, as a form of 'experimentation' associated primarily with a quest for self-definition rather than intimacy.

Wendy and Rex Stainton Rogers suggest that before the 1980s clear distinctions were drawn between childhood and adult sexuality, with the former seen in terms of innocent childish explorations. Adult/child sexual relations, while proscribed, were seen as rare aberrations (Stainton Rogers and Stainton Rogers, 1999, p.188). From a Freudian perspective 'memories' of adult/child sex and rape could be interpreted as wish-fulfilling fantasies. But by the 1980s such an approach was falling into disrepute, with a growing awareness of the sexual abuse of children in policy circles and the public imagination. While in an earlier era techniques were developed to identify the *self-abusing child*, at this point attention shifted to the identification of the *sexually abused child*, with masturbation recodified as a potential sign of the presence of abuse. The 1983 Children and Young People's Act made possible a range of interventions in family life that we now think of as constituting the practice of child protection work. Scott (2001) has noted the important role of the Women's Liberation Movement in the 'rediscovery' of child sexual abuse, with feminism having a direct impact on the consciousness of professionals and there being a fit between feminist analyses of power and the family systems focus that characterized professional expertise in the area.

Think about the following terms that are used in relation to sexuality: 'experimentation', 'harassment', 'play', 'abuse', 'exploration' and 'exploitation'. Can these terms be applied to both adults and children?

The unresolved legacy of these competing views is reflected in contemporary constructions of childhood sexuality which view the child as simultaneously asexual, sexual and sexualized. Anxieties about the potentially corrupting effects of sexual knowledge, played out in debates over sex education and young people's access to contraceptive services, can be seen as the most recent in a long series of modern moral panics over childhood sexuality. In this latest version professionals and the state struggle to regulate young people's access to sexual knowledge in the face of a media-saturated consumer culture in which young people are competent participants (Bragg and Buckingham, 2002). The proliferation of sexual imagery and information in the popular media – what **sexualization of** McNair (2002) calls the **sexualization of social life** – confounds attempts to **social life** regulate its consumption. Children and young people learn about sex from adult-oriented media sources – for example, confessional television shows such as *Jerry Springer* – and from more specialized media targeted directly at them, such as pop music and videos and teenage magazines.

risk anxiety

Sue Scott and colleagues suggest that, in contemporary society, children become the bearers of a generalized **risk anxiety** which is sexualized and fed back to children in the form of the 'idea that sexuality *per se* is inimical to children's well being' (Scott et al., 1998, p.702). From this perspective they suggest that childhood is seen to be 'at risk from pressures towards early maturity, conspicuous consumption and precocious sexuality', a concern which in turn legitimates moves to deny children knowledge about sex.

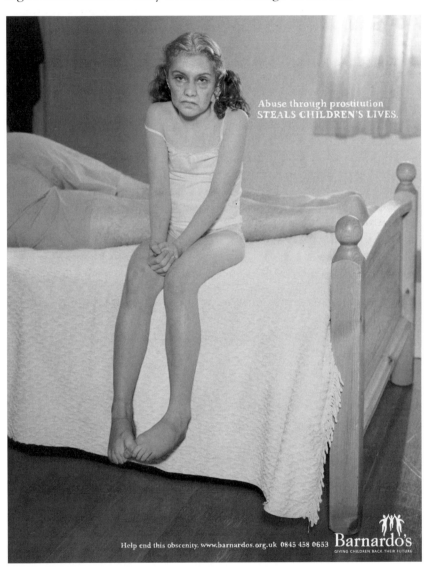

Figure 3.2   Images from this campaign against child prostitution make an explicit link between sexualization and the loss of childhood

2.2   The changing character of youth

Why is it then that the boundary between childhood and adulthood has become such a site of concern and regulation? Popular debates about morality and sexual behaviour are fuelled by a range of social changes that impact on the family, the relations between men and women and between adults and children.

Figure 3.3   The 'truth' about teenage sexuality?

The 1970s saw a reversal of a long-term trend towards earlier childbirth and marriage, which coincided with an improvement in young women's earnings relative to young men and a decline in young men's earnings relative to adult men. Sarah Irwin (1995, p.184) has argued that 'patterns of delay in family formation are bound up with changes in gender related inequalities'. For example, the increasing importance of women's paid employment, which is contributing to increased affluence for families, means that young people can afford to stay on in education for longer. As the importance of young women's earnings increases compared with those of young men, the meaning of 'setting up home' transforms into a shared and extended project.

The dramatic historical changes that have affected the expectations of women (and in the process all intimate and family relations) are illustrated well by an interview-based study conducted by Norwegian researchers Harriet Bjerrum Nielsen and Monica Rudberg. In this study they interviewed three generations of women about their transition to adulthood, following eight 'generational chains': grandmothers (born between 1910 and 1927), mothers (born between 1940 and 1948) and daughters (born between 1971 and 1972). They observe important shifts in the gender subjectivities of these women across the generations while also accounting for the ways in which each generation responds to the lives of the generations before them. They are also able to

sequencing   identify clear, if uneven, changes in the **sequencing** of the key steps towards adult life: working, leaving home and establishing a sexual relationship:

> For the rural grandmothers the order was *work, moving out, sex.* For the urban grandmothers and most of the mother generation, both urban and rural, the order changes to *moving out, sex, work.* For the youngest generation the order seems to have become *sex, moving out, work.* The image of the modern girl in the family may be a bit paradoxical. On the one hand she exhibits independence with regard to education, sex and position towards the parents. On the other hand all this is framed by a context where they are still children and have few adult responsibilities. Their many travels out in the world, which are at least partly financed by their parents, presuppose a home to return to and to call up if something should go wrong. One could also ask in what respect sex is a criterion of adulthood when it takes place in the teenagers' bedroom in the house of the parents?
>
> (Bjerrum Nielsen and Rudberg, 2000, p.443)

ACTIVITY 3.1

Take a moment now to think about a family you know.

- What changes exist over three generations in the sequencing of the key steps to adulthood?

- Try comparing the transitions of the men and the women. Are the changes in the sequencing of the women's lives more obvious than those of the men?

- To what extent are the changes tied up with processes of social and geographical mobility?

---

extended
dependency

Despite diversity, the overall trend is that young people are staying on longer in education and living longer in the family home. This **extended dependency** does not simply point to an extension of youthfulness. Rather, there has been a fragmentation in the markers of adulthood, with some accessed earlier (for example, independent consumption) and others accessed later (for example, economic independence). In this process sexual activity has become one of the more accessible forms of being 'grown up' available to young people. Moore and Rosenthal (1998, p.54) suggest that what they term 'sexual initiation' has become 'the *rite de passage* of modern adolescents' providing 'an opportunity to move to adult roles that are substantially delayed for them in other areas such as career choice and economic independence'.

fragmented
transition

Youth researchers have described these changes in terms of a shift from a unitary transition between childhood and adulthood to a **fragmented transition** within which there are distinct but interdependent 'strands' such as housing, education and intimacy (Jones, 1995). It is increasingly difficult for young people to achieve adult status simultaneously in each strand. Different strands are associated with common-sense understandings of what it means to be 'grown up' and structured by a range of different age limits enshrined in legislation. Jones and Bell (2000) argue that these age limits are in turn based on different and competing criteria, including age, competence, vulnerability and understanding.

ACTIVITY 3.2

Consider Table 3.1 which outlines the different age limits enshrined in UK legislation. Which of the limits do you think are based on criteria of competence and which might be based on criteria of vulnerability?

COMMENT

There are some clear examples here of legal limits based on criteria of vulnerability which seek to protect children from exploitation (such as limits on child employment) and of those based on competence which refer to a child's ability to act independently and to understand the consequence of their actions (age of criminal responsibility). Yet each of these age limits has a particular historic legacy. The age of sexual consent, for example, was established in 1885 as an attempt to protect young working-class women from the predatory sexual advances of older men. Over time the law has been amended, each time on the basis of new arguments, and most recently to bring the law for heterosexual and homosexual sex into line.

The history of the age of sexual consent shows that notions of competence and protection, themselves highly gendered, are always in play in the construction and reform of the law (Waites, 1999; Thomson, 2000a).

Table 3.1   Some ages in legislation

Age	Rights/responsibilities acquired
8	Criminal responsibility (Scotland)
10	Criminal responsibility (England and Wales)
13	Child employment
16	Can leave school
	Can contribute to national insurance (NI) and pay income tax
	Age of sexual consent
	Can marry with parent's consent in England and Wales (without consent in Scotland)
17	Can drive car
18	Age of majority
	Can marry without parent's consent in England and Wales
	Can vote
	Can sign tenancy (16 in Scotland)
	Can buy alcoholic beverages
	Can claim NI (including unemployment benefit)
	Can claim social security (at 18–21 rate)
22	Adult minimum wage rate
25	Adult rates of income support and housing benefit

Source: adapted from Jones and Bell, 2000, p.3

There are important national differences in the character of the transition to adulthood, as we have already seen in Bjerrum Nielsen and Rudberg's research discussed above. For example, in Spain it is still usual for young men and women to remain economically dependent on their parents and be living at home until the age of 30, leaving only to get married. The UK is both a multicultural and a multinational society, and in such a culture the kind of 'national patterns' described for Norway and Spain may be less easily identified. So, for example, although the age at which women have their first baby has been rising progressively, in the UK a small but significant minority buck this trend. We could understand these young people as reordering the normative sequence of adulthood by having children young while living with their parents and returning to education at a later stage as part of a process of establishing economic independence. However, such responses are not considered to be 'different but equal' to the prevailing norm within the current policy agenda that constructs teenage parenthood primarily in terms of social exclusions. Although evidence from young mothers suggests that they see the benefits and costs from a different perspective, their personal experiences are positioned discursively as a problem, which inevitably impacts back on the way in which the personal is interpreted (Phoenix, 1991).

In order to understand differences in sexual cultures (both within the UK and between the UK and other countries) it is important to consider the relationship between dependence and independence in the different arenas of young people's lives and why it makes sense for some young people to invest heavily in sexual relationships or in parenthood. These investments are mediated by local cultures, as well as social class, religion and ethnicity. Thomson (2000b) has found striking differences between the sexual values of young people living in different communities: for example, sexual experience and parenthood is considered to be a sign of 'maturity' in one economically deprived housing estate and a sign of 'immaturity' in an affluent home counties commuter town. In each there exist distinct moral economies within which sexuality and parenthood have meaning and which in turn are shaped by economic and educational opportunities. Within these local moral economies young people's decisions about the sequencing of adulthood have, in Bourdieu's terms, their

logic of practice   own '**logic of practice**' (Bourdieu, 1977). Therefore it 'makes sense' for one young woman to enter parenthood in her teens as a first stage towards acquiring responsibility, and some authority within her community. Likewise it 'makes sense' for another to defer the complications of heterosexual attractions and sexual relationships until she has managed to secure her entry into higher education. In Bourdieu's terms, in 'choosing' what is available to us, the personal emerges in the context of place structured within or against particular normative standards.

It should be clear by now that there are tensions between and within policy discourses on young people's sexuality as well as contradictions between these and the different lay understandings that characterize different sexual cultures. Yet these contradictions make sense if we understand them as responses to uneven social conditions and unresolved social change. On one hand, young people appear to be pursuing sexual relationships as a means of experiencing a sense of autonomy; for some this translates into early parenthood, for others it is associated with an extended 'youth' and economic dependence on parents. At the same time we find that young people are constructed by social policy as children and thus in need of protection from sexualization of adult society and the sexual advances of adults. The fragmentation of the different markers of adulthood increases uncertainty about what it might mean to be adult, fuelling anxieties about transgression of the borderlands of childhood. These contradictions have provided the impetus for the enduring controversies that have surrounded public policy-making in this area since the mid 1980s. Such policy responses to young people's sexuality need to be understood as engaged with a wider cultural narrative about social change and the detraditionalization of gender, sexuality and generation.

3   Researching sexual cultures: evidence of the personal in the public

According to the Kinsey Report
Ev'ry average man you know
Much prefers to play his favourite sport
When the temperature is low
But when the thermometer goes 'way up
And the weather is sizzling hot
Mister Adam
For his madam
Is not

Cole Porter (from 'Too Darn Hot', quoted in Kimball, 1983)

In this section we will sketch a picture of young people's contemporary sexual cultures, drawing on a base of social research. In doing so we want to encourage you to be aware of the ways in which research has an impact on its audiences and how researchers play a strategic role in the evolution of sexual politics and policy-making. In her overview of the modern history of sex research, Liz Stanley reminds us that 'perceptions of change can be an artefact of the research process' (Stanley, 1995, p.235). Sex research, then, needs to be understood as a cultural intervention that exists within and not outside the social. The works of Havelock Ellis (1937), Kinsey et al. (1948, 1953), Masters and Johnson (1966) and Shere Hite (1976) represent important moments in sexual politics, each reflecting the particular concerns of their authors and their times. These studies also make visible aspects of the personal in the public sphere and transform what ordinary people 'know' about sex – be it the notion that 'one in 10 are gay', the location of the 'G spot', or women's dissatisfaction with penetrative sex. More recent 'discoveries' such as the pleasures of sexual risk-taking also need to be understood as contributing to and reflecting the concerns of contemporary sexual politics.

3.1   The bigger picture? Trends, patterns and quantitative sources

The advent of HIV and AIDS in the early 1980s revitalized research into sexuality in the UK. Although much of this research was fuelled by anxieties about the sexual activities of 'risk groups', in practice the research had the effect of drawing attention away from stigmatized sexual *identities* towards risky sexual *practices*. In the same way that the research of Havelock Ellis and Alfred Kinsey had questioned the boundaries between 'normal' and 'deviant' sexual behaviour, this generation of research demonstrated the extent of sexual diversity and the health risks of conventional sexual behaviour. One of the primary sources of information on the sexual behaviour of the UK population can be found in the National Survey of Sexual Attitudes and Lifestyles (Natsal) conducted in 1990 and repeated in 2000 (Johnson et al., 1994; Wellings et al., 2001). The first wave of the study was planned as part of a major government-funded research programme into HIV and AIDS in the late 1980s. However, promises of funding were withdrawn due to the study's 'sensitive nature', and the study was picked up by the charitable wing of an international drugs company. The second wave of the study was funded by the Medical Research Council with support from the Department of Health and other UK government bodies.

Fears about the sexualization of children mean that studies that seek to document the sexual practices of the young are beset with political and ethical problems. These include demands by funders and ethics committees for researchers to secure parental consent for young people's participation and difficulties in ensuring confidentiality to participants in the face of child protection procedures. Problems associated with interviewing those under the age of sexual consent resulted in the Natsal study only sampling adults over the age of 16. However, this did not prevent the researchers commenting on teenage sexuality as they were able to report on the past sexual experiences of adults, and thus to point to changes in sexual practices over time. Three main trends were identified (Johnson et al., 1994, p.69):

1   a progressive reduction over the years in the age at which first intercourse occurs;

2   an increase in the proportion of young women who have had sexual intercourse before the age of sexual consent;

3   a convergence in the behaviour of men and women.

The authors interpreted these changes as coinciding 'with a period in which the traditional constraints on early sexual expression ... have gradually been lifted in the context of liberalizing legal reforms, a relaxation of sexual attitudes and advances in medical technology' (Johnson et al., 1994, p.106).

The study also pointed to the existence of different sexual cultures, with early intercourse being associated with lower social class and educational level, although this trend was found to be weakening over time. Ethnicity and religious affiliation were also found to have an influence on adolescent sexual behaviour 'through cultural or contextual mechanisms', with the 'median age at first intercourse being higher for Asian groups and lower for blacks, compared to whites' (Johnson et al., 1994, p.83) and those reporting no religious affiliation being more likely to experience intercourse before the age of 16.

The second wave of research conducted in 2000 identified further changes taking place in young people's sexual cultures over a 10-year period. The authors (Wellings et al., 2001) point to:

■   the continuing convergence of age of first intercourse at 16 for young men and women;

■   a rise in numbers of sexual partners;

■   an increase in risk-reduction practices;

■   an overall increase in 'sexual competence'.

The story told by the research was one of liberalization, manifest through the erosion of gender difference towards the male norm. This 'historical' perspective found resonance with wider discussions of social change within the culture. The research was used by both sides in the debate over youth sexuality, with the moralists using it as evidence of moral decline and the liberals as evidence of progress.

The emergence of a measure of 'sexual competence' is an interesting example of how research can contribute directly to social policy categories. The measure was constructed by combining four variables relating to the circumstances in which sexual encounters take place: regret, willingness, autonomy and contraception at first intercourse. Data on individuals were collected for each of these variables. Where an individual's practice was characterized by regret, coercion and unprotected sex they would score poorly on a scale of sexual competence. Here we see how highly personal and subjective experiences can be translated into social facts through the methodology of social research.

So defined, 'sexual competence' proved to be a powerful measure, with the authors finding that sexual competence at first intercourse had increased during the past three decades (despite a decreasing age at first intercourse), and that sexual non-competence was much higher among young people who left school at 16 without qualifications, for those whose main source of information about sex was not school or parents and for young women who were younger than 13 at first menstruation. The authors also found that 'although sexual competence decreases substantially with age at intercourse, more than a third of young women for whom sexual intercourse occurred at age 15 years were sexually competent, and more than a third of those aged 18–24 years at occurrence were not' (Wellings et al., 2001, pp.1849–50). In creating this category the researchers shift policy attention from the absolute age at which young people are sexually active towards an understanding of individual development and social norms. In this way highly personal experiences can be translated into policy-relevant 'facts'.

ACTIVITY 3.3

Table 3.2 details the variables that contribute to the measure of sexual competence. Spend five minutes 'reading' the table.

- Can you see how levels of sexual competence increase with age at first intercourse?
- Can you see gender differences in sexual competence?

Sexual behaviour is difficult to research, being one of the most hidden aspects of our personal lives. Our knowledge of the 'big picture' in terms of trends and patterns is largely dependent on official statistics that measure the medical outcomes of sexual behaviour such as rates of terminations, teenage conceptions and sexually transmitted infections (STIs). From these we are able to gain some insight into the existence of underlying sexual cultures. For example, we know that terminations of pregnancy are more common among middle-class than working-class young women (Smith, 1993), that there are high levels of STIs in particular ethnic minority groups in inner city locations (Low et al., 2001) and that teenage parenthood is associated with socio-economic deprivation, doing badly at school and being the child of a teenage mother (NHS Centre for Reviews and Dissemination, 1997). What we cannot know from such

Table 3.2 Prevalence of contextual factors surrounding first intercourse, 16- to 24-year-olds

| | Age (years) at first intercourse | | | | | | p. trend with age at first intercourse |
	13 or 14	15	16	17	18–24	All	
Men*							
Regret							
Wish waited longer	41.8 (33.6–50.4)	26.3 (19.8–34.0)	19.0 (14.0–25.2)	11.8 (7.0–19.2)	8.2 (4.9–13.6)	20.4 (17.7–23.4)	<0.0001
Willingness							
Respondent more willing	5.7 (2.8–11.2)	2.5 (0.9–7.1)	3.2 (1.4–7.3)	2.5 (1.1–5.7)	1.7 (0.6–4.8)	3.0 (2.0–4.5)	0.022
Partner more willing	9.0 (5.2–15.1)	6.8 (3.8–11.7)	6.7 (3.7–12.0)	5.6 (2.7–11.2)	5.3 (3.0–9.2)	6.6 (5.0–8.7)	0.283
Contraception							
No condom	31.2 (23.8–39.7)	19.4 (13.6–26.9)	18.6 (13.9–24.5)	17.8 (12.1–25.4)	19.5 (14.2–26.3)	20.9 (18.3–23.8)	0.115
No contraception	17.9 (12.3–25.2)	9.8 (5.5–16.7)	7.7 (4.7–12.4)	3.0 (1.2–7.2)	7.1 (4.0–12.1)	8.8 (7.0–11.0)	0.016
Status of partner							
Met for first time	2.5 (1.0–6.4)	0.9 (0.3–2.5)	4.7 (2.6–8.3)	7.8 (3.9–15.1)	6.4 (3.4–11.8)	4.6 (3.3–6.4)	0.002
Main reason							
Peer pressure	9.2 (5.3–15.6)	9.9 (6.0–16.0)	8.1 (5.1–12.5)	8.8 (5.0–15.2)	4.8 (2.5–8.8)	8.0 (6.2–10.2)	0.086
Drunk	11.8 (7.0–19.1)	6.7 (3.3–13.1)	3.8 (2.0–7.1)	12.1 (7.1–19.7)	10.4 (6.3–16.8)	8.5 (6.6–10.8)	0.392
Not sexually competent	66.6 (58.0–74.2)	46.4 (38.2–54.8)	43.2 (36.3–50.4)	38.0 (30.1–46.6)	38.6 (31.8–45.9)	45.7 (42.2–49.2)	<0.0001
Number unweighted, weighted	165,195	179,212	262,320	162,195	201,268	969,1190	—

Women*	Age (years) at first intercourse						p. trend with age at first intercourse
	13 or 14	15	16	17	18–24	All	
Regret							
Wish waited longer	84.3 (77.4–89.4)	49.1 (42.1–56.2)	34.0 (28.7–39.9)	33.8 (26.4–42.1)	19.3 (14.2–25.7)	41.8 (38.5–45.2)	<0.0001
Willingness							
Respondent more willing	0.7 (0.1–4.8)	1.5 (0.4–5.6)	1.1 (0.2–4.8)	0	0	0.7 (0.3–1.9)	0.034
Partner more willing	32.9 (25.6–41.2)	26.0 (20.5–32.5)	19.9 (15.4–25.3)	16.4 (11.5–23.0)	18.1 (13.1–24.4)	22.1 (19.5–24.9)	<0.0001
Contraception							
No condom	33.6 (26.1–42.1)	16.5 (11.8–22.6)	19.5 (15.3–24.4)	21.2 (15.4–28.3)	21.1 (15.4–28.1)	21.5 (18.9–24.3)	0.060
No contraception	21.7 (15.7–29.2)	10.0 (6.4–15.2)	8.6 (5.9–12.3)	7.9 (4.5–13.5)	10.2 (6.2–16.5)	10.9 (9.1–13.1)	0.005
Status of partner							
Met for first time	5.3 (2.5–10.8)	3.1 (1.4–6.7)	2.3 (0.9–5.7)	0.8 (0.2–3.5)	4.1 (1.8–9.1)	2.9 (2.0–4.3)	0.440
Main reason							
Peer pressure	13.0 (8.3–19.8)	13.7 (9.5–19.3)	7.4 (4.9–11.1)	4.8 (2.1–10.2)	3.2 (1.4–7.0)	8.3 (6.6–10.4)	<0.0001
Drunk	6.9 (3.7–12.4)	7.4 (4.5–11.9)	5.5 (3.1–9.4)	4.7 (2.4–9.1)	5.3 (2.8–9.7)	5.9 (4.5–7.6)	0.218
Not sexually competent	91.1 (85.3–94.7)	62.4 (55.1–69.1)	49.7 (43.9–55.6)	48.6 (40.7–56.6)	36.6 (29.4–44.4)	55.8 (52.4–59.2)	<0.0001
Number unweighted, weighted	167,164	229,224	352,362	195,193	196,188	1139,1130	—

Note: All data are % respondents unless indicated.
*All respondents aged 16–24 who have had heterosexual intercourse and with non-missing values for all variables.

Source: Wellings et al., 2001, p.1847

research is how or why such patterns exist – insights more readily available from qualitative sources. The Natsal study, however, is unusual in the detail and sophistication of its methods of data collection, analysis and interpretation, and for the ways in which it builds on insights gained from qualitative research.

3.2   The view from below: identities, meanings and qualitative sources

Qualitative research in this area has generally been smaller in scale, drawing on a wider disciplinary and funding base. Although many of the same obstacles to researching sexuality still exist, such methods have the advantage of being sensitive to sexual meanings and identities. As always, methodological constraints shape the focus of the research. Researchers have tended to rely on young people's reports of their experiences or observations of the informal sexual cultures of the classroom and playground. This inevitably leads to a focus on language, peer group relations and the institutional context of the school.

This body of research is also characterized by a closer relationship to theory, with analysts concentrating on the identification and interpretation of sexual **discourses** in the language used by young people. At one level it is possible to understand a particular discourse as 'representing the social construction of language and knowledge, organizing the ways in which we think about the world and what we come to regard as appropriate, valid and true' (Connolly, 1998, p.11). Following the work of Foucault many researchers have also sought to draw links between the language that young people use to talk about sex and wider social structures, seeking to understand how power reaches 'into the very grain of individuals, touches their bodies, inserts itself into their actions and attitudes, their discourses, learning processes and everyday lives' (Foucault, 1980, p.39).

discourses

Recent qualitative research on young people's sexuality has also been influenced by feminist theory which questions the inevitability of a **gender order** (Connell, 1987) predicated on a model of heterosexuality that presumes an active masculinity and a passive femininity. Many researchers have been influenced by the work of Judith Butler who has described heterosexuality in terms of a performance that takes on the appearance of being natural through acts of repetition (Butler, 1990). Moving away from feminist perspectives which seek to privilege different sites of oppression, it is possible to understand that sex and gender identities are constantly and contingently created through a matrix in which class, gender, 'race' and locality are always in play in a non-hierarchical or determining fashion. From this perspective a plurality of sexual and gender identities can be recognized which are irreducible in their difference, while also demonstrating well-worn patterns of gendered inequalities – the performance of which contributes to the **institutionalization of heterosexuality** in practices, relationships and identities through which it is constructed as a 'coherent, natural, fixed and stable category: as universal and monolithic' (Richardson, 1996, p.2; see also Chapter 1 of this book).

gender order

institutionalization of heterosexuality

The relationship between this kind of research and policy is not as direct as is the case with the kind of quantitative material discussed, but it provides insights into *how* and *why* patterns in sexual cultures exist. Researchers have explored the interplay of gender, 'race' and sexual identities from early childhood (Connolly, 1998; Frosh et al., 2002), illustrating the ways in which social policy discourses contribute to the lived sexual identities of young people (Epstein and Johnson, 1998), and perhaps most importantly providing a voice for young people within policy-making processes (Sharpe, 2001).

I only have space here to draw attention to one study in which I was involved with colleagues over a number of years. The Women, Risk and AIDS Project (WRAP) and the Men, Risk and AIDS Project were large-scale qualitative investigations of young people's heterosexual cultures, undertaken in the early 1990s at a time when concerns about the potential for the heterosexual spread of HIV/AIDS began to enter the public health agenda. The initial study was funded under the same government research programme of which the original Natsal study was designed to be part. Focusing on young people aged between 16 and 21 living in Manchester and London, the studies sought to explain the initial findings that conventional heterosexual masculine and feminine sexual identities were at odds with sexual health. These revealed that many young women found it difficult to insist on condom use in a sexual relationship and tended to define sexual encounters as 'steady', irrespective of circumstance. To insist on condom use was to openly recognize the relationship as transitory, and in doing so to place a young woman's sexual reputation in danger. Young women tended to 'trust to love', seeing relationships as potentially serious, with 'safety' constructed in terms of the maintenance of conventional feminine identities rather than sexual health:

> If you want to have relationships then you've got to trust them. Otherwise it's no good from the start. You have to believe what they tell you. You just hope they tell you the truth. You can't find out if it's lies or not. (young woman aged 20, white, working class)
>
> (Thomson and Holland, 1998, p.68)

In contrast, the young men tended to approach sexual relationships in a more instrumental way. For many young men the primary objective of early heterosexual experiences was to have a 'story' that could be told to their male peers. Their anxieties centred on their own performance and subsequently on the positive sexual reputation that this could generate for them. So not only were masculine and feminine sexual identities constructed in opposition to each other, but the desires of young people were, in gendered terms, mutually exclusive. Central to this oppositionally constructed view of sex is the notion that sex is something that a man *does* to a woman and that a woman *gives* to a man. Young men and young women are then constructed as active agents and passive objects respectively, and these early sexual encounters take place within a 'war of attrition' where young men are expected to persuade and young women to resist and finally cede. Here a young man questions his partner's claims to virginity on the basis of her unseemly lack of resistance to his advances:

Q: Was it her first time?

A: She said it was but I – I don't know whether it was or not. Because like it was too quick like for her like, for a girl to say it was, like a couple of hours. It would have been more if like she was a virgin, so I reckon she wasn't. (young man, 18, white working class)

(Thomson and Holland, 1998, p.62)

These findings may appear to contradict the trend towards gender convergence over time found by the Natsal study. The WRAP researchers did in fact find a widespread desire for mutuality, but intentions and practices were often at odds. We found some young people negotiating more equal relationships in which female sexual pleasure and male vulnerability were expressed. However, these relationships appeared to be possible only where young people were able to negotiate some privacy within a couple relationship. For those who were younger, the norm was to socialize primarily in same-sex or peer groups. Other researchers have demonstrated the ways in which homosocial peer groups give rise to oppositionally constructed gender relations in which difference is 'othered' and eroticized and in which a gendered double standard underpins the construction and policing of sexual reputations (Frosh et al., 2002).

While young men were found to have most of the power within early heterosexual relationships, young women were found to bear the main responsibility for negotiating sexual safety. The study showed that young women engaged in a range of creative strategies in order to practice safer sex while not disrupting the gender relations of the encounter, the most common of which was being on the pill but using its invisibility as a cover to request condom use on the basis of a fear of pregnancy. Some young women also sought to establish relationships with young men who were significantly less mature or experienced than them (against the typical cultural trend) in order to bolster their negotiating position. The difficulty here was that, in a cultural context in which gender difference is eroticized, young women struggled to find these 'nice guys' desirable. We found that a small but significant minority rejected a view of heterosex based on mutually exclusive gender identities. This entailed challenging a definition of sex structured by expectations of men's needs and, in doing so, rejecting the implicit constraints to safer sex such as spontaneity, loss of control and trusting to love:

A: Safe sex is as pleasurable an experience as actual penetration. Oral sex, just things like touching somebody else's body in a very gentle way. Kissing. Appreciating one another's bodies. I think it's just as much fun, if not more. You concentrate on each others needs a lot more, you're more aware of them. You're aware of each other's bodies a lot more. Instead of twenty minutes of bang, bang, bang, you've got a whole night; you watch the dawn come up and you're still there.

Q: Have you had to convert your partners?

A: Yes, I've said 'I don't want to do that' or 'why don't you try this?' Before they know it they're converted, and they suddenly realise – 'well I haven't actually done it – well I'm tired now' – Haven't you had a good time. You can change a lot of people's ideas'. (young women, 18)

(Thomson and Holland, 1998, pp.73–4)

Unfortunately, few young people have the confidence, self-awareness or privacy necessary to engage in this kind of negotiation when they begin their sexual relationships. This may be the case especially when young people are seeking these relationships as a way of acquiring maturity, autonomy and an emergent sense of adulthood. While adult sexual cultures may increasingly be influenced by notions of empowerment, pleasure and self-interest, the sexual negotiations of young people remain largely unspoken and dominated by conventional notions of masculinity and femininity. In this way we can see how the personal is constituted at the level of the individual, the couple and wider collectivities, and how these negotiations and resistances are embedded in socially structured relations of power.

ACTIVITY 3.4

Take a moment to reflect on both the qualitative and quantitative research presented here.

■   What are the strengths of the two approaches?

■   What are their weaknesses?

■   To what extent do you think that the two approaches work to complement and contradict each other?

■   What kind of authority do you think each approach has in relation to the policy process?

COMMENT

The WRAP study was unusually influential for a qualitative research study. Recent moves towards an 'evidence-based' approach to policy-making have privileged quantitative approaches, struggling to fit qualitative research into a paradigm for which the randomized controlled trial is the 'gold standard'. Yet qualitative research continues to be influential with practitioners who can make direct links with their practice. Ideally the two approaches can be complementary, used in conjunction to generate and extend knowledge and critical insight.

In this section we hope to have encouraged a *dynamic* understanding of the relationship between personal lives and the public sphere, in which representations of personal lives (such as by research) are centrally important. In the absence of public representations of the ways in which personal lives are actually lived, social policies will tend to promote normative ideals – ways of living that are unrealistic and which in turn regulate the identities of those subject to them. In this context, social research can be a transgressive intervention, telling new sexual stories that make visible different kinds of sexual subject and turning personal conflicts into public problems (Plummer, 1995). By making visible hitherto hidden aspects of personal lives, such interventions can result in a form of recognition that makes the personal a less excluded space. It is to this dynamic and situated understanding of the personal within social policy-making that we now turn.

4 Policy case study: sex education in schools

The regulation of sex education has been one of the key sites through which social policy has engaged with the sexual cultures of the young. In the following case study we will trace the historical evolution of current debates and policies on sex education, pointing to processes of politicization, centralization and codification in statutes and official guidance. The case study will focus on changing policy discourses and the practices through which these discourses construct policy subject positions and contribute to lived sexual cultures.

4.1 Historical roots: from sex hygiene to sexual health

Prior to 1986, school-based sex education was not mentioned in any primary legislation. Since that time it has been the subject of a proliferation of law, official guidance and, increasingly, evaluation. The roots of modern sex education lie in concerns that surfaced at the turn of the twentieth century over the spread of sexually transmitted diseases. These in turn became associated with the development of eugenics as a medico-moral movement in which education for 'sex hygiene' was promoted as a means to strengthen the physical and moral health of the nation (see discussion of eugenics in Chapter 1, section 5). Campaigns to include 'race' and sex hygiene in school curricula gathered pace in the first decades of the twentieth century, in which 'a broad and often uneasy coalition of medics, clerics, social purists, eugenists and some feminists campaigned to raise the question as a matter of vital national and even imperial concern' (Mort, 1987, p.162). The activities of such progressives were not without risk. Frank Mort (1987) provides a description of a national sex education scandal in 1913, in which a progressive teacher influenced by eugenic and feminist philosophies sought to introduce sex education to her class at Dronfield Elementary School in Derbyshire. Mort suggests that the subsequent scandal (in which working-class fathers denounced the interventions of an upper-class woman) was not an isolated incident, but was characterized by the competing forces of class and gender conflicts which made sex education so important in public debates in the early years of the twentieth century.

In the post-war years sex hygiene became embodied in the emerging welfare state. Joanna Bourke describes 'the tortuous progression of widening access to sexual information' effected by a series of government reports (including the 1959 Crowther Report, the 1963 Newsom Report and the 1964 Cohen Report) in which a pro-natalist philosophy was promoted which sought to achieve social cohesion through the development of the family (Bourke, 1994, p.37). Education about 'healthier family life' was encouraged, including home economics, child development and 'the facts of life'. But provision remained voluntary with responsibility delegated by government to the National Marriage Guidance Council, the Family Planning Association (FPA) and the discretion of local education authorities (LEAs) (Meredith, 1989). In the 1970s and 1980s the influence of new social movements such as second wave feminism, lesbian and gay equality and anti-racism, began to be felt in local government, and more formalized pockets of 'progressive' practice arose, typified by the Inner London Education Authority Sexuality Unit. Throughout this whole period there was no formal curriculum framework for sex education, and while local education authorities had the responsibility of providing guidance to schools in this as in other areas, the definition of good practice was not a concern of central government.

4.2 The politicization of sex education

A debate in the House of Lords on the funding of the FPA in 1976 marked the end of this period of consensus and subcontracting. Throughout the Conservative administration of Margaret Thatcher, sex education (and in particular the excesses of what were coined 'loony left' councils) became the focus of a popular concern. Through an alliance of moral lobby groups, the press and members of the government, anxieties were raised about the potentially corrupting influence of state intervention, portrayed as undermining the exercise of the 'natural' authority of the family.

The Education Act 1980 ushered in a new era of consumerism in education which focused on the preferences of parents rather than young people, despite the emergence of a competing discourse of children's rights made available through the Children Act (Fergusson, 1998; Pinkney, 1998).

Key policy moments in this process were:

- the 1986 Education Act in which control of sex education was taken out of the hands of local education authorities and placed into the hands of school governors (a previously neglected group in social policy terms);

- the inclusion in the 1988 Local Government Act of restrictions on how homosexuality could be presented in the classroom (Section 28) (see Chapter 1, section 4.1).

Martin Durham (1991) has argued that Thatcherism employed moral politics in an *instrumental* way, in order to rally populist fears and gain support for other, often radical structural reforms. The paradox of the Thatcher administration was that, although it met moralist demands on sex education, it did not give way to them on other issues such as abortion, under-16s' contraception and embryo research where public health and scientific opinion was privileged. One of the most important policy battles in this area was the 1985 House of Lords ruling against moral majority activist Victoria Gillick. She had challenged West Norfolk and Wisbech Health Authority over the right of general practitioners to provide contraceptive advice to under-16s without parental knowledge or permission.

"My name is Betty Sheridan.

I live in Haringey.

I'm married with two children.

And I'm scared.

If you vote LABOUR they'll

go on teaching my kids about

GAYS & LESBIANS instead of

giving them proper lessons."

E Sheridan

Committee for a Free Britain

Figure 3.4   An advertisement paid for by the Committee for a Free Britain and placed in the *Sun* and *Evening Standard* newspapers on 8 June 1987

Ultimately, a majority opinion expressed support for doctors to give under-16s contraceptive advice in 'exceptional circumstances', provided that doctors deem them competent to consent to treatment following guidelines laid out by Lord Fraser in the ruling. The notion of '*Gillick* competence' was seized on by progressive campaigners who unsuccessfully sought to generalize the guidelines to include education professionals. The outcome of the case was complicated, generating anxiety among professionals about the legal consequences of young people disclosing sexual activity, while also confirming the superior standing of health professionals over those in education in this respect.

Thomson describes this ambivalence in social policy relating to young people's sexuality in terms of tensions between 'moral authoritarianism' and 'public health pragmatism', tensions which became increasingly acute under the administration of John Major (Thomson, 1994). In the area of sex education, two contradictory policies were running in parallel. Consistent with a public health agenda, aspects of sex education were included in the national curriculum for science, and health targets were set for reducing under-16 pregnancies. Yet at the same time John Major launched a moralist 'back to basics policy' which was thwarted by scandal over the personal lives of government ministers and a growing recognition of the UK's poor standing when compared internationally on measures of sexual health. 'Nationhood' has always played a symbolic part in the sex education agenda. Initially conceived of in eugenic terms, the sexual health of the nation increasingly became cast in terms of comparative league tables generated by global bodies such as the World Health Organization, the International Planned Parenthood Federation and UNAIDS. Along with the USA, the UK was identified as an international example of bad policy practice, with a series of comparative reports drawing connections between high levels of teenage pregnancy, deprivation and punitive policy measures. In contrast, northern European countries with low rates of teenage pregnancy, such as the Netherlands and Sweden, were identified as models of progressive practice associated with a liberal and tolerant approach towards risk reduction (Jones et al., 1985).

The moral lobbies unleashed during Thatcherism continued to be influential and the tabloids' interest in sex education meant that the practices of teachers, school nurses and voluntary organizations were subject to 'an atmosphere of intimidation' (Esptein and Johnson, 1998, p.14), resulting in considerable self-censorship. Moreover, the legal framework for sex education was in a mess: sex education was a compulsory part of the curriculum, yet in effect it was optional, being in the hands of school governors to decide if and how it was taught. In the summer of 1993 the Department for Education issued guidance for consultation, seeking to clarify these anomalies. Before the consultation period was over the guidelines were rendered redundant by a parliamentary ambush in the House of Lords, when an amendment to the Education Bill was tabled and accepted, effecting a parental right of withdrawal from sex education.

Figure 3.5

Do you think that parents should have a legal right to withdraw their children from sex education classes? What might be the arguments for and against this provision?

4.3　A new consensus? Social exclusion, effectiveness and teenage pregnancy

The law on sex education in schools has not changed since the 1993 Education Act, yet the climate has transformed, with attention paid less to *whether* sex education should happen, and more to the *quality* and *targeting* of provision. A symbolic shift has been a change of name – to Sex and Relationships Education (SRE) – in all official documents. SRE is now a compulsory subject separate from the national curriculum and parents have a legal right to withdraw their children from it, though few do. Since 1993 sex education has also formally been inspected and reported on by OFSTED and it is increasingly included in teacher training. The change of government in 1997 brought with it a new policy language. Where the focus of debate had previously been on boundaries of authority between the state, professions and the family, new terms began to dominate the agenda: social exclusion, targets and effectiveness.

International evidence has been used strategically in order to coalesce a new consensus, which can be seen most clearly in the influential report by the Social Exclusion Unit on teenage pregnancy that resulted in a government Teenage Pregnancy Strategy and Teenage Pregnancy Unit (SEU, 1999). At the time of writing, the goals of the strategy are to halve the rate of conceptions among under-18-year-olds in England by 2010 and to achieve a reduction in the risk of long-term social exclusion for teenage parents and their children by getting more teenage parents into education, training and employment. Teenage pregnancy is seen as the result of social exclusion (occurring in deprived communities among young women who are educational under-achievers) as well as a central cause of social exclusion (associated with low birth weight and other negative social and health indicators). The government takes a characteristically 'joined up' approach to addressing this problem, with the Teenage Pregnancy Unit having a cross-departmental brief, and the strategy dovetailing with Sure Start (a programme to support under-fives and their families in deprived communities) and Connexions (a programme to support post-16 transitions into education, training and work).

subject positions

In the New Labour agenda, interventions are targeted at those considered to be either 'at risk' or 'risky'. This marks a significant break with the approach of previous Conservative administrations which employed populist terminology such as 'parental rights' and 'the health of the nation', effectively cutting across social class divisions. The return of deprivation into the policy lens has brought with it new stigmatized **subject positions** implicit in terms such as the 'teenage mother', the 'school excludee', the 'care leaver' and those 'not in employment, education or training'.

A concern with the moral 'effects' of sex education that dominated under the previous administrations has increasingly become a concern with 'effectiveness' defined in terms of outcome, in both behaviour (falling teenage pregnancy rates, less unsafe sex, later first sex) and cost-effectiveness (demonstrating that the cost

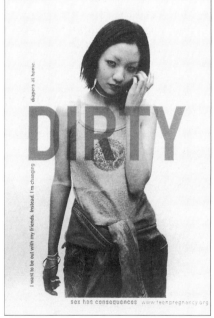

Figure 3.6   These images, used in the US National Campaign to Prevent Teenage Pregnancy, typify an approach to the prevention of teenage pregnancy that emphasizes social exclusion

of prevention is less than treatment). The influence of 'public health pragmatism' has endured, and the moral agenda has taken a new incarnation in which behaviours and identities associated with state dependence are more clearly placed beyond the pale. Ironically, the New Labour government has been unable to exorcize the ghosts of the previous administration. This is most clearly the case in relation to attempts to repeal Section 28 of the Local Government Act. Yet formal moves have been made to address homophobia with the Local Government Act 2000 (Section 104), stating that teachers must take steps to prevent any form of bullying, 'including homophobic bullying', reinforced by guidance on peer bullying 'related to sexual orientation'. Old arguments have not been resolved so much as laid over with a new policy discourse, in the course of which many of the policies for which sex education campaigners fought during the 1990s have been secured.

4.4   The changing language of policy discourse

A number of researchers have sought to trace the processes that have, over time, constituted the policy agenda for sex education. One of the most productive research approaches to sex education policy during the 1990s used textual analysis of policy documents, parliamentary debates and media representations. By treating documents as texts it was possible to identify tensions between the ways in which different policy discourses make available contradictory subject positions. For example, in an analysis of the 1994 Department for Education Guidance to schools, Daniel Monk explored the contingency of legal constructions of the child by observing discrepancies in the position of young people in the locations of 'health' and 'education'. He concluded that:

> In the health context the child is constructed in law as a *patient*, independent and potentially sexual while in the education context the child is a *pupil*, dependent, non-sexual and ideally heterosexual on obtaining adulthood. In this way the legal structure enables conflicting practices or expertise, to operate simultaneously and in this way, in a limited sense, resolves the political conflict.

(Monk, 1998, p.304, emphasis added)

ACTIVITY 3.5

Extracts 3.1 and 3.2 are taken from government guidance to schools on sex education issued in 1987 (under Margaret Thatcher's Conservative Government) and in 2000 (under Tony Blair's 'New Labour' Government). Each extract addresses the question of providing contraceptive advice to young people, constituted initially as 'pupils'.

Take a moment now to identify the main changes and the continuities between the extracts.

■   How does the language reflect changes in the overarching policy discourse in which the 'problem' of teenage sex is situated?

■   Are the differences of substance or only of tone?

Extract 3.1   Official guidance on 'sex education at school'

Good teachers have always taken a pastoral interest in the welfare and well-being of pupils. But this function should never trespass on the proper exercise of parental rights and responsibilities. On the specific question of the provision of contraceptive advice to girls under 16, the general rule must be that giving an individual pupil advice on such matters without parental knowledge or consent, would be an inappropriate exercise of a teacher's professional responsibilities, and could, depending on the circumstances, amount to a criminal offence.

(DES, 1987, p.5)

Extract 3.2   Official guidance on 'sex and relationship education'

2.9 In England in 1998 there were over 100,000 conceptions to teenagers, of which over 8,000 were to girls under 16. This is clearly totally unacceptable. Not only are there obvious risks to health, but this also leads to greater dependence, undermining potential achievement in education and further employment, placing greater stress on the young person and their family, and denying choices available to others. ... It is therefore appropriate for secondary schools to provide education about contraception.

2.10 Knowledge of the different types of contraception, and of access to, and availability of contraception is a major part of the Government's strategy to reduce teenage pregnancy. Effective sex and relationship education in secondary school has an important part to play in achieving this.

2.11 Trained staff in secondary school should be able to give young people full information about different types of contraception, including emergency contraception and their effectiveness. Pupils may wish to raise further issues with staff arising from discussions in the classroom. Trained teachers can also give pupils – individually and as a class – additional information and guidance on where they can obtain confidential advice, counselling and, where necessary, treatment.

(DfEE, 2000, p.15)

COMMENT

By tracing the rhetorical shifts between these texts it is possible to see the way in which pressure groups, civil servants and politicians employ language as a means of constructing a policy problem and how this changes over time. Here we see the 'problem' shifting from the infringement of parental authority, to a national problem of teenage pregnancy. Behind this shifting rhetoric it is possible to discern the ways in which different governments respond to the changing face of family life and intimate relations.

4.5 An integrated perspective on the personal in policy

A focus on texts can be helpful in deciphering the centrality of language to the strategic moves that mark shifts in social policy. However, it is also important not to 'over-read' them. An exclusive focus on texts can eclipse an understanding of their place within professional and institutional cultures and how they may be deployed as part of wider struggles over authority and influence. Table 3.3 outlines the different spheres within which it is possible to understand sex education policy as constituted: the national and local spheres and the formal and informal spheres of the school. Within each sphere it is possible to identify the key *texts*, the *actors* seeking to influence and interpret these texts, and the *techniques* that are used in order to translate policy into practice. Each sphere represents a lived culture in which the 'personal' has importance – civil servants, lobbyists and journalists operating at the national level share physical and symbolic spaces in much the same way as do the participants of a school. Moreover the spheres interact. Research or consultation may bring evidence of young people's sexual cultures into the national policy-making sphere. Levels and gatekeepers can be circumvented (a young person may ring a sexual health helpline) and texts are reinterpreted according to local conditions and interests. So one teacher may be happy to interpret Section 28 as meaning that she is 'not allowed' to teach about homosexuality, while another may actively challenge homophobia using official guidance on bullying as a resource to this end.

Table 3.3   A model of the spheres of sex education policy-making

National	
Texts	Legislation, official guidance, national curriculum, health strategy/targets, inspection framework
Actors	Pressure groups, national media, government departments, Teenage Pregnancy Unit, professional bodies (for example, British Medical Association, teaching unions)
Techniques	Research evidence, international models of good practice, public opinion, professional opinion, legal opinion relating to national and international frameworks
Local	
Texts	Local teenage pregnancy strategies, LEA policies for schools and youth work
Actors	Health and education professionals, teenage pregnancy co-ordinators, voluntary sector personnel, local media
Techniques	Resources, services, professional networks, local models of good practice, scandal and local popular opinion
Formal school	
Texts	School sex education policy, school curriculum, government guidance to schools on implementation

Formal school *(continued)*	
Actors	Governors, teachers, parents, school nurse/doctor, 'visitors', school council
Techniques	Lesson plans, teaching resources and methods, self-censorship, professionalism
Informal school	
Texts	Teenage magazines, graffiti, gossip, television
Actors	Young people, popular media, parents, teachers
Techniques	Reputations, popularity, embodied femininities and masculinities, resistance

Attempting to bring this picture together within one conceptual frame, Epstein and Johnson observe that the effect of an intensified political control of sex education has been to increase the distance between public policy and everyday life, noting that 'there has been a determined minority attempt to narrow the terms of sexual recognition while at the everyday level and in entertainment and youth-related media, sexual categories have become more fluid' (Epstein and Johnson, 1998, p.130). At the level of the school they see this reflected in a split between the student sexual culture and the official sexual regime focused on the regulation of make-up, etc. (Epstein and Johnson, 1998, p.128).

Mary Jane Kehily (2002a,b) has conducted extensive research into the provision and reception of sex education at the school level, including the interaction between the formal school and the informal sexual cultures of teachers and young people. In order to make sense of what happens in a sex education class she draws attention to the *cultural* ways in which sexuality is experienced within schools. Kehily notes that, while policy approaches stress the importance of certain pedagogic approaches and curriculum documents which 'strike the right note', these formal models fall apart in practice where success depends on a contingency of factors that cannot necessarily be accounted for at the level of policy:

> Mr Carlton, for example, is unlikely to match the selection criteria drawn up in a person specification for the post of sex educator. Rather, his profile as rugby-playing, heavy-drinking lad would place him beyond the bounds of desirability for the teaching of a subject which requires sensitivity and understanding, especially in relation to issues of gender politics. However the success of Mr Carlton's approach ... indicates that other factors might be at play in the development of 'good practice'. Mr Carlton's identification as local, working class, speaker of the regional dialect and part of the community gives him a grounding which facilitates the development of positive and mutually affirming pupil–teacher relations.
>
> (Kehily, 2002a, p.230)

Not only do teachers' pedagogic strategies need to be understood in relation to their own sexual and gender biographies (for example, Miss Green the 'good girl' who didn't get pregnant and Mr Carlton a local man who 'treats them the way their parents treat them'), but the ways in which students receive and resist these interventions need to be understood in terms of the particular class, 'race' and cultural dynamics of the particular teacher/pupil binary. Kehily cites comments such as 'she's always doing that', 'so bloody what?' and 'I bet she knows the Queen' as capturing 'the feelings of resentment, tedium and derision characteristic of many responses' voiced to her by students (Kehily, 2002a, p.216).

Other researchers have captured similar dynamics at play. Debbie Weekes (2002) cites a group of young black women's rejection of a white teacher's attempts to forge a personal link with them, in which the young women sexualize and 'other' the teacher in the process:

> [I got in trouble] and Miss Brown went [to me]. 'I know what it's like to be Black, I have Black friends' [I said] 'excuse me?' 'I know what it's like, I have Black friends' And then she had the nerve to say to [Nia] 'when you're going to Jamaica Nia, could you give this letter to my friend in Kingston?' You know I would've took the letter and I'd read it and tell everyone how it was to her lesbian friend. (Francine, 16)
>
> (Weekes, 2002, p.258)

And Thomson and Holland (2002) have observed that young people are distrustful of teachers who seek entry into their 'personal' worlds:

Richard: She tries too hard. It's like, she actually – Mr Levis relates to us. But she tries to be one of us. She's like oh ... she pries into our lives. She's like – oh I heard about you and

Lorna: At that party at the weekend. And you think, how did she find that out, you know. She's just so nosy. And Mr Levis, like you can sit down, and you can work and you can have a chat with him at the same time. She like comes over and the first thing she says: 'Did anyone see EastEnders last night?'. And it's like oh, shut up.

Richard: She tries to be really cool.

Lorna: But she just tries too hard. She's just annoying.

(pair interview, home counties school, age 14–15)

(Thomson and Holland, 2002, p.108)

ACTIVITY 3.6

Did you receive any sex education at school? If you did, try to write a brief description of a memorable moment of sex education.

- What most vividly marks this memory?
- How important was it in your own process of learning about sex?
- Now try to imagine the situation from the point of view of the teacher involved. What might it have felt like for them?

It is clear from the young people's views above that policy-making does not simply produce compliant subjects and that it does not always have the outcomes that it intends. Foucault (1980, p.142) has written that 'there are no relations of power without resistance', and power and resistance interact with each other in a continuing and unending spiral. Kehily suggests that, in the context of increased regulation of school life through testing and monitoring, young people's sexual cultures may become a site of resistance – 'adult-free and education-free zones in which students can collectively negotiate what is acceptable, desirable and what is "too much"' (Kehily, 2002b, p.207).

Sex education is quite different from learning about sex. The former is the outcome of political and institutional battles between national and local agents over what it is possible to 'tell'. Learning about sex is part of each individual's biography, beginning in earliest childhood. School sex education is likely to be one small part of that process, and research suggests that it is remembered primarily as an entertaining disruption in the life of the school, where it is possible to turn the tables on the teachers, to embarrass them, to make the lived sexual culture of the school playground and the staffroom explicit (Thomson and Scott, 1991; Kehily and Nayak, 1996). As one young woman interviewed commented: 'Oh yes, we asked him plenty of questions, we had him very embarrassed. We asked him, but he didn't answer any', 'Show us Sir, what do you mean?' (Holland et al., 1998, p.60).

5   Conclusion

In this chapter we have:

- traced the development of a social policy context in which the sexuality of young people is both denied and constructed as a 'problem';

- located this within a historical account of the changing character of youth and the fragmentation of different strands of transition to adulthood, suggesting that sexual experience needs to be understood in terms of levels of dependence and independence available to young people;

- looked at the relationship between social research and representations of sexuality in the wider culture, seeing how these contribute to what we 'know about sex' as well as the construction of social policy categories and problems;

- sketched, through a case study of sex education, the relationship between the development of social policy in the area of young people's sexuality, the social and cultural forces that contribute to it and its impact on the sexual cultures that it seeks to address.

In conclusion, it is possible to identify an enduring tension between competing social policy agendas that might be called protectionist (in which young people are designated as children, asexual and in need of protection) and an emergent agenda rooted in a notion of sexual citizenship (in which sexuality of young people is recognized and in which issues of rights, responsibilities and competence, rather than age, are stressed). The position of both feminist and health discourses have an uncertain relationship to these two agendas. A feminist concern with power relations and abuse in sexual relationships has been associated with aspects of a protectionist position, although feminist research that gives voice to young people's complex experiences has formed the foundation to understandings of sexual citizenship. Likewise, a sexual health perspective has been important in recognizing the existence of young people's sexuality and in countering the censoriousness of moralists who would prefer to deny it. Yet health perspectives are also limited and limiting, tending towards utilitarian solutions and having little interest in the sphere of the intimate as an arena of identity, self-expression and empowerment.

The balance of forces between these two policy agendas is highly contingent, depending on the activities and influence of a range of social actors including pressure groups, politicians, civil servants, professional opinion, the popular media and the contributions of social researchers. For social policies to gain support they must provide a compelling narrative – identifying a problem and suggesting a solution that has resonance with ordinary people's understandings. This chapter has shown how these narratives can change over time and how new constituents can be brought into the process of their definition. The stage on which these narratives are forged is increasingly international as processes of globalization intensify the exchange and consumption of information as well as the movement of people around the globe. While the agenda of sexual citizenship has relatively weak roots within the UK, it is able to draw strength from international policy discourses of children's and human rights. Nevertheless, the policy tensions between protectionism and sexual citizenship, and between the competing criteria of age, vulnerability and competence, are deeply rooted and are likely to shape policy in this area for some time.

Further resources

If you want to think more about the historical evolution of our ideas about sexuality, a good place to start is Jeffrey Weeks' *Sex, Politics and Society* (1989). Frank Mort's *Dangerous Sexualities: Medico-moral Politics in England Since 1830* (1987) will tell you more about the history of sex education; and Mary Jane Kehily's *Sexuality, Gender and Schooling: Shifting Agendas in Social Learning* (2002b) will bring you right up to date. For an in-depth picture of young people's sexual cultures, see *The Male in the Head: Young People, Heterosexuality and Power* by Janet Holland and colleagues (1998).

Useful websites include the following:

Social Exclusion Unit (SEU): www.socialexclusionunit.gov.uk (accessed 22 August 2003).

A cross-government unit that has produced a number of important reports identifying priority areas for intervention, including teenage pregnancy. Reports available at this site. The SEU report *Teenage Pregnancy* is available at www.socialexclusionunit.gov.uk/published.htm (accessed 22 August 2003) and at the Teenage Pregnancy Unit website below.

The Teenage Pregnancy Unit: www.teenagepregnancyunit.gov.uk (accessed 22 May 2003).

Established following the publication of the SEU report in 1999, responsible for implementing the Government's Teenage Pregnancy Strategy. Site includes information on the structure and remit of the unit, up-to-date information on conception rates, the evaluation of the strategy and useful links.

The Sex Education Forum: www.ncb.org.uk/sef/index.htm (accessed 22 May 2003).

Umbrella body bringing together a range of organizations promoting sex education. Includes links to member organizations' websites, newsletter, project information and publications.

The International Planned Parenthood Federation: http://www.ippf.org/ (accessed 22 May 2003).

International umbrella for family planning organizations, which operates at both national and international levels. Website provides up-to-date information on international policy agenda as well as national and regional profiles.

References

Beck, U. and Beck-Gernsheim, E. (1995) *The Normal Chaos of Love*, Cambridge, Polity Press.

Bjerrum Nielsen, H. and Rudberg, M. (2000) 'Gender, love and education in three generations: the way out and up', *The European Journal of Women's Studies*, vol.7, pp.423–53.

Bourdieu, P. (1977) *Outline of a Theory of Practice*, Cambridge, Cambridge University Press.

Bourke, J. (1994) *Working Class Culture in Britain 1890–1960: Gender, Class and Ethnicity*, London, Routledge.

Bragg, S. and Buckingham, D. (2002) *Young People and Sexual Content on Television*, London, Broadcasting Standards Commission.

Butler, J. (1990) *Gender Trouble: Feminism and the Subversion of Identity*, London, Routledge.

Connell, R.W. (1987) *Gender and Power: Society, the Person and Sexual Politics*, Cambridge, Polity Press.

Connolly, P. (1998) *Racism, Gender Identities and Young Children: Social Relations in a Multi-Ethnic Inner-City Primary School*, London, Routledge.

DES (Department of Education and Science) (1987) *Circular 11/87: Sex Education at School*.

DfEE (Department for Education and Employment) (2000) *Sex and Relationship Education Guidance*.

Durham, M. (1991) *Sex and Politics: The Family and Morality in the Thatcher Years*, London, Macmillan.

Ellis, H. (1937) *Studies in the Psychology of Sex*, Vols I–III, New York, Random House.

Epstein, D. and Johnson, R. (1998) *Schooling Sexualities*, Buckingham, Open University Press.

Erikson, E. (1968) *Identity, Youth and Crisis*, New York, Norton.

Fergusson, R. (1998) 'Choice, selection and the social construction of difference: restructuring schooling' in Hughes, G. and Lewis, G. (eds) *Unsettling Welfare: The Reconstruction of Social Policy*, London, Routledge.

Foucault, M. (1980) *Power/Knowledge: Selected Interviews and Other Writings, 1972–77* (edited by C. Gordon), London, Harvester Wheatsheaf.

Foucault, M. (1990) *The History of Sexuality, Volume 1: An Introduction*, Harmondsworth, Penguin.

Frosh, S., Phoenix, A. and Pattman, R. (2002) *Young Masculinities*, Cambridge, Polity Press.

Giddens, A. (1992) *The Transformation of Intimacy: Sexuality, Love and Eroticism in Modern Societies*, Cambridge, Polity Press.

Hite, S. (1976) *The Hite Report on Female Sexuality*, London, Macmillan.

Holland, J., Ramazanoglu, C., Sharpe, S. and Thomson, R. (1998) *The Male in the Head: Young People, Heterosexuality and Power*, London, Tufnell Press.

Irwin, S. (1995) *Rites of Passage: Social Change and the Transition from Youth to Adulthood*, London, UCL Press.

Jamieson, L. (1998) *Intimacy: Personal Relationships in Modern Societies*, Cambridge, Polity Press.

Johnson, A., Wadsworth, J., Wellings, K. and Field, J. (1994) *Sexual Attitudes and Lifestyle*, Oxford, Blackwell.

Jones, E., Darroch Forrest, J., Goldman, N., Henshaw, S., Lincoln, R., Rosoff, J., Westoff, C. and Wulf, D. (1985) 'Teenage pregnancy in developed countries: determinants and policy implications', *Family Planning Perspectives*, vol.7, no.2, pp.53–63.

Jones, G. (1995) *Leaving Home*, Buckingham, Open University Press.

Jones, G. and Bell, R. (2000) *Balancing Acts: Youth, Parenting and Public Policy*, York, York Publishing Services for Joseph Rowntree Foundation.

Kehily, M.J. (2002a) 'Sexing the subject: teachers, pedagogies and sex education', *Sex Education*, vol.2, no.3, pp.215–33.

Kehily, M.J. (2002b) *Sexuality, Gender and Schooling: Shifting Agendas in Social Learning*, London, Routledge.

Kehily, M.J. and Nayak, A. (1996) 'The Christmas kiss: sexuality, story-telling and schooling', *Curriculum Studies*, vol.4, no.2, pp.211–27.

Kimball, R. (ed.) (1983) *The Complete Lyrics of Cole Porter*, London, Hamish Hamilton.

Kinsey, A.C., Pomeroy, W.B. and Martin, C.E. (1948) *Sexual Behaviour in the Human Male*, Philadelphia, PA, and London, W.B. Saunders and Company.

Kinsey, A.C., Pomeroy, W.B., Martin, C.E. and Gebhard, P.H. (1953) *Sexual Behaviour in the Human Female*, Philadelphia, PA, and London, W.B. Saunders and Company.

Low, N., Sterne, J. and Barlow, D. (2001) 'Inequalities in rates of gonorrhoea and chlamydia between black ethnic groups in south east London', *Journal of Sexually Transmitted Infections*, vol.77, no.1, pp.15–20.

Masters, W.H. and Johnson, V.E. (1966) *Human Sexual Response*, Boston, MA, Little, Brown.

McNair, B. (2002) *Striptease Culture: Sex, Media and the Democratization of Desire*, London, Routledge.

Meredith, P. (1989) *Sex Education: Political Issues in Britain and Europe*, London, Routledge.

Monk, D. (1998) 'Sex education and HIV/AIDS: political conflict and legal resolution', *Children and Society*, vol.2, pp.295–305.

Moore, S. and Rosenthal, D. (1998) 'Adolescent sexual behaviour' in Coleman, J. and Roker, D. (eds) *Teenage Sexuality: Health, Risk and Education*, Reading, Harwood Academic.

Mort, F. (1987) *Dangerous Sexualities: Medico-Moral Politics in England Since 1830*, London, Routledge and Kegan Paul.

Phoenix, A. (1991) *Young Mothers?*, Cambridge, Polity Press.

Pinkney, S. (1998) 'The reshaping of social work and social care' in Hughes, G. and Lewis, G. (eds) *Unsettling Welfare: The Reconstruction of Social Policy*, London, Routledge, pp.250–90.

Plummer, K. (1995) *Telling Sexual Stories: Power, Change and Social Worlds*, London, Routledge.

Porter, R. and Hall, L. (1995) *The Facts of Life: The Creation of Sexual Knowledge in Britain, 1650–1950*, New Haven, CT, and London, Yale University Press.

Richardson, D. (1996) 'Heterosexuality and social theory' in Richardson, D. (ed.) *Theorising Heterosexuality*, Buckingham, Open University Press.

Sage, L. (2000) *Bad Blood*, London, Fourth Estate.

Scott, S. (2001) *The Politics and Experience of Ritual Abuse: Beyond Disbelief*, Buckingham, Open University Press.

Scott, S., Jackson, S. and Backett-Milburn, K. (1998) 'Swings and roundabouts: risk anxiety in the everyday worlds of children', *Sociology*, vol.32, no.4, pp.689–707.

SEU (Social Exclusion Unit) (1999) *Teenage Pregnancy*, Norwich, HMSO.

Sharpe, S. (2001) *More Than Just a Piece of Paper? Young People's Views on Marriage and Relationships*, London, National Children's Bureau.

Smith, T. (1993) 'Influence of socio-economic factors on attaining targets for reducing teenage pregnancies', *British Medical Journal*, vol.306, pp.1232–5.

Stainton Rogers, W. and Stainton Rogers, R. (1999) 'What is good and bad sex for children?' in King, M. (ed.) *Moral Agendas for Children's Welfare*, London, Routledge.

Stanley, S. (1995) *Sex Surveyed 1949–1994: From Mass-Observation's 'Little Kinsey' to the National Survey and the Hite Reports*, London, Taylor and Francis.

Thomson, R. (1994) 'Moral rhetoric and public health pragmatism: the contemporary politics of sex education' *Feminist Review,* vol.48, pp.40–60.

Thomson, R. (2000a) 'Legal, protected and timely: young people's reflections on the age of heterosexual consent', Monk, D. and Bridgeman, J. (eds) *Feminist Perspectives on Child Law*, Cavendish Press.

Thomson, R. (2000b) 'Dream on: the logic of sexual practice', *Journal of Youth Studies*, vol.4, no.4, pp.407–27.

Thomson, R. and Holland, J. (1998) 'Sexual relationships, negotiation and decision making' in Coleman, J. and Roker, D. (eds) *Teenage Sexuality: Health, Risk and Education*, Reading, Harwood Academic.

Thomson, R. and Holland, J. (2002) 'Young people, social change and the negotiation of moral authority', *Children and Society*, vol.16, pp.103–15.

Thomson, R. and Scott, S. (1991) *Learning About Sex: Young Women and the Social Construction of Sexual Identity*, London, Tufnell Press.

Thomson, R., Bell, R., Henderson, S., Holland, J., McGrellis, S. and Sharpe. S. (2002) 'Critical moments: choice, chance and opportunity in young people's narratives of transition to adulthood', *Sociology*, vol.6 no.2, pp.335–54.

Waites, M. (1999) 'The age of consent and sexual citizenship in the United Kingdom: a history' in Seymour, J. and Bagguley, P. (eds) *Relating Intimacies: Power and Resistance,* London, Macmillan.

Weekes, D. (2002) 'Get your freak on: how Black girls sexualize identity', *Sex Education*, vol.2, no.3, pp.251–63.

Weeks, J. (1989) *Sex, Politics and Society: The Regulation of Sexuality Since 1800* (2nd edn), London, Longman.

Wellings, K., Nanchahal, K., Macdowall, W., McManus, S., Erens, R., Mercer, C. H., Johnson, A.M., Copas, A.J., Korovessis, C., Fenton, K.A. and Field, J. (2001) 'Sexual behaviour in Britain: early heterosexual experience', *The Lancet*, vol.358, pp.1843–50.

CHAPTER 4

Silencing Sexuality: The Regulation of the Disabled Body

by Margrit Shildrick

Contents

1   Introduction

This chapter shows – through analysing a range of theoretical perspectives and empirical material – how normative assumptions about sexuality impact on the personal lives of people with disabilities, especially in relation to the discourses and practices of social policy.

Our purposes in working through the text can be summarized as follows:

Aims
- To open up the field of sexuality and disability to a critical analysis that challenges hitherto unquestioned attitudes, beliefs and values.

- To uncover the effects of the material processes and policies that organize lives.

- To consider the modes of representation that lie behind the so-called 'facts of the matter'.

This emphasis on discursive issues takes on some of the theoretical features of post-structuralism (see Chapter 1), and provides a new way of thinking about the issues of disability and sexuality. The point is always to question how meanings are constructed.

binary oppositions
A principal characteristic of Western thought is that what we 'know' is organized according to a series of **binary oppositions**. With regard to disability, the most obvious split is between those who are able-bodied and those who are not, which gives rise to the crude identification of the categories of 'us' and 'them'. Most of us, in the light of our own embodiment, know which side of the divide we fall on. Turning to sexuality, a conventional split occurs between hetero-sexuality and homosexuality; while in the area of social policy, there is a putative split between what is seen as either private or public, which in terms of social welfare feeds into the distinction between needs and desires. Nonetheless, by focusing on a particular group whose very forms of embodiment are the site of various more or less 'public' interventions, what is shown is that personal lives are never outside the discursive structures of society. The way in which the sexuality of people with disabilities is shaped and given meaning by a combination of sociocultural assumptions, the physicality of the body, the personal experience of desire, the operation of social policy, and so on, indicates the highly constructed nature of all sexuality. And while it is extremely important to acknowledge the specific consequences of differential embodiment, we should reflect too on the rigidity of the apparently common-sense division between those who are able-bodied and those who are disabled. If we take seriously the notion of constructionism (see Chapter 1), then perhaps none of our familiar categories should be taken for granted.

One major obstacle is the widespread use of the reductive term 'the disabled' which encourages planners and lay people alike to lump a large variety of disabling conditions into a single category which denies the individuality of each person's life. Despite the use of the wheelchair symbol to represent disability generally, there are very significant differences between having restricted mobility, for example, and being sight or hearing impaired, or having a congenital body anomaly. As the chapter will illustrate, words do matter, and the kind of discourse we engage in is highly influential in framing our expectations about those who differ from the norms of embodiment. Notice how 'anomaly' is a less loaded term of difference than the more familiar word 'deformity'. Consider too how the dehumanization implicit in the term 'the disabled' allows our society to cover over what are seen as the more personal aspects of everyday life.

silence   This is nowhere more apparent than in the relative **silence** about the sexuality of disabled people, and it would be fair to say that many professionals and even some activists in the field do not see it as a priority. But although the dominant discourse that frames disability has little to say about sexuality, and perhaps even deliberately avoids it, the point is that even in absence sexuality still plays a significant role in forging personal and social identities. In other words, sexuality is never simply a matter of what a person *does*, but more importantly it is to do with who he or she *is*. That is not to say that identities are ever fixed: because sexual practices change and develop over a lifetime and divergent meanings are attached to a person's sexuality, identity itself is always in a *process* of construction. As the chapter will show, personal identity, sexuality and disability alike are constructed not only by a web of determining factors, but are mutually constitutive. By focusing on the experience of disabled people, then, we shall explore the interconnections between personal and social identity, sexuality, the body, and – just as importantly – the assumptions about all those which underlie social policy.

2   Some preliminary definitions and grounding issues

To define something is never the neutral act that it might seem, because it always involves making choices about where the boundaries lie and about who or what is included or excluded from any particular category. It is about putting people, behaviours and bodies into boxes that are more amenable to order, control and management, about knowing the place of everyone and everything. In both bureaucratic society and personal lives alike this has the advantage of simplifying relationships with others and speeding up the structural processes to which we are all subjected. Definition is always an exercise in closing down some possibilities in favour of others, and although any orderly society cannot do without it, we should remember that it is not simply an unbiased description of how things really are. Right from the start, it is important to bear in mind that the terms we use are open to reinterpretation and change. It may help you to think of categories as being somewhat leaky rather than closed and watertight.

2.1   What counts as disability?

Many competing definitions of disability exist (Hughes, 1998) which give different emphasis to functional incapacities, to stigmatization, to physical or mental abnormality, to the condition of dependency, to the loss of social opportunities, or to the external restrictions that those with non-normative bodies may meet. All these tend to concentrate on the consequences of disability, but what is going on for the body itself? Not surprisingly, this is equally complex, for disability may include not only congenital impairment or the effects of trauma but also temporary or chronic disease, longstanding pain or, for most of us, the predictable effects of ageing. In a similar way, although the needs and interests of physically disabled and learning disabled people do overlap somewhat, the distinctions between them mean that any catch-all approach is bound to be seriously limited. We need to be clear that it is always an oversimplification to talk about disability as though it were a coherent category. Given the limits of space, this chapter concentrates on physical disability, but it is important to remember that what gets left out always deserves further thought.

Both physical and mental conditions are alike, however, in that the disabled person is deemed to have fallen short in some way of the normative standards of embodiment. To use the crude stereotype, he or she is 'not like us', where 'us' reflects the narrow parameters of a supposedly naturally given category of 'normality'. This in part may explain why there is a relative failure to research the experiences of minority ethnic groups. Given a social norm of whiteness, black bodies are already marked out as different, and disability is no longer seen as the significant difference from the dominant standard. It is important to acknowledge, then, that whatever the statistical norms to which some, and perhaps even a majority of, bodies approximate, there are nonetheless very wide variations. There are never just two clear-cut categories of either able-bodied or disabled into which we can neatly fit ourselves or, more likely, be fitted by others. For many people a disabling condition can be invisible for most of the time – epilepsy, for example, may be well controlled by medication, or the weakness and fatigue of multiple sclerosis may be intermittent and variable in intensity. Any one of us, moreover, can be unexpectedly incapacitated by accident or sickness, and as we grow older our bodily capabilities, such as sight, hearing, mobility, sexual performance and rationality, are likely to diminish. The division between those who are and are not disabled is by no means self-evident, and some disability activists have suggested the term **temporarily able-bodied** (TAB) as a more accurate description of the status of the majority. It reminds us all that at the very least the boundaries between categories are far more fluid than our everyday understanding and use of the term disability indicates.

temporarily able-bodied

2.2 Competing models

In recent years there has been a highly influential move from the traditional **medical model** to the **social model of disability** (SMD), suggested initially by activists (Oliver, 1990; Hughes, 1998, pp.77–86). Instead of seeing a range of disabling conditions as medical problems centred on individual bodies and susceptible to individual rehabilitation or alleviation (such as the use of hearing aids, speech therapy, prosthetic limbs or wheelchairs), activists argue that people are disabled by the social response to bodily impairments rather than by any individual problems. For instance, congenital blindness is an impairment but it is disabling only in so far as society fails to accommodate it by, for example, providing a full range of listening books in libraries, or marking the intersections of pavements and roads with a different surface that can be felt

medical model
social model of disability

easily with a guide stick. As the Union of the Physically Impaired Against Segregation definition asserts, the meanings of 'impairment' and 'disability' are not the same:

> *impairment* – 'lacking part or all of a limb, or having a defective limb, organism or mechanism of the body'
> *disability* – 'the disadvantage or restriction of activity caused by a contemporary social organization which takes no or little account of people who have physical impairments, and thus excludes them from the mainstream or social activities'.

(UPIAS, 1976, pp.3–4)

One important consequence of the SMD – and its political relevance – is that if the problems encountered by those with impairments are not just private but *socially constructed*, then changes in social policy can give a better quality of life.

ACTIVITY 4.1

Read Extract 4.1, written by the Minister for the Disabled and taken from a 1998 White Paper which introduced plans for the Disability Rights Commission. Identify what the Government's priorities are, the kind of discourse that expresses them, and what is left out.

Extract 4.1   Disability Rights Commission

The continuing extent of discrimination against disabled people and the exclusion of so many disabled people from the opportunities that they ought to have to contribute to our economy and our society are shaming. Not only is it ethically unacceptable that disabled people should experience prejudice and discrimination as they do, but it is foolish and to the detriment of the interests of all of us that it should be so.

We believe that a Disability Rights Commission will make a large contribution to ending discrimination against disabled people. It is not our intention that the Disability Rights Commission should work in an adversarial or oppressive way. We do not believe there should be any tension between the interests of disabled people and the interests of employers or of providers of goods and services; rather the contrary. We intend that the role of the Disability Rights Commission should be as much in educating and promoting good practice as in enforcement.

(DfEE, 1998, p.4)

COMMENT

In this extract, the White Paper shows concern with the *external* barriers, values and constraints that limit participation in social, economic and political citizenship. The appeal to a rights discourse based in such participation is therefore very important. The notion of social construction implicitly alluded to here – and an important theme throughout this chapter – is increasingly deployed at the level of social policy, in contradistinction to, or alongside, the older medical model.

The SMD itself attracts some criticism for its tendency to cover over the often very real effects of *bodily* difference. For example, if someone experiences an uncontrollable pain in their legs, then no level of removing social obstacles to mobility will allow them to experience directly the pleasures of running on the beach. In concentrating on social effects, it is as though the body itself is unimportant and that we could theorize disability without reference to it. Several writers have picked up this shortcoming (Crow, 1996; Shildrick and Price, 1996) and it is worth considering its special relevance to sexuality. Because in our discursive tradition sexuality is understood primarily in terms of private bodily pleasures and face-to-face physical and emotional relationships, its problems have not been addressed by the SMD. As Tom Shakespeare (2000, p.162) says, 'A social constructionist approach that loses contact with the physical does us no favours. I think we have to have a position that recognizes difference and limitation, and the very real problems which disabled people may have with their bodies and their lack of function'.

More recently, however, theorists, welfare professionals and disability activists alike have become more aware that sexuality itself is also subject to social construction and that, like the category of disability, it too is defined in terms of normative values.

ACTIVITY 4.2

Close your eyes and imagine yourself in a different body, with disabilities other than those you may have already. For example, imagine being 50 pounds heavier or being old and frail. Imagine having a mobility disability that requires the use of a wheelchair, or being unable to move or use your hands and arms. Perhaps you have a speech impediment or involuntary muscular spasms or facial expressions. Or it could be a sensory impairment of hearing or sight. Perhaps your imagined disability is hidden, but you must wear a catheter.

Now ask yourself a series of questions (adapted from Galler, 1984):

- How would you feel coming into a room full of strangers?
- If you were invited to a party by a new acquaintance, would you feel comfortable going?
- Would you join a group going to the pool? Could you let your body show?
- Suppose someone new wanted to sleep with you. How would you respond in your imaginary body? How would you feel about undressing in front of them? How would you relate sexually? How do you imagine your new partner would react?

COMMENT

The exercise may expose how uncomfortable we are with difference, including our own differences. It makes us confront internalized normative values and the limitations they place on our understanding of bodies and sexuality. Self-esteem is highly tied up with bodily form, and even the smallest anomaly, let alone larger ones, can be deeply undermining. This exercise also illustrates that normative assumptions have emotional as well as social implications.

2.3   A radical view of embodied difference

To insist that disability is always about embodiment opens up a more radical understanding of how the categorizations of normal and abnormal are used to inscribe and structurally advantage some people above others. Regardless of recognized disability status, most of us acknowledge that our bodies are far from the ideal that society promotes. Widespread concerns with issues such as weight, the appearance of our skin, physical fitness, and the growing use of cosmetic surgery to radically alter appearance, all make clear that the body is seen as highly malleable and that our normative standards are constructed rather than given. At the same time, what counts as a desirable form of embodiment varies both historically and culturally. Consider the old Chinese tradition of foot binding, or the wasp waists aspired to by British Victorian women that so constricted breathing that fainting fits were commonplace. From present-day perspectives we probably see both practices as productive of disability, yet they once constituted normative standards of feminine beauty. In other words, the idea of normality that we take for granted is not a natural biological given but marks instead a discursively constructed set of meanings and values that are always open to significant changes.

None of us lives up to the normative ideals precisely because the categories of difference that organize our lives are never really fixed and distinct, but fluid and unstable (Shildrick, 1997). This idea enables us to deconstruct – take apart the operation of – many forms of oppositional binary thinking including that of able-bodied/disabled, us/them, sexual/asexual, and to think instead in terms of a continuum (see Figure 4.1). Nonetheless, though *fixed* categories are illusionary, we do, for the most part, act as though the differences between people are mutually exclusive. Indeed, our society puts a great deal of stress on marking out boundaries, even at the cost of ignoring our everyday experiences. The rigid separation of masculinity and femininity or heterosexuality and homosexuality, for example, simply overrides men's 'feminine side' or the commonality of homoerotic dreams in convinced heterosexuals.

3   Sexuality, disability and control

Let us turn now to constructions of sexuality, and to how issues of sexuality are dealt with (or not) in the sphere of disability and in the relevant areas of social policy.

Figure 4.1   Alexa Wright's photo images challenge the distinction between 'us' and 'them' by using her own face on the bodies of women with disabilities

3.1   The construction of normative sexuality

Like disability, the notion of sexuality is highly complex and can be given many different and sometimes competing meanings, which should again alert us to the idea that it is socially and culturally constructed rather than natural or biologically fixed (Saraga, 1998). Throughout life, sexual expression is highly bound up with normative expectations – that it is, for example, wrong or dirty for young children, exploratory and exciting for adolescents, reproductive in heterosexual coupledom, and somewhat distasteful in older age. All make clear that sexuality is never a neutral fact of life, but can only be understood within the specific context in which it occurs. Moreover, although the term is used to mean individual sexual practices and personal relationships, it also covers the social expression of those practices and relationships. As such, it is no surprise that the state maintains a clear public interest in regulating the sexuality of its citizens. Even in the realm of what we think of as private sexual behaviour – in lay terms what goes on in the bedroom – sexuality is subjected to a web of regulatory controls. These range from strictly legal constraints about such things as consent, incestuous relationships, rape, child abuse, and so on, to the less formalized but no less powerful sociocultural standards that determine what is acceptable and valued, and what is not (see Chapter 1).

For our society those standards are centred on the monogamous heterosexual relation between two putatively equal adults whose sexual practice is primarily genitally based and conducted in private. Yet despite a putative distinction between **public and private** and a belief that certain areas are primarily a matter of individual choice and agency beyond the reach of state concern, sexuality is rarely, if ever, under personal control. The material controls of familial, religious, community and social rules and regulations may be resisted, but they are fundamentally inescapable. And at the same time, the power of discursive norms – the values, beliefs and traditions of any group – play an equal part in problematizing the public/private binary. Those who reject the normative standards are seen as a threat to the very fabric of society. People who challenge our sense of sexual propriety or morality do not simply meet public censure but may find themselves – as, for example, in some expressions of homosexuality – crossing into illegality. And remember, it is not just that norms are imposed on a fixed sexuality after the fact; rather, they are a major force in organizing and managing sexuality.

public and private

In *The History of Sexuality*, Foucault (1979) shows how these processes first emerged during the eighteenth century. And he goes on to outline how sexuality is constructed and controlled through the operation of what he calls **disciplinary practices** (see Chapter 1). We will return to this in section 3.3.

disciplinary practices

3.2   Disability and the silencing of sexuality

What, then, of those who cannot – because of bodily difference – meet the normative standards of sexuality: people unable to experience genital effect or verbally communicate their needs and desires; women who will never conceive, or men who cannot produce sperm; those whose institutionalized lives allow for little privacy; sexual partners who require the physical support of third parties;

or those whose ageing bodies are no longer fertile? The experience of disability covers a huge range of differences, which can have anything from a profound physical effect on sexuality to virtually none at all. Yet, because so little attention is paid to the particularity of each person, nearly all disabled people suffer from the general tendency to dismiss the idea of their sexuality altogether. A comprehensive collection of articles on feminism and sexuality (Jackson and Scott, 1996), for example, makes no mention of disability, while perhaps more surprisingly *The Disability Studies Reader* (Davis, 1997) is scarcely less silent on the subject of sexuality, unless linked to reproduction. Similarly, the Government-sponsored *Practical Guide for Disabled People* (DoH, 2002) devotes eleven pages to work and nine to education but only three to 'personal and sexual relationships'.

In popular culture we are surrounded by images of sexuality, which both construct and reflect a powerful series of social norms. Just as gender and ethnicity, for example, are stereotyped, so too is disability – and in a highly negative fashion, as Figure 4.2 illustrates. Part of the difficulty is that what counts as sexually attractive is confined to a fairly narrow band.

ACTIVITY 4.3

Before reading further, consider the issues raised in Extracts 4.2 and 4.3. Think about how sexuality cannot be boxed off, but has important consequences for self-esteem in general.

Extract 4.2   Desiring Michael

I'm a very independent guy. I'm intelligent, I'm funny, and thanks to the miracles of hair-products, I daresay I am able to attract a decent share of admiring looks when I put in the effort to do so. All in all, a pretty good package, one I feel comfortable presenting to the world on most days. Then my disability reaches out and smacks me, just to make sure I don't forget what I really am, and all of that hard-won (and carefully crafted) confidence goes flying out the window.

Who was I kidding? Michael is handsome and strong and desirable. Then there's me, the helpless, clumsy cripboy who can't even manage to walk down the street without making a spectacle of himself. How could I ever hope to compete against all the other bodies that are so much closer to perfect than mine will ever be? Will I still be attractive to him after he's had to pick me up off the ground for the umpteenth time? Will he grow tired (or worse, ashamed) of my limp, my scuffed shoes, my scraped knees?

(Aguilera, 2002)

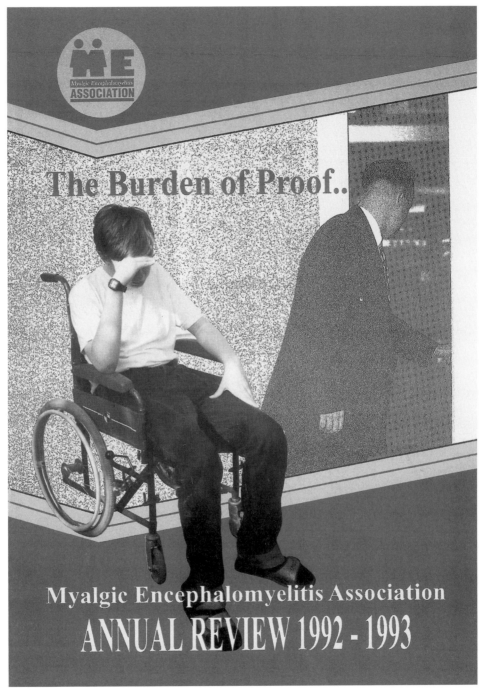

Figure 4.2   An older image of disability that still persists in our cultural tradition

Extract 4.3   Sexual value and disability

It's difficult for some of us to stare back at an airbrushed image of physical perfection, say in Playboy or muscle magazines, and not start contemplating deeper issues of self-worth. We keep telling ourselves that the quality of our lives and our attractiveness should have nothing to do with flawless skin and bodily virtue – but they seem to anyway.

In the realm of disability, these issues are even more intensely felt. They go right to the heart of sexual self-esteem for those of us struggling to maintain visibility within a culture that imposes ruthless standards for attractiveness and desirability. The mandate, or so it would seem for individuals with disabilities, requires a sort of physical legitimacy in order to obtain love and acceptance, with a certain sexual model as the gateway to both.

We are overwhelmed with television, magazine, and billboard ads using conventionally beautiful bodies to sell everything from jeans to taco chips. Sexual value has a certain cultural look that typically does not include people with disabilities. When was the last time you saw an attractive woman in a wheelchair selling Slim-Fast, or a Paralympic athlete posing for a Gap ad?

(Tarricone, 2000)

In the light of your own experience, spend a few moments reflecting on images that involve people with disabilities, whether in the media presentation of 'real life' narratives, television and film dramas, the visual imagery of advertisements, or in fiction.

What is striking is not just the paucity of positive representations, but the almost complete absence of examples portraying a sexual context. At the time of writing, we can think of Carrie in *ER*, who is mobility-impaired, and the deaf character Joey Lucas in *The West Wing*, but each is highly unusual in having a sexual life that is not dependent on her disability. More often, there is an implicit pity stemming from the assumption that disabled people have either lost or never experienced sexuality. The actor Christopher Reeves, for example, who came to fame as Superman, is widely admired for his fortitude since suffering traumatic spinal cord injury, but he is no longer seen as a sexual being. His oft-stated determination to regain mobility encourages the media to mark him out as what disability activists scathingly refer to as a 'supercrip' – someone who fits the 'heroic' narrative of overcoming misfortune. The alternative, less gushing view is that the purported supercrip is unable to accept bodily difference. But it is hardly a private matter. It is society at large that has trouble with difference and you may find yourself thinking that the general negativity of the imagery simply reflects the facts of life for disabled people. Even those of us who are acutely aware of the construction of gender, class or 'race' bias may regard disability as an unchanging unnatural condition, in which sexuality in particular is not an issue. The point is that so strongly is 'proper' sexuality associated with one particular set of standards that there is very little recognition that those outside the standards have any sexuality at all. In other words, disabled people are seen – implicitly and explicitly – as sexless.

Where the sexuality of a person with disabilities is portrayed, it is rarely as just one ordinary facet of life, and is more likely to be seen as 'improper', or even perverted. As Robert Murphy (1987, p.83) comments: 'The sexual problems of the disabled are aggravated by a widespread view that they are either malignantly sexual, like libidinous dwarfs, or more commonly, completely asexual, an attribute frequently applied to the elderly as well'. The same point is made by Kirsten, who as a blind woman shows that it is not only overt bodily anomalies that elicit a negative response. In her experience, the image of people with disabilities is:

> Very unsexy, but also ... slightly monstrous and very perverted. Which always makes it a bit of a challenge being a lesbian actually, because they just think you are being utterly perverse and perverted. The image of a disabled person is not a sexual being, it's not someone attractive and beautiful.
>
> (quoted in Shakespeare et al., 1996, p.69)

In general, it seems that if sexual practices do not fall within the normative range, they are either delegitimized – as in interracial, or lesbian and gay relationships – or simply not recognized at all. There is usually no problem in acknowledging the existence of loving and caring relationships involving those with disabilities, but that operates alongside a widespread disbelief or denial that sexual pleasure is part of it, still less that sex could be valued for its own sake. The evidence indicates that the majority of able-bodied people quite literally believe that sexual function disappears in many instances of disability – that men with spinal cord injury cannot achieve erection, that women with congenital skeletal disorders do not experience orgasm, or that those with cerebral palsy cannot give birth. In fact none of these assertions is true, and in any case, loss of sexual function is not the same as having no sexuality. Yet even professional carers can make such assumptions. As Sarah Earle (1999, p.317) remarks: 'The perception of the severity of an individual's impairment seemed to be associated, not necessarily with asexuality, but with an incorrect belief that it habitually relates to a physical inability to engage in sexual activity'. Such sincere but inaccurate beliefs, and widespread lay prejudices alike, are generalized across the bodies of all disabled people.

infantilization

Another factor is at work here too. As medical sociologists have long recognized, anyone who suffers illness, and to some extent becomes more dependent, is likely to be subjected to **infantilization** – treated as though he or she were a child. It is no different for people with impairments (Morris, 1993; Shakespeare et al., 1996) and they often complain – with good reason – of being patronized. More to the point, childhood sexuality, as we know, is either denied or suppressed in our society (see Chapter 3), so it is a short step to doing the same to disabled people.

3.3   Social policy and silence

When we turn to the operation of social policy it is clear that one of its major effects concerns the organization of social knowledge around the split which sets standards of normativity against putative or real vulnerability, dependency, deviancy, and so on. Like the media, social policy is both reflective of existing power/knowledge attitudes and discursively constructs those attitudes through what Foucault calls **power/knowledge** (see Chapter 1).

As Foucault understands it, any authoritative discourse exercises power by claiming to speak the truth – which in turn imposes the parameters of accepted knowledge. Many different types of discourse are at work in the operation of power/knowledge but, according to Foucault, medicine and to a lesser extent education are at the forefront. Although he does not link these to social policy, such policy is fully implicated in his analysis. Foucault himself was particularly interested in the effect of power/knowledge on bodies and his major concentration falls on how sexuality is constituted, disciplined and regulated:

> [Sexuality is] not a furtive reality that is difficult to grasp, but a great surface network in which the stimulation of bodies, the intensification of pleasures, the incitement to discourse, the formation of special knowledges, the strengthening of controls and resistances, are linked to one another, in accordance with a few major strategies of knowledge and power.
>
> (Foucault, 1979, pp.105–6)

One of Foucault's most important claims is that the strategies of construction and control work through the setting up of normativities which lay out the boundaries of the operative categories. In other words, each of us operates within a strictly bounded category that to a large degree determines how we can name ourselves, what we can 'know', and the limits of appropriate behaviour. To see oneself as heterosexual, for example, makes it difficult to acknowledge same-sex desire. As we have already seen, the categories of normal and abnormal are opposed to one another, but both are subjected to disciplinary controls that keep their boundaries in place. This is achieved in a variety of ways, but Foucault is less concerned with the power of material force than with the power of **surveillance** and even **self-surveillance**. To use his example, it is not a matter of physically punishing masturbating children so much as subjecting them to a gaze that will find them out if they transgress sexual normativities. Even when such external surveillance is absent, people internalize its disciplinary power, and impose self-regulation. In other words, modern power is discursive: it works both through defining the boundaries of our normative categories and by policing them through an all-seeing knowledge.

surveillance
self-surveillance

How do all these considerations manifest themselves in the discourse and practices of social policy? Although the explicit aims are to alleviate need and to compensate for vulnerability, social policy is concerned also with the containment and management of those it identifies as its clients. For instance, in order to benefit from welfare payments, potential recipients must give a full accounting of their lives and are likely to be subjected to continual surveillance and disciplinary controls. Unemployed claimants, for example, are required to sign on regularly, attend job clubs, and report any absences from home. All this is so familiar that we scarcely notice the level of intervention into both the public and private aspects of life that it implies. In a similar way a Foucauldian analysis can help throw light on social policy initiatives with regard to disability and sexuality, even though the issue of sexuality is most notable for its absence. The extensive Disability Living Allowance (DLA) application forms, for example, run to dozens of pages and demand a highly detailed and differentiated personal accounting of bodily function in relation to cooking, mobility or toilet needs, among others, but there is no mention of sexuality or sexual needs. The explanation cannot be reticence about so-called personal matters, for other similar areas covered by the questions exhibit a high degree of what might be considered intrusive.

ACTIVITY 4.4

Consider Figure 4.3 – a single page of the DLA forms – and try to work out what explicitly and implicitly might be behind the questions.

COMMENT

For those who frame policy, the justification for such questions might be that they need to have a full picture of the highly differential needs of each claimant before they can formulate appropriate interventions. As the form itself states: 'The more you can tell us, the easier it is for us to get a clear picture of the type of help you need' (section 2.1). Indeed, some pressure groups for disabled people have welcomed the very specific nature of the questions as being more responsive to individual needs than an approach that lumps all sorts of disabilities into the same category. But given that there are limited options – either in the form of financial benefits, or goods and services – that are provided to those with disabilities, is such a detailed accounting really necessary? Note too that completion of the form extends the reach of regulatory knowledge by requiring each individual to provide a personal accounting. In other words, it relies on self-surveillance and effectively pushes the person involved into fitting himself or herself into a category. In one important sense the whole process is part of the construction of disability. And it exemplifies exactly that demand to know – the operation of power/knowledge – which Foucault predicts.

The question, then, is whether the disappearance of sexuality from the surveillance process is just as significant as the over-accounting of other aspects of personal life. Foucault certainly thought that silence was significant:

> Silence itself – the things one declines to say or is forbidden to name, the discretion that is required between different speakers – is less the absolute limit of discourse ... than an element that functions alongside the things said ... [silences] are an integral part of the strategies that underlie and permeate discourses.
>
> (Foucault, 1979, p.27)

But can we apply his insight here? Remember that what the DLA process shows is that social policy is not after all bound by any public/private split. And it is not simply that policies operating in the public sphere inevitably filter down to have effects on personal lives, it is more that there are direct interventions. Any notable absence, then, surely conveys a meaning that plays its part in constructing the category from which it is excluded. In this case, it implies that any assessment of sexuality is missing because people with disabilities are being actively constructed as non-sexual. Now this is a very strong claim, and we

Washing, bathing and looking after your appearance

Do you have problems washing, having a bath or shower, or looking after your appearance?   No ☐

Some examples might be   Yes ☐
• getting into or out of the bath or shower
• cleaning your teeth
• washing your hair
• shaving
• checking your appearance
• personal hygiene
• coping with periods.
Or something else.

Does someone have to tell you, remind you or encourage you to wash or take a bath or shower?   No ☐

Yes ☐

Describe in your own words the problems you have and the help you need washing, bathing or showering, or looking after your appearance. If you need to wash or bath or shower more than once a day, please tell us why. If you have bed baths, tell us how long they take.

☐

Tell us about any equipment you use to help you with washing, bathing or showering, or looking after your appearance. Tell us how the equipment helps you and how useful it is. Tell us if someone helps you use the equipment.

☐

How long on average does it take you to wash or to have a bath or shower?

☐

How many days a week do you need help with washing, bathing or showering, or looking after your appearance?

☐ days a week

How many times a day do you need help with washing, bathing or showering, or looking after your appearance?

☐ times a day

Figure 4.3   Page from Disability Living Allowance application form (Source: Benefits Agency, 2001)

should be aware that few if any social policy-makers would readily agree to its veracity. If challenged, they are more likely both to reiterate the rigidity of the public/private split that supposedly exempts personal concerns from policy mandates, and to point to the fundamental belief that social policy's remit is to answer to needs not desires. In such reckonings, the agencies of the state have no concern with sexuality (see Chapter 1).

need and desire   If there is such a binary distinction between **need and desire**, how far do we as a society believe that desires as well as needs should be met by public policy? There is little doubt that existing social policies are singularly lacking in any acknowledgment of pleasure as such, but does that overlook the fact that pleasure is a highly consequential aspect in the quality of life? In a situation of inevitably scarce resources we might decide that only basic needs should be funded, but if the aim is to achieve some kind of equitable value to life – in this case between differently abled people – how can we say that some people do not need to experience the pleasure freely available to others? As far as sexuality is concerned, the strategy of denying or ignoring the sexual needs or desires of disabled people simply sidesteps the issue. Recent moves within social policy to **independent living**   support what is termed **independent living**, which is intended to give a higher degree of autonomy to disabled people to decide their own priorities and organize their own lives, may mean, however, that the question of sexuality cannot be long postponed.

4   Challenging the stereotypes

In this section, we explore some relatively recent developments within the disability community itself and in social policy. Faced with a long history in which sexuality has been put to one side, consciously or not, what are the signs that the silence may finally be breaking?

4.1   Voices from the disability community

Given the very evident power of the discourses that construct both disability and sexuality, it is hardly surprising that even those with personal experience of disability have been locked into a system of generalized categories bounded by highly normative expectations. None of us is able to stand outside the various discourses that construct our sexuality. Until recently, material coming from the disability community would not have indicated that there were any major issues to address around either sexual practices or sexual identities. Like the rest of the population, disabled people by and large maintained a silence about the subject or saw themselves as others saw them: that is, as having severely compromised or even absent sexual expression. As one female polio survivor remembers: 'I always felt like a neutral sex. It's like I'm not a woman, not a man. I don't know what I am because I was never approached like a woman' (Nosek et al., 2001, p.5). And Eddie, who has spina bifida, recalls: 'When I fancied a girl, I wouldn't tell her. I was seen as a really good guy, you had a good laugh, I would always listen. Most women saw me as a big brother, rather than a boyfriend' (Shakespeare et al., 1996, p.63).

Yet recent empirical studies give a very different perspective. One qualitative study on 14 men with moderate to severe cerebral palsy found that, despite an array of painful social and emotional obstacles to establishing sexual intimacy, most had been sexually active and all were acutely sexually aware (Shuttleworth, 2002). Similarly, a recent study of women with disabilities reveals the hitherto unacknowledged extent of disabled sexuality (Nosek et al., 2001). Like their able-bodied peers, well over 90 per cent of the women had experienced a sexual relationship in their lifetimes, though the finding that fewer (a ratio of 49 to 61 per cent) were currently in a relationship reflects the reduced opportunities for sexual engagement that disabled women face. The most challenging result, however, was not in the differences but in the similarity. As the authors note: 'We found significant differences in the level of sexual activity, response, and satisfaction, with women with disabilities reporting much lower levels. There were no differences, however, between the groups on sexual desire' (Nosek et al., 2001, p.20). You will be asked to think more about this survey in section 5.2.

Although the push for greater rights has long been a focus of resistance to the stereotyping that society – including social policies – imposes, the activist SMD centres on external issues such as access to education and employment and to public facilities. It has little place for the body, still less for the emotional and psychic components that play such a large part in sexual relations, or for the sense in which sexuality is tied up with identity. Apart from some individual voices, the rethinking of sexuality has not been considered a priority. Now, however, some sections of the community are beginning to challenge the representation of disability and sexuality and to see it as another area in which specific campaigns can make a material difference. Of course, like the population in general, not all disabled people place a high value on sexual expression, but sexuality has become an area of discussion in newsletters, websites, cultural events, conferences, and, to some extent, in academic texts.

One highly influential source is *The Sexual Politics of Disability* (Shakespeare et al., 1996) which for almost the first time discusses the issues from the perspective of people with disabilities. Several years on, there has been relatively little development of its themes. The book explodes many of the myths and prejudices around sexuality and makes clear that disabled people, like everyone else, have a range of sexual preferences and attitudes towards normative sexual expression. By highlighting the term 'sexual politics' the authors directly challenge the presumption that sexuality is a private matter. As feminists have long since discovered, the personal *is* political.

4.2   Rethinking sexual stereotypes

gender difference   One important advance in the disability community concerns how **gender difference** is fed into the question of disability and sexuality. The two autobiographical passages in Extract 4.4, given by a woman named Selma, begin with her childhood in India and then move on to her adult life in the UK.

Extract 4.4   Selma's story

I lost my sight due to meningitis at the age of four. My whole family was in mourning for several months as a result of this 'tragedy'. It was thought especially tragic because of my being a girl. If I had been a boy, it would not be 'half as bad', as on reaching marriageable age they could find a woman to look after me and I would have been 'all right'. My being a girl meant that I was a burden on the family for the rest of their lives, for no man was going to want me. Especially as I would not be able to fulfil my role of keeping a home and bearing children (how could I – I was blind) ... Women are still expected to be the carers in a relationship, and therefore would be happy to marry a disabled man, but not the other way round.

...

I enjoy being a woman, and various men have always told me how attractive I am, but I also know that my disability, especially with Asian men, always stops them from getting involved with me. As one non-disabled man, a vicar who is a colleague in the equal opportunities field, recently said to me, 'It is very important to a man to have an attractive woman as his partner and one who isn't disabled in some way, because it is a question of pride for him as men compete with each other for the prettiest woman on their arm ... ' Women are sexual objects to boost the male ego as ornaments of his masculine pride, and disabled women are flawed objects.

(quoted in Shakespeare et al., 1996, pp.146, 152)

Whatever your own bodily status, pause for a moment to think about your personal expectations of gendered sexual behaviour, and how those might impact on people with disabilities. What evidence is there, both in the extract and in your own reflections, that Selma's experience of sexism around her disability is hardly culture-specific (see Figure 4.4)?

In common with wider societal norms, the presumption is that loss of sexual function is of greater importance for a man than it is for a woman. Our expectations of normative masculinity and femininity are very closely related to sexuality: stereotypically men are expected to be active, dominant and able to take the initiative, while women are passive receivers. In many forms of popular culture old attitudes towards gendered behaviour are shifting, albeit in a limited way, but there is little sign that such changes are reflected in the discourse surrounding disability and sexuality. In consequence, discussion of impaired sexual capacity and function has been heavily skewed towards the male experience. Although the disability community itself has recognized that disabled men are far more capable of sexual feelings and activity than the stereotype allows, the putative loss of self-directed independence has been seen as the most salient point. In contrast, in lay terms and to a large extent within disability politics itself, the 'tragedy' of disability for a woman has been perceived not as the assumed effect on sexual activity but on her ability to become a mother.

Could less traditional models of gendered relations offer more hope? Many disabled women, often supported by feminist ideals, have long since challenged

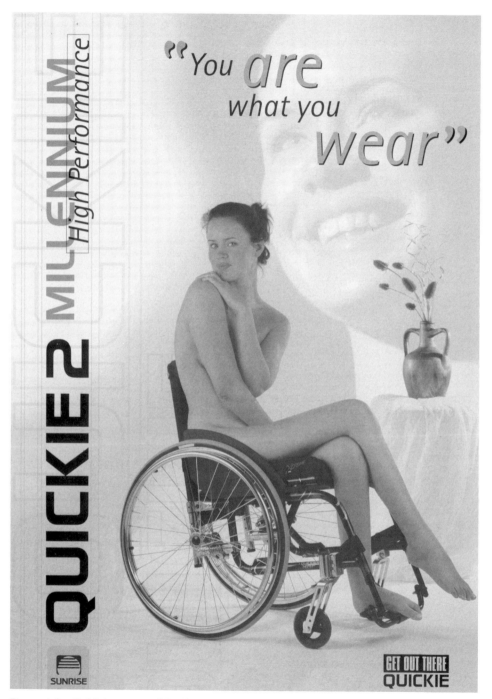

Figure 4.4   Publicity material for high-performance wheelchair

the normative view, but it is only recently that the community as a whole has
begun to contest the rigidity of the masculine/feminine binary. Just as HIV-
positive men and women have been forced to break with gender and sexual
stereotypes in the search for 'safe sex' practices, so too those with disabilities
have rethought their modes of sexual expression. If full physical autonomy is

impossible, then one way forward is to challenge the convention of male-dominant heterosexuality.

There is now a growing acceptance that masculinity and femininity need not be reliant on traditional patterns of sexual behaviour: it is not necessary for men to be in control in order to enjoy their sexuality, and women need not be always on their backs. Moreover, if conventional intercourse is painful or difficult to achieve, then disabled people are exploring a range of alternative sexual pleasures – such as oral sex, stroking, fantasy and finding sexual expression through other forms of intimacy such as emotional closeness and touch. It requires courage to challenge sexual normativities, particularly by those perceived as 'weak', but as David, who has a speech impairment, puts it: 'people on the fringe – and we are – need to position themselves not in the secure mainstream but they need to be on the edge and they need to take risks and gamble' (Shuttleworth, 2002, p.118). In resisting dominant meanings, disabled people can reconstruct themselves as sexual beings. For many gays and lesbians with disabilities, and some others who have already rethought the conventions, much of this is familiar, but for more conservative heterosexual men and women, and particularly those who associate sexuality primarily with reproduction, it may break new ground and open up the possibility of satisfying sexual lives. This new thinking is highly relevant to the type of care or assistance that those with disabilities receive. So long as there is a physical need for external services, the very evident breakdown between private and public means that changing attitudes and values in one sphere has implications for the other. In the next section we will look more closely at how social policy has responded to the challenges.

5   Social policy and the negotiation of sexuality

Before reading further, pause to remember that sexuality is not just about sexual function. It is about how we understand our embodiment; about masculinity and femininity; about the experience of pleasure and desire; and about self-identity and identifications. And rather than simply being the property of an individual, the import of sexuality is always both personal and social.

To reiterate, social policy has a constitutive effect on all these things. That is to say, it does not simply reflect a predetermined view of a person's sexuality, but actually plays a part in constructing it in a particular way. If someone with disabilities receives no recognition as a sexual being, then that view becomes internalized with a probable resultant loss of self-esteem. Equally, if people with disabilities redefine their sexuality better to fit their bodily experiences, then that reconstruction feeds back into how the wider society understands both disability and sexuality and will shift normative expectations. The mutually constitutive process is an example of the operation of Foucault's notion of power/knowledge. Let us now further explore the social policy side of the interaction.

5.1   The reach of social policy

All through the chapter the idea that there are neat little boxes housing well-defined categories has been challenged and, as you might anticipate, social policy too is far more fluid than traditional accounts suggest. The values, decisions and operative policies flow into all areas of life, and contrary to expectations have a deep influence in personal life.

ACTIVITY 4.5

Consider now the areas in which social policy exercises its power in the lives of disabled people, and think about how it operates in relation to sexuality. Inevitably there will be several overlapping categories, and you may want to expand this brief list.

Access

■   For many disabled people access is highly restricted unless facilitated by mechanical and human aids. The Disability Discrimination Act 1995 enforces accessibility to many leisure facilities (as well as to shops, offices and work places), but it does not cover existing private clubs or other venues where disabled people might meet potential sexual partners. And remember, access for some severely disabled people means being able to freely invite others into their place of residence.

Education

■   Despite huge strides towards fully integrated education – for physically disabled children at least – discrimination remains. Sexuality may be seen as a problem and implicitly discouraged by excusing disabled adolescents from sex education classes at worst, or by failing to address their differential needs. As a result many disabled people are left unaware of both the pleasures and dangers of sex.

Biomedicine

■   The medicalization of disability gives authoritative justification to many restrictions placed on sexuality. The history of eugenics, with its stress on purity, positions disability as a contamination. The elimination of less-than-perfect bodies remains evident now in the abortion of foetuses that show congenital deformities and in technologies – such as germ line therapy – that permanently eliminate genetic disabilities.

Financial independence

■   Having sufficient cash to spend as one wants is an important prerequisite for self-governance, and that includes exploring sexuality. Both the limitations on welfare benefits and the relative exclusion from paid employment have a knock-on effect on sexual choices.

Control of everyday living

■   See below.

5.1.1 Study focus: control of everyday living

The way in which social policy is implicated in shaping the less public aspects of personal lives is difficult to pin down. It is also harder to resist effectively, and by and large the energies of disability activists have been directed towards challenging structural restraints on the quality of life. Moreover, the specific difficulty in identifying controls over sexuality make it easier to campaign for better employment prospects than for a better sex life. Underneath, however, both issues are concerned with the same demand: that people with disabilities should have the same quality of life as other adults. That does not deny the very real need for physical assistance in many cases, but rather makes the point that although all of us have bodily imperfections to some degree, most non-disabled people can take for granted that they will be able to maximize their own physical capacities and manage their own lives. We do not, for example, treat someone who is short-sighted as disqualified from sexuality, yet there is little hesitation in intervening in the sexual life of someone who is blind. The major problem in many cases is not that disabled people are physically incapable, but that they are thoughtlessly treated as objects of pity or concern who have no say in the conduct of their own lives.

In the past, and to a lesser extent today, social policy towards those with disabilities has been demonstrably paternalistic. In other words, it has made decisions on behalf of its clients instead of facilitating their own decisions, and at worst has acted in a quasi-parental role. As we have seen, social policy mobilizes a range of regulatory techniques which are justified as necessary and beneficent, intrinsically concerned with the assumed best interests of the client. Indeed, some procedures do provide an important protective function for those unable to exercise appropriate agency on their own behalf – as with some learning disabilities. However, a lack of agency is too often assumed. Although it is administratively convenient to categorize people and treat them all alike, that approach denies the individuality and specific circumstances of each person. The problem is the widespread tendency to infantilize disabled people as though they had no capacity to make choices, including sexual choices, for themselves. Carers may go on supervising or intervening in the social – and potentially sexual – contacts of people with disabilities well into adulthood. Despite a need to protect a certain minority, who are unable to defend themselves either physically or mentally against sexual abuse, for example, is there any justification for a more general surveillance of sexual activity? It seems that one predominant approach to the sexuality of disabled people is often to reduce it to a difficulty to be managed, with the result that intrusive controls preclude alternative ways of responding to the needs of disabled people. At the same time, the accounts of people with disabilities suggest that, for many carers, the preferred outcome would be the silencing and disappearance of sexuality. However, it may be that social policy approaches to disabled people's sexuality produces the very problems it fears. For example, over-enthusiastic sexual expression in a learning disabled person might be the result of a lack of education about sexual conventions.

Granted that no-one escapes the discursive control of sexuality and that the putative public/private divide is often breached, disabled people are especially unable to claim private space in the more intimate areas of personal life. In institutions or sheltered housing, where monitoring is a way of life, the problem is likely to be greatly exacerbated. People in residential care may find that their visitors are scrutinized, sexual relationships are heavily discouraged or even forbidden – particularly if they do not fit normative patterns of heterosexuality – and that even where outside partners are tolerated they are unable to stay overnight. One care worker in a national charity-run home reports that the usual excuse is that the other residents 'wouldn't like it', despite a lack of any obvious disapproval. Even where disabled people who are less physically dependent have been moved to more secluded bungalows in the grounds, they are still closely monitored for sexual behaviour, and care workers are asked to report any vehicles that remain outside a residence overnight (personal communication).

Like a lot of other evidence about institutional care, the report is anecdotal, but that should not detract from its validity if it is backed up by similar accounts. It alerts us to the fact that at least some care homes are actively engaged in limiting the sexual expression of their residents, as shown in Extract 4.5. The research difficulty is that, in the somewhat nebulous area of personal lives, in which attitudes and values are often the mobilizing factor rather than more material obstacles such as lack of money, there are practically no formal nationwide policies that can be analysed. Decisions deeply affecting people with disabilities may be made on a highly local and ad hoc basis, and it is often only through autobiographical narratives that they come to light. Here Andrew recalls his own adolescent experience: 'At the residential college, because it was like an institution with a lot of rules, visitors had to leave by half ten. You were allowed to have one late pass a term to be up at midnight, it was quite rigid like that' (Earle, 1999, p.312).

Extract 4.5   'Tender love – and care'

Building a loving relationship is difficult enough, but for disabled people in residential care and in the community, it can be even more challenging. ...

When Carl Holmes fell for his care worker, he knew there might be problems with her employers. He was thrilled when she told him she felt the same. But sure enough, his residential care providers frowned on the relationship. The couple stuck to their guns. Diane, 34, said she would leave if they were not allowed to continue seeing each other.

Carl, 28, who needs 24 hour support and relies on a ventilator, now lives in a bungalow in Colchester provided by a different provider, the charity John Grooms. They see each other regularly and if Diane stays over, she takes on caring responsibilities for Carl. 'We just clicked, really. It is very good,' he says.

Carl has his bungalow through the Treetops High Dependency Centre which also provides residential care. Sheila Flynn, centre nurse manager, says: 'Our attitude is if somebody wants to conduct a relationship with a member of the opposite sex or the same sex, it is their own business.' But she concedes that John Grooms, too, does not encourage relationships between clients and members of staff.

Marion Norman had a relationship while in a Leonard Cheshire home in 1998. Marion, 67, of Newcastle, has cerebral palsy. She claims relationships were not encouraged there and that staff would start laughing if she and the man in question started kissing. 'Things were just as bad when he moved into a bungalow. I was not allowed to stay beyond ten o'clock,' she says. She has since moved out and married another man, Paul.

The charity says that its staff are trained to support relationships and the sexual needs of its clients. It has 2,000 residential places and 12,000 clients in the community. Fiona Street, director of services at Leonard Cheshire, says: 'There are a significant number of service users living in our residential services that are having relationships with other service users, people in the community and with staff. We have examples of service users visiting prostitutes. They have been given the support to do that.' But staff cannot make the arrangements. While she admits the charity has only 24 double rooms in residential settings, she says double beds have been put in other rooms.

...

Concerns remain about the residential care sector in general. Anne Macfarlane, a disability equality trainer, says staff in any care home can stop disabled people from having relationships. 'They just won't sit them next to the person they want to talk to'. Only a few years ago, she says, she met a couple who were told they could not buy an engagement ring by staff. Simon Parritt, director of the Association to Aid the Sexual and Personal Relationships of People with a Disability (SPOD) says: 'Staff don't really know how to handle relationships in residential homes.' SPOD gets calls from staff worried about an inexperienced resident getting into a relationship or concerned about what will happen if relationships fail. But it gets more calls from people in the community and their care staff asking, for example, how much support they should give.

There is no doubt that there is a long way to go before disabled people living in care and many in the community can have the relationships that others take for granted.

(Hermeston, 2002)

Parents and professional carers can exercise enormous control over sexuality not only by restricting access to specific venues such as pubs and clubs, but also by simply failing to respect the privacy of those with dependent needs. Since the NHS and Community Care Act 1990, much greater emphasis is put on keeping people in their own homes, but this does not necessarily mean more independence for those with disabilities. In many cases the home in question is the parental home, which throws up particular problems around sexuality. After giving years of care, parents can become over-protective and find it difficult to accept young peoples' needs for sexual independence. The difficulties for gay and lesbian disabled adolescents and adults in exploring their sexuality are especially acute as they may be faced not only with moral disapproval from either parents or paid assistants, but with material obstructions to any sexual fulfilment. Potential partners may be refused access to the parental home, and even where the disabled person has their own space, essential support – such as help with getting undressed – may be withheld. Normative attitudes on the part of helpers are often repressive: 'A not uncommon scenario ... is disabled men being threatened with the removal of home care because staff found pornographic magazines and videos' (Valios, 2001, p.20). Part of the problem, identified by Jenny Morris (1995), is that where helpers are provided by the statutory services, they have increasingly seen their task as one of care (in the sense of looking after), not of assisting the disabled person to achieve their own wishes. The result is a conflict of interests and a battle over control.

5.2   The problem of sexual abuse

Consider now how the lack of appropriate sex education can underlie several serious problem areas for people with disabilities. Many things come to mind – how relative ignorance can limit sexual confidence, for example, or obstruct the possibilities of pleasure or the experience of desire, or extend even to putting people in danger. An important part of contemporary sex education is to promote sexual health and to alert young people to the risks of unwanted pregnancy and sexually transmitted diseases. Yet as long as education is silent about the sexuality of disabled people it leaves them ill-equipped to protect themselves or to know where to seek help. The negotiation of clinics for sexually transmitted diseases, or contraceptive advice, is often fraught with material and emotional difficulties, and a lack of prior knowledge is an additional burden. Even more worrying is the evidence that relative ignorance of sexuality can leave both young people and adults vulnerable to sexual abuse. As one informant puts it: 'A young woman of 14 who had a disability was raped by her teacher ... because she had no sex education or values clarification, she didn't know that she didn't have to submit to this, and so she just went along' (Begum, 1997, p.81).

Although many progressive disability activists complain that the discussion of sexuality is too often negative, with little emphasis given to the potentially positive pleasures, all agree that sexual abuse is too prevalent to ignore. There is a wealth of anecdotal and autobiographical evidence of disabled people being abused, particularly in institutional care where power inequalities are at their strongest, and a sense of isolation and low self-esteem can build. Margaret Kennedy (1996, p.127), for example, claims that the risk is two to four times higher than in the community. The few extant surveys indicate that an exceptionally high proportion of adult women with disabilities have experienced abuse at some point, often by sexual partners, family members or statutory carers, rather than by outsiders. Shakespeare et al. (1996) draw on a Sexual Health and Equality Project to cite a figure of 48 per cent (and claim that men experience similar levels of abuse).

It is worth looking again at the US study conducted by Nosek, which is based on 31 qualitative interviews with physically disabled women, and then a quantitative follow-up of almost 1,000 women divided evenly between disabled and able-bodied groups. The results show little variation between the groups with regard to abuse, with 40 per cent and 37 per cent respectively suffering strictly sexual abuse, while the overall figure for emotional, physical and sexual abuse combined is 62 per cent for each group. But does this simply indicate experience in common? The authors go deeper:

> Women with disabilities face the same risk of abuse that all women face, plus additional risks specifically related to their disability ... It is notable that women with disabilities tended to experience abuse for longer periods of time, reflecting the reduced number of escape options open to them due to more severe economic dependence, the need for assistance with personal care, environmental barriers, and social isolation. It is difficult to separate the effects of disability from the effects of poverty, low self-esteem, and family background in identifying the precursors to violence against this population. There is much more that we need to know about how women with disabilities escape or resolve abuse situations.
>
> (Nosek et al., 2001, p.27)

The study demonstrates the importance of comparative figures. It highlights the extent of abuse in general, but it also makes clear that women with disabilities had extra problems and showed lower self-esteem than their non-disabled counterparts. So does abuse 'cause' loss of self-esteem? Not necessarily – it may be that those with low self-esteem more readily endure abuse without acting to stop it. Like Nosek, we must be cautious about assuming cause–effect relations just because two or more factors show a strong correlation. In this case both financial and family factors may play a part. On a wider level, too, we would need to look carefully at how the sample was put together and whether we can really generalize from these experiences to draw conclusions about *all* physically disabled women. As it happens, the women here either volunteered or were recruited through centres for independent living (see section 6), which might suggest that they were likely to have higher self-esteem than is usual. It might be that the recorded levels of abuse are in fact lower than in the wider population of disabled women. Even the most careful quantitative research is open to interpretation, and many researchers prefer to use qualitative approaches which, in recording the voices of individuals, are more open about the impossibility of delivering a definitive result that applies to everyone.

On the basis of their combined methodology, the authors of the US survey feel justified in calling for policy initiatives to tackle the problem of abuse. The contrasting work of Jenny Morris, who uses a more qualitative approach, makes a similar point:

> For any disabled person experiencing abuse there will be particular difficulties in disclosing the abuse when the abuser is also the person on whom they rely for the practical assistance which makes daily survival possible. These difficulties are only compounded by a failure of statutory organizations to recognize disabled people's aspirations for independent housing and assistance.
>
> (Morris, 1995, p.82)

The question, then, is how far social policy is responsive to the growing demand of people with disabilities for greater independence and control over their own lives.

5.3   Contemporary trends in social policy

Although 'care' for those who are disadvantaged is a legitimate aim of any social policy, we should reflect on the fact that the meaning of the term is uncertain, and that even in a single society there are conflicting discourses (**Fink, 2004**). With that in mind, consider the change in emphasis in social policy from the generalized provision of care and assistance with little regard to individuality to

care plans   the formulation of personal **care plans** that are tailored to meet each person's unique needs. The move is from imposing services on a take or leave it basis to giving a higher degree of autonomy to disabled people to decide their own priorities. When, however, we consider how each package is assessed, it becomes clear that there is a built-in presumption concerning those priorities. In the questionnaires that accompany any application for a care plan, the emphasis on *needs* assessment precludes mention of sexuality. Although the claimant has more say in the relative weighting of tasks, it is implicit that the services are there to support basic needs only. While care for bathing is provided without question, it is inconceivable that sexual services would be part of the package. Inevitably a lot of discretion remains with the carer, and because he or she is employed directly by social services or by an agency rather than by the disabled person, the dynamic of control is little changed from the older model. If the task is to assist with shopping, then a trip to the supermarket is acceptable, but if the disabled person wants to prioritize a visit to a sex shop, there may be problems.

Although contemporary social policy may claim to address desires as well as needs, it has not yet been worked out how to incorporate sexuality into the calculation. Much of the help given by carers involves an intimate handling of the client's body, but there is often confusion on both sides as to what can be legitimately expected. As Shakespeare and colleagues note:

> Many disabled people require assistance to get into particular positions in order to facilitate sexual activity. However, they may well experience resistance, or outright refusal to help, from carers who believe disabled people should not be sexual ... This outright denial of disabled people's right to be sexual is unacceptable, and agencies that provide individual assistance have a responsibility to ensure that assistance is exactly that, assistance, and that no judgements are made about the nature of the assistance required.
>
> (Shakespeare et al., 1996, p.38)

You will notice how this quotation circumvents the needs/desires debate by referring instead to rights, but is that plausible? Is sexuality a right?

One avenue that might be explored by disability activists is the extent to which the UK is bound by European protocols and legislation. Although the specific issue of sexuality and disability is nowhere explicit in the regulations, it could be argued that it is covered under broader areas. Two articles of the European Convention on Human Rights (ECHR) are particularly promising. Article 12 refers to the right to found a family, while Article 8 enshrines recognition of self-determination through an individual right to privacy. Could these formal and legalistic discourses be invoked by those disabled people who are denied sexual expression?

For activists, the goal for people with disabilities should be to achieve independent living, and there is some irritation that social policy-makers have co-opted the phrase to describe measures already on offer that allow only a limited degree of control to disabled clients. Although the care package is an advance, many people would prefer to be in full financial control and directly employ their own helpers. Rather than care worker, the term for such an
personal assistant   employee is **personal assistant** (PA), someone who is primarily responsible to the disabled person rather than to statutory or agency services. Under this development there is far more flexibility for the disabled employer to set the terms of the contract in advance and specify exactly what assistance is required. After an initial assessment of the level of disability, the person is allocated a regular sum of money which must be spent on buying services (rather than goods) without further direct interventions from statutory agencies – although monitoring at a distance still occurs.

6   Independent living and sexual dilemmas

In Western society autonomy is given an extremely high value, but it is worth remembering that we are all situated on a continuous spectrum of dependency and all fall short of the ideal of total independence. The vulnerabilities of people with disabilities are clearly more in evidence than those of able-bodied people, but it is a difference in degree not kind. Given that we are socially engaged and gain a sense of identity, purpose and pleasure from our mutual interactions with others, perhaps we should be cautious about over-emphasizing the value of complete autonomy. For anyone requiring assistance in their personal lives, independent living means *maximizing* autonomy, not aiming for full self-reliance. The model enhances self-worth while accepting the limitations of the body.

Following the lead from the USA, where independent living was first mooted, disabled people in the UK have been pushing for a system that does not impose external values, but instead prioritizes their individual choices and enables a less regulated lifestyle. One essential step in the process has been to gain control over statutory financial support which, since the late 1980s, has included not only direct payments but also the Independent Living Fund. The purpose of the fund – and similar provisions made by some charitable bodies – is to top up other state income available to disabled people. Neither type of payment is a right available to all, and those with impairments must make individual application without guarantee of success.

Despite such criticisms, the advantages of the scheme are widely recognized by
facilitated sex   people with disabilities, not least in the area of what is called **facilitated sex**. As an employer, the disabled person is in a far stronger position to hire only those assistants who seem comfortable with sexual issues and are aware that they may be asked to provide forms of sexual assistance. For many assistants this might cover the fairly routine tasks of helping with makeup, undressing the employer, or bathing after sex. Given the contemporary – and particularly masculine –

construction of sexuality in terms of the active pursuit of sexual pleasure, however, some activists go further. They argue that assistance should include things such as giving help with masturbation if requested by someone who cannot achieve it for himself, accompanying the employer to sex clubs, negotiating prices and services with sex workers, and supporting disabled employers in the position in which they can best achieve sexual satisfaction with a partner. These largely male-generated demands may seem extreme in the context of the UK, but note that the use of trained sex workers for disabled people is already subsidized by the state in the Netherlands (Valios, 2001).

ACTIVITY 4.6

The moral and social complexities of such situations are difficult to gauge, and, as Sarah Earle (1999) found in her small-scale qualitative study, the success of contractual arrangements relies heavily on pre-existing attitudes. Try to analyse your own responses to the remarks of both disabled students and PAs given in Extract 4.6.

Extract 4.6   'Facilitated sex'

Personal assistants seem most likely to be reluctant to facilitate sex when the sexuality of disabled people deviates from the generally accepted norms of conventional heterosexuality and sexual restraint. Luke found it difficult to facilitate sex for the student he worked for, who liked to cruise gay nightclubs and engage in casual sexual encounters. ...

Luke [PA]: What he does sexually is his personal business ... I had voiced my concerns to other people that I was not prepared to [go to gay clubs] ... you are just going to be there for getting off. It's quite repulsive.

Andrew [student]: One of my partners lives locally and I see a lot of him, so I get quite a lot of sex that way. But in the long holidays I don't see him so someone else does it [masturbates] in the holidays for me, so I get relief. ...

Alison [PA]: If his boyfriend comes round and they want to have sex or some thing I have to put him on the bed and take his clothes off and then leave him so that they can do what ever they want to do ... Also, he's got more than one partner ... I think they sometimes make threesomes, but I don't know the details they like try and tell me to shock me ... I thought, well I'm not really being asked to partake in the act, and I can understand him wanting to have the same sex life as anyone else, so it's an understandable request. ...

Derek [PA]: I just think well, if you've never been able to do it for yourself, you won't know what you're missing sort of thing. ...

Sebastian [student]: You've got to be clear right at the beginning about what you want and what you expect from your carer. To me, sexuality must be treated the same way as any other thing.

(Earle, 1999, pp.312, 314, 316, 317, 319)

It is difficult not to make implicit distinctions between public and private, between needs and wants, and between acceptable and unacceptable sex. Whether you are able-bodied or disabled, you may find the idea of facilitated sex shocking, commendable or immoral. It may make a difference to your response to reflect on the specific context in which many disabled people find themselves in so far as it can entail social, and indeed economic, relations of power between the 'client' and 'worker' that are far removed from the norm. While we might agree that no-one is entitled to coerce PAs who are unwilling to get involved, should there be a proper policy to train helpers in specifically sexual support? Should individual views determine the part played by social policy? If, as I have been arguing, personal lives and social policy are always intertwined and mutually constitutive, then we must accept that our individual values and expectations are already actively implicated in policy directives. It is just that the dominant discourse of normative sexuality has silenced minority voices. One thing is sure: however we view the dilemmas, the idea of facilitated sex does force us all to acknowledge the sexuality of disabled people.

The issue is highly controversial even within the disabled community, but it raises the question of how far it is justifiable to exclude certain people from the expression of their sexuality where the situation could be alleviated. Some of the problems are to do with legality, where arranging a visit from a sex worker, for example, could open a PA to prosecution for procurement, or with the risk of sexual abuse, which could occur on either side. A further important issue, in which class and racism cannot be ignored, is that many assistants are themselves exploited as workers by a care system that gives them little control of their lives. Commenting on the situation in Canada, a public health nurse explains:

> Attendants are a wonderful group of people ... Unfortunately, they would make more if they were feeding the penguins in the zoo. The attendant isn't well-educated, isn't well-paid, isn't well-valued, isn't well-trained. And then they're confronted with something that nobody in our society is all that comfortable with. So they lapse into a parental type – 'I'm not going to help you with that. I'll clean up your shit because it's normal, but I won't clean up your come.'
>
> (quoted in Stoner, 1999)

Like other commentators she believes that better training – leading to a shift in the meaning of care – is the way forward.

The point made by activists is that people with disabilities should not be denied sexual citizenship, which they see as a right on the same level as political citizenship. As it stands, most arrangements involving the facilitation of sexual activity are made directly between the employer and the personal assistant, but what would happen if funding bodies demanded an accounting of how money for independent living is spent? And should 'public' money be allocated for the purchase of sex aids – things like no-hands vibrators, for example, would greatly help those without upper limbs – as well as for services? Given that other intimate areas of personal life are increasingly monitored, can sex be far behind? The worry shared by many activists is that if policy guidelines were ever issued, facilitated sex would become prohibited. At present, sex is still a deeply taboo subject and, so far, social policy has largely exempted itself from such problematic questions by failing to engage directly with the sexuality of disabled people at all.

7   Conclusion: sexuality and identity revisited

Earlier in the chapter, the point was made that sexuality is not just a matter of what a person does, but of who he or she is. In contradistinction to the classical split between mind and body where identity lines up with mind and sexuality with the body, a more considered understanding of the self stresses that we exist only as fully embodied beings. In other words, the form and capacities of the body are inextricably interwoven into a sense of identity. But as we have seen, the body itself is in a continual process of discursive construction, defined within or against prevailing normativities, and subjected to a range of regulatory practices and policies that enforce particular meanings and identities. As part of that process, Foucault names sexuality as the prime site in which identity is inscribed. As he puts it: 'How has sexuality come to be considered the privileged place where our deepest "truth" is read and expressed? For that is the essential fact: ... "To know who you are, know what your sexuality is"' (Foucault, 1988, pp.110–11). For Foucault, sexuality is not a potentially pleasurable bonus but the very heart of self-becoming. To strip it of significance or silence it is, then, to do damage to the very notion of being human. This has profound importance for the issue of disability and sexuality.

In the West at least, the cultural devaluation of the anomalous body, and the degree to which the conjunction of sexuality and disability is silenced, makes it all the more difficult for disabled people to have a positive self-identity. It is only by challenging prevailing sociocultural values, and the binaries of normal and abnormal, that people with disabilities are able to resist normative constructions of themselves as dependent, asexual or deformed, and begin to forge new identities. If everything was fixed in advance – if biology and bodies were a given, and identities unchanging – then the task would be hopeless, but once we recognize that our knowledge of the world is a matter of constituted meanings, not solid facts, then there is always the potential for change. As we have seen, body is not simply a material reality but a complex and fluid mix of corporeal, psychic and social components. And the interrelated notions of the self/ sexuality/body are all in a process of construction, so that changes to one area are inevitably reflected in the others. To suffer a disabling accident that restricts normative sexual expression will indeed have a profound effect on one's sense of self, but that newly experienced disjunction is not then fixed. The changed experience of the body can lead to new forms of sexuality and self-identity that enhance, rather than diminish, self-esteem.

Once it is accepted that sexuality, body, self-identity and social norms are all connected, then social policy has a high responsibility, as much ethical as practical. It is not just a matter of enhancing putative rights (as the SMD and recent calls for sexual citizenship suggest), but of recognizing that the wider well-being of people with disabilities is at stake. The power exercised by social policy is not simply in strategies that manage and control the external conditions of disability but, as we have seen, extends to constructing the very category itself with all its limitations on the significance and meaning of sexuality. Social policy both operates in the social interactions of the 'public' sphere and infiltrates the most intimate areas of personal life. It displaces the boundaries between public and private, and profoundly affects every aspect of our sense of self. Rather than better procedures of assessment that can only encourage yet more surveillance, perhaps social policy requires a greater sensitivity to all the differential needs *and* desires of people with disabilities. It is a question of working out how to acknowledge difference without devaluing it.

Further resources

Aside from the material mentioned in the text, there are several other resources, particularly websites, that are beginning to address the issue of disability and sexuality. *Disability Now Newsletter* (http://www.disabilitynow.org.uk) offers news and views across a range of disability concerns, as does the site http://www.independentliving.org which gives details of several resources dealing with sexuality. More specifically, SPOD (Sexual Support for Disabled People) gives advice, counselling and support, and can be reached by email on spoduk@aol.com.

References

Aguilera, R. (2002) 'The boy I used to be', unpublished paper, Queer Disability Conference, 2002.

Begum, N. (1997) 'Disabled women and the feminist agenda', *Feminist Review*, vol.40, pp.70–84.

Benefits Agency (2001) *Disability Living Allowance – For a Person Aged 16 or Over*, (DLA1), Department of Social Security.

Crow, L. (1996) 'Including all our lives: renewing the social model of disability' in Morris (ed.) (1996).

Davis, L.J. (1997) *The Disability Studies Reader*, London, Routledge.

DfEE (Department for Education and Employment) (1998) *Promoting Disabled People's Rights: Creating a Disability Rights Commission Fit for the Twenty First Century*, Cm 3977, London, HMSO.

DoH (Department of Health) (2002) *A Practical Guide For Disabled People*, London, HMSO.

Earle, S. (1999) 'Facilitated sex and the concept of sexual need: disabled students and their personal assistants', *Disability & Society*, vol.14, no.3, pp.309–23.

Fink, J. (ed.) (2004) *Care: Personal Lives and Social Policy*, **Bristol, The Policy Press in association with The Open University.**

Foucault, M. (1979) *The History of Sexuality, Vol.1*, London, Allen Lane.

Foucault, M. (1988) *Politics, Philosophy, Culture: Interviews and Other Writing, 1977–1984*, London, Routledge.

Galler, R. (1984) 'The myth of the perfect body' in Vance, C. (ed.) *Pleasure and Danger: Exploring Female Sexuality*, London, Pandora Press.

Hermeston, R. (2002) 'Tender love – and care', *Disability Now*, February, p.24.

Hughes, G. (1998) 'A suitable case for treatment? Constructions of disability' in Saraga (ed.) (1998).

Jackson, S. and Scott, S. (1996) *Feminism and Sexuality: A Reader*, Edinburgh, Edinburgh University Press.

Kennedy, M. (1996) 'Sexual abuse and disabled children' in Morris (ed.) (1996).

Morris, J. (1993) *Independent Lives? Community Care and Disabled People*, London, Macmillan Press.

Morris, J. (1995) 'Creating a space for absent voices: disabled women's experience of receiving assistance with daily living activities', *Feminist Review*, vol.51, pp.68–93.

Morris, J. (ed.) (1996) *Encounters with Strangers: Feminism and Disability*, London, The Women's Press.

Murphy, R. (1987) *The Body Silent*, London, Dent.

Nosek, M.A., Howland, C., Rintala, D.H., Young M.E. and Chanpong, M.S. (2001) 'National study of women with physical disabilities: final report', *Sexuality and Disability*, vol.19, no.1, pp.5–39.

Oliver, M. (1990) *The Politics of Disablement*, London, Macmillan.

Saraga, E. (1998) 'Abnormal, unnatural and immoral? The social construction of sexualities' in Saraga (ed.) (1998).

Saraga, E. (ed.) (1998) *Embodying the Social: Constructions of Difference*, London, Routledge in association with The Open University.

Shakespeare, T. (2000) 'Disabled sexuality: toward rights and recognition', *Sexuality and Disability*, vol.18., no.3, pp.159–66.

Shakespeare, T., Gillespie-Sells, K. and Davies, D. (1996) *The Sexual Politics of Disability: Untold Desires*, London, Cassell.

Shildrick, M. (1997) *Leaky Bodies and Boundaries: Feminism, Postmodernism and (Bio)ethics*, London, Routledge.

Shildrick, M. and Price, J. (1996) 'Breaking the boundaries of the broken body', *Body & Society*, vol.2, no.4, pp.93–113.

Shuttleworth, R. (2002) 'Defusing the adverse context of disability and desirability as a practice of the self for men with cerebral palsy' in Corker, M. and

Shakespeare, T. (eds) *Disability/Postmodernism: Embodying Disability Theory,* London, Continuum.

Stoner, K. (1999) 'Whose job should it be to help disabled people make love?', www.eye.net/issue/ (accessed 6 October 2002).

Tarricone, L. (2000) 'Sex and disabilities, part 1: model behaviour', www. accessibility.com.au/news/articles/ (accessed 6 October 2002).

UPIAS (1976) *Fundamental Principles of Disability,* London, Union of the Physically Impaired Against Segregation.

Valios, N. (2001) 'Desire denied', *Community Care,* 20 September, pp.19–21.

CHAPTER 5

Personal Lives, Public Policies and Normal Sexualities?

by Jean Carabine

Contents

1   Introduction

In this book we have considered some of the ways in which personal lives and sexualities are constituted in and through social policy. Our aim has been to open sexuality, personal lives and social policy to critical analysis and in so doing challenge the normative and taken-for-granted assumptions about sexuality that inform the discourses and practices of social policy. The chapters have illustrated how these assumptions about sexuality impact on personal lives in a variety of different contexts and ways. The aims of the book have been:

Aims
- To centre personal lives and sexuality in social policy, and to show how sexuality and social policy are mutually constitutive.

- To expose the assumptions about sexuality that pervade contemporary thinking in the UK.

- To show that these assumptions occupy a normative position in social policy discourses and practices.

- To demonstrate that certain kinds of heterosexuality have come to occupy a position of 'normal' and that this is linked to heteronormativity.

- To illustrate that heteronormative discourses and practices are the product of a series of complex intersections between heterosexuality and social differences and divisions such as gender, age, dis/ability, 'race', ethnicity and class.

- To show that what we 'know' about sexuality is socially constructed and that heteronormative dominance is open to contestation and change.

Above all, the focus of the book has been the complex links between sexuality, personal lives and social policy.

A clear purpose of the chapters in this book has been to uncover, not just the material effects and processes of the policies that organize our lives, but also the knowledge, values and attitudes which inform taken-for-granted assumptions about sexuality. We have seen how ideas about family, marriage, parenting and the body are central to understanding normal sexuality. We have focused upon how heterosexuality is privileged in social policy, and how it intersects with discourses and practices of difference, especially in regard to gender, 'race', disability, age and class. We have explored an understanding of sexuality as primarily private, having to do with bodily pleasures and both physical and emotional intimacy. For these reasons sexuality is simultaneously central and marginal to the concerns of social policy for, while social policy confirms and reinforces a norm of heterosexuality, it also asserts that sexuality is an individual and private matter. This, together with a focus on agency and on recognizing individuals as active agents, emphasizes the way in which encounters between personal lives and social policy are mutually constituting.

In this final chapter we explore how the aims have been developed in each of the four preceding chapters. In section 2 we review the theoretical approaches through which the aims are explored, and in section 3 we focus on some of the different and complex ways in which the dynamic of sexuality, personal lives and social policy is illustrated in the book. This dynamic will be explored in relation to the following themes that run through the book:

- personal lives and social policy;

- public and private;

- personal biographies;

- contesting social policy.

2 Theoretical perspectives and key concepts

The themes of the book have been explored mainly through the use of Foucauldian post-structuralist and feminist perspectives. These perspectives centre concepts of sexuality, power, knowledge, discourse, heteronormativity, normalization and difference, and look at gender relations, bodily autonomy, gendered and sexual identities, and historical and cultural specificity.

2.1 Foucauldian post-structuralism

A post-structuralist approach is most in evidence in Chapters 1 and 4, and it is in these chapters particularly that the importance of questioning the taken-for-granted nature of knowledge is stressed. From a Foucauldian post-structuralist perspective, knowledge is linked to power. According to Foucault, 'there is no power relation without the correlative constitution of a field of knowledge, nor any knowledge that does not presuppose and constitute at the same time, power relations' (Foucault, 1991, p.27). In these chapters sexuality is seen as a system of knowledge, and what dominates as the 'truth' of sexuality at any given moment is both influenced by power relations and is power itself. Chapter 1 focused on the dominance of essentialist ideas about sexuality as 'natural', which privilege heterosexual marriage, the family and childrearing. Chapter 4 emphasized the influence of medical and scientific knowledges on how we think about disability.

Chapter 3, on the other hand, adopted both a feminist and a post-structuralist approach and concentrated on those knowledges which form our contradictory and competing constructions of childhood. From a post-structuralist perspective, all knowledge is socially constructed and therefore so too is what we 'know', for example, about sexuality, disability and childhood. (Indeed, in all the chapters sexuality was interpreted as being socially, culturally and historically constructed.) As a result, meanings, words, texts and other forms of representation 'matter' and are understood as being influential in framing our expectations and assumptions about sexuality, bodies, gender roles, age, 'race' and ethnicity. For this reason, Margrit Shildrick showed in Chapter 4 how '"anomaly" is a less loaded term of difference than the more familiar word "deformity"' (Chapter 4, section 1). In focusing on how meanings are constructed, particular attention has been paid to discourses and discursive formations and their role in positioning and constituting welfare subjects. In Chapter 1 examples were given of how discourses of the Poor Law and supplementary benefit constituted single women and unmarried mothers, albeit in different ways, as sexually immoral. Chapter 4 showed how medical discourses generated a relative silence around the sexuality of disabled people, constituting them as asexual or as incapable of sex.

The role of knowledge – or, to put it another way, its power effects – especially scientific, medical and professional knowledge, in constituting difference through categorization based on binary opposites has been highlighted. Binary divisions, such as heterosexual/homosexual, white/black, male/female, adult/child, abled/disabled and sane/mad, produce linguistic, social and structural hierarchies and inequalities. These hierarchical oppositions and the meanings associated with them shape social practices as they become institutionalized in mass culture; therapeutic and welfare regimes; gender, sexual and racialized relations and conventions; and so on. However, as all the chapters have shown, the meanings attached to binary categories, although presented to us as fixed, are unstable, contradictory, shifting and contested. Central, then, to understanding the relationship between sexuality, personal lives and social policy is to question how meanings are constituted. The discourses that are available about sexuality, and in which we engage, are highly influential, not only in framing our personal lives and the choices open to us, but also in influencing social policy – its analyses, provisions and priorities.

2.2   Feminism

Chapters 2 and 3 drew more overtly on a feminist perspective, although, as mentioned in the previous section, Chapter 3 also used aspects of a post-structuralist perspective, particularly for analysing discourses. In these chapters gender was the central dimension, and the significance of gender relations and identities for understanding normative constructions of heterosexuality was underscored. Chapter 2, for example, used a feminist perspective to emphasize the unequal nature of gender relations in the late nineteenth and early twentieth centuries, the role of gendered power and the importance of representing actors as active agents in accounts of history. Common to both Chapters 2 and 3 was a concern to address directly the negotiations which take place, usually overtly but sometimes silently, between men and women in heterosexual relationships. The aim was to explore and understand how agency and power operate differentially in gendered personal relations. Each chapter, albeit in different historical moments and social contexts, was concerned with the connections and negotiations within and between personal lives and social policy, particularly in the context of changing or reshaped gender relations. Chapter 2 focused on the gendered negotiations of couples to restrict reproduction, and Chapter 3 on safer sex. Both chapters linked these negotiations back to the wider context of social policy.

2.3   Heteronormativity

As we have seen, social policy foregrounds the married monogamous heterosexual relationship as the preferred social–sexual arrangement. In this way, social policy performs a normalizing role when it reinforces and asserts heteronormative constructions of sexuality as acceptable sexuality. The most significant aspect of heteronormativity is the way in which it is constituted by a number of unequal and institutionalized binary oppositions. Conventionally, these are those between heterosexuality and homosexuality and between men and women, which are intersected by other binary oppositions organized, for example, around black/white, abled/disabled and adult/child.

Think back and identify where each of these oppositions was considered in the chapters.

These oppositions locate us in the society in which we live through a series of belongings and exclusions which are marked by difference. Normalization, or rather the effects of normative constructions, operates in hierarchically coded ways which are variously affirmative, regulatory or punitive and which variously centre, marginalize or exclude certain groups. One aspect of the marginalizing or exclusionary effects of normalization can be seen in Chapter 4 in the processes Shildrick referred to as the 'silencing' of disabled people's sexuality. She asked:

> What, then, of those who cannot – because of bodily difference – meet the normative standards of sexuality … ? … The point is that so strongly is 'proper' sexuality associated with one particular set of standards that there is very little social or individual recognition that those outside the standards have any sexuality at all. In other words, disabled people are seen – implicitly and explicitly – as sexless.
>
> (Chapter 4, section 3.2)

In Chapter 3, section 4.3, Rachel Thomson provided us with an example of the regulatory aspects of normalization processes in her discussion of New Labour policy responses which problematize and devalue young people who choose to have children instead of pursuing higher education. Rather than seeing such decisions as equal but different, she argued that the tendency is for policy to represent a preferred route for young people of delaying sexual activity and pregnancy until after higher education and training.

Heteronormative discourses affect us all – heterosexual and gay or lesbian, black and white, male and female, with or without disabilities, and whatever our age – organizing and constituting the physical and social spaces we inhabit. At one and the same time heteronormativity encourages and discourages us from certain bodily activities and relationships and from inhabiting particular personal and sexual identities. We take these subject positions and work within and against them, sometimes accepting while at other times resisting or subverting them. This is what Thomson referred to when she said that 'it is possible to understand that sex and gender identities are constantly and contingently created through a matrix in which class, gender, "race" and locality are always in play' (Chapter 3, section 3.2). She gave an example from her

Women, Risk and AIDS Project (WRAP) research which illustrates how individuals simultaneously resist and accept normative identities and roles. Her research found that 'young women engaged in a range of creative strategies in order to practise safer sex while not disrupting the gender relations of the encounter' (Chapter 3, section 3.2).

Social policy discourses and practices are therefore a means through which acceptable sexualities, populations, gender relations, families and relationships are spoken about at any given time. Sexuality is produced in part through social policy. This is a mutually reinforcing process because what we know as sexuality at any given time also constitutes social policy in specific ways that reflect the power/knowledge relations centred on sexuality as they are intersected by discourses of gender, 'race', disability, class and age. Chapter 2, for example, highlighted in particular the ways in which sexuality is a gendered concept. From a historical perspective, Megan Doolittle illustrated how the intersection of gender and sexuality produces unequal power relations which are in turn reflected in and reinforced by social policy. She also highlighted the role of gender and power in reshaping parenthood and sexuality in social policy and personal lives, as well as the particular ways in which late nineteenth and early twentieth-century sexuality discourses were gendered. The chapter showed that what counts for heterosexuality has come to be differently constituted and can mean different things in different times and contexts. Indeed, that all four chapters have emphasized the various competing and contradictory views and discourses about sexuality, reproduction, childhood and disability illustrates the constructed basis of these categories and concepts. From a social constructionist perspective nothing, not even knowledge itself, can be taken for granted or at face value.

In all the chapters the importance of recognizing individuals as active agents with desires and emotions has been emphasized. While Doolittle illustrated some of the effects of ignoring this in traditional historical accounts of fertility decline, Thomson signalled agency when she called our attention to the importance of recognizing the role of what Bourdieu (1977) termed individual 'logic of practice' in young people's sexual decision-making and through which they make sense of their lives (Chapter 3, section 2.2). Shildrick pointed us to the demands of people with disabilities for the right to be seen as sexual and autonomous beings by policy-makers and welfare and medical practitioners (Chapter 4, section 6).

In the next section we explore a core theme of the book – personal lives.

3   Personal lives, sexuality and social policy

Throughout this book the importance of the personal has been emphasized and we have seen that sexuality is a highly personal experience. Our specific focus on personal lives has been to understand how the personal and the sexual are produced, inhabited and resisted and with what effects. The chapters have focused on some of the ways in which our lived experiences are central to how we think about, encounter, experience, participate in and influence social policy. We, all of us, shape social policy. Think back, for example, to the previous chapter and the discussion of how care homes limit or facilitate residents' freedom to express their sexuality or to develop sexual relationships. In that same chapter, the discussion of personal care assistants and facilitated sex illustrated one way in which some disabled people's personal needs and experiences have been used to influence social policy. These are just two examples of the ways in which we can link personal lives and social policy. What they show is that this relationship contains a two-way or double dynamic, so that, just as our personal lives influence how we experience social policy, so too does social policy influence the shape of our personal lives. From our experience of these a third dynamic emerges which is concerned with challenging and transforming social policy. Indeed, it is precisely this that the chapters in the book have demonstrated. They have shown that, when analysed through the lens of sexuality, the personal is:

- simultaneously private and public;

- experienced in relation to and affected by other people's personal lives;

- inextricably linked with social policy – impacting on and influenced by it (that is, the two are mutually constitutive);

- affected by power relations;

- socially, structurally, locally and nationally, culturally and historically constituted;

- fluid, creative, active and changing, transformative, contesting and challenging.

This has helped us to see that our individual biographies – what we think of as uniquely 'ours', as private and outside social concerns – are simultaneously influenced by and impact upon the wider social world. Let us explore these points further.

3.1   Private lives, public lives

In what ways should social policy be concerned with personal lives, especially where sexual, physical and emotional intimacy is involved? You may think that intervention into our social lives is an intrusion into our most private feelings and relationships. We tend to think about the personal – particularly in relation to sexuality – as being firmly located in the private realm. Indeed, sexuality, perhaps more than any other area of our lives, is the consummate signifier of the private and the personal. In one sense, as we saw in Chapter 1, this idea of sexuality as private and outside of the concern of the law and policy is encapsulated in the rationale of the Report of the 1957 Wolfenden Committee on *Homosexual Offences and Prostitution*, popularly summarized as 'whatever we do in private is our own business'. But as all the chapters in this book have demonstrated, our sexual lives are far from being an entirely private matter, especially when those sexual lives fall outside of the norm, as the examples of cohabitation, homosexuality and lone motherhood in Chapter 1 showed. During the period between 1860 and the 1920s, as we saw in Chapter 2, the most personal of negotiations about family size became a concern of the nation and a target of public intervention. Further, as we saw in Chapter 4, the topic of disability illustrates one way in which the relationship between the public and the private is reconfigured. As Shildrick pointed out, despite the dominance of the idea of sexuality as personal and private, people with disabilities are more likely to find it difficult to claim private space in their personal lives either because they live in residential settings (and any sexual behaviour might therefore be subjected to close monitoring) or because they require the assistance of another to have sex.

State intervention in the private realm may not be new, but, as Chapter 2 illustrated, it is a relatively recent development. Previously, the public and the private were seen as more rigidly delineated. Doolittle pointed out that, unlike today, very little legislation or policy directly addressed the private sphere of marriage and the family and that, for the most part in the nineteenth-century family, sexuality and personal lives were seen as occupying a very different sphere from the state, and as having little to do with social policy. The rigid separation between private and public during this period was a socially constructed one which functioned partly to delineate male and female roles and responsibilities by positioning men in the public realm and by restricting women to the private. Although the public and private may have been discursively constructed as separate, evidence from the early part of the nineteenth century suggests that these boundaries were not so distinct in practice, especially where the sexual lives of the poor and of women were concerned. A plethora of policies concerned with health, disease and poverty sought to regulate the sexuality of the working classes and poor women (Mort, 1987, on sexuality, health and disease; Carabine, 2001, on poverty and sexuality).

As Weeks (2000, p.164) points out: 'Nothing is straightforward when we try to think or speak of sexuality. It is both the most private and personal of activities, and the most public'. Indeed, when it comes to sexuality our personal lives can be said to straddle the public/private divide, being simultaneously of private and public concern. Viewed through the lens of sexuality, we find that the boundary between private and public is blurred and unstable rather than fixed or distinct and separate. It is constantly being redefined, redrawn, challenged and breached – that is, it is far less firm than popularly assumed – and this is one way in which we can think of it as discursively produced. Indeed, when analysed through the combined lenses of personal lives, sexuality and social policy, the public/private divide disintegrates. Instead, it is revealed as a normalizing process – a dynamic of power – governing and regulating the relationship between the state and the individual. There are, however, additional dimensions to the construction of the boundary between the public and the private and these illustrate further how much our 'personal lives' are subjected to processes of normalization, binary division and intervention.

In the context of personal lives, sexuality and social policy, the relationship between the public and private realms is a contradictory and complex one and, as indicated above, the boundary between the two is continually shifting and contested. There are many publics and many privates and what counts as public or private has been shaped in and through history. What we mean by public and private is also open to different interpretations. When we say that sexuality is private, this can refer to:

- the idea of sexuality as a personal and private matter and as something which should take place in private, as in the Wolfenden Report and more recently in *Protecting the Public: Strengthening Protection Against Sex Offenders and Reforming the Law on Sexual Offences* (Home Office, 2002);

- the way in which some sexualities are privatized or hidden and are not publicly or legally recognized, as with homosexuality, disabled or young people's sexualities, transsexuality, and cohabitation, for example;

- the way in which some sexualities have their privacy assured or protected and are less likely to be subjected to state, legal or policy intervention or regulation, as with normative married monogamous heterosexual relationships.

Some sexualities may also be considered 'public' and therefore as legitimately subject to public scrutiny and legal and social regulation. As we have seen in this book, this has been the case for non-normative or 'unacceptable' sexualities (those of lesbians and gays, lone mothers, young people, pregnant teenagers, disabled people, or cohabiting or birth-controlling couples) and violent or dangerous sexualities.

In the context of sexuality, the role of social policy has been to publicly affirm normal heterosexual married family relationships, while preserving for these a privileged location in the private sphere relatively free from policy interventions. At the same time, unacceptable sexualities are marginalized, subjected to greater public scrutiny and policy intervention, and awarded little or no public affirmation. Thus, we can see how the wider social world of the law, the state and social policy works to construct a shifting boundary between the public and the private, and that this in turn impacts upon and shapes individual personal lives, creating legitimate and illegitimate sexualities. The maintenance and construction of this boundary is inextricably intertwined with the construction and regulation of normative sexuality. This means that, while on the one hand sexualities are subject to intervention, scrutiny and regulation, on the other they are simultaneously ignored, elided and marginalized. At one and the same moment social policy both speaks of sexuality and is silent about it.

3.2   Personal decisions, public consequences

Our personal lives are very much at the heart of social policy and it is possible to identify four ways in which this connection works. First, social policies prescribe and proscribe (legitimate or problematize) certain kinds of sexual behaviour and sexuality. Second, and in a way that indicates a flow of influence in the opposite direction, is that people's decisions about how to practise their sexuality undermines or contradicts the normative assumptions about sexuality that are embedded in social policy. Third, sexualities and sexual practices that are neither normalized nor designated as dangerous or pathological, are simply ignored. Fourth, our experiences of social policy can generate a different encounter – arising from our resistance to the ways in which we are constituted in and by social policy – which results in individual or collective demands for change. Each of these links to how the connections between sexuality, personal lives and social policy 'work'. This is because they are part of a discursive formation of normative and normalizing assumptions and discourses which mark out those forms of sexuality that are subjected to direct intervention and those that are designated 'private'.

The decisions we do or do not make concerning our sexuality – such as whether and when to have sex and with whom, or whether to have children – can transform our personal lives, identities, close relations and even the opportunities open to us. Such choices can also affect how we are positioned by social policy – as married, heterosexual, teenage or lone mother, lesbian or gay, 'normal' or a 'problem'. They can also impact on social policy. Decisions made by young people about when to have sex or the age at which to have their first baby can result in them being discursively positioned by social policy in different ways which in turn impact on how the personal itself is experienced and interpreted. If young people choose to delay sex and wait until their late teens or early twenties before having a baby, then current policy constructs them as socially responsible adults and active welfare-independent citizens. If, however, they decide to have their first baby in their early teens, then they are discursively positioned as a problem and are seen to contribute to their own social exclusion and welfare dependence. It does not follow that because someone is discursively positioned as a problem that they will readily accept that positioning. Deciding to have your first child in your teens can be seen as offering certain opportunities. For young people whose access to adulthood is increasingly being delayed or denied by extended dependency on family or as a result of prolonged education, it can be a means of obtaining a sense of autonomy and adult status and an identity as a mother and partner (see Chapter 3, particularly section 2.2). It can also limit the opportunities open to young people if it means giving up on or postponing obtaining qualifications or training.

Furthermore, personal decisions about sexuality can result in direct intervention or regulation by the state through social policy. As we have seen, not only were unmarried mothers of the New Poor Law discursively positioned as irresponsible, so too were birth-controlling couples and, more recently, pregnant teenagers, and social policies were or have been introduced to regulate or change their behaviour. Under the 1834 New Poor Law unmarried fathers were absolved of all legal and financial responsibility for their children. The full financial responsibility was placed instead upon unmarried mothers with the intention of making having illegitimate children onerous. British governments of the early and mid nineteenth and early twentieth centuries, concerned about falling birth rates and population decline, directed social policies, albeit unsuccessfully, at restricting the use of birth control methods and at encouraging the 'right sorts' of couples to have children. By the end of the twentieth century, fears about rising numbers of pregnant teenagers led to the publication of the *Teenage Pregnancy Report* (Social Exclusion Unit, 1999) and, since then, the implementation of a range of local and national schemes aimed at delaying teenage sexual activity and pregnancy and at improving educational attainment and labour market involvement.

The relationship between personal lives and social policy is not simply a one-way process whereby policy is imposed on individuals. As the examples of birth-controlling, cohabiting and same-sex couples; young people; lesbians and gay men; and disabled people in this book show, the ways in which we choose to live our sexualities, and challenge or transgress heteronormativity, can generate significant policy debate which in turn shapes and transforms the social policy formations within which we find ourselves. Sometimes this has resulted in a relaxation of controls (the repeal of the Contagious Diseases Acts in the nineteenth century, or the so-called 'permissive moment' of the 1960s), while at other times it has resulted in a tightening of regulation (as with Section 28 of the Local Government Act 1988). In this way personal lives and social policy intersect and can be said to be mutually constitutive of each other.

Changes in sexuality, sexual cultures and practices at a wider societal level do not just happen. They are the product of personal negotiations and changes in personal lives. Nor should they be straightforwardly understood as the outcome or an effect of social policy. Instead, as the example of the couples in Chapter 2 shows, they are the products of multiple *individual* negotiations and changes in personal lives and sexual practices and relationships. The form these personal and wider social changes take are themselves influenced and framed by local as well as national, cultural, economic and structural contexts, as we saw in the discussion of individual 'logics of practice' and 'moral economies' in section 2.2 of Chapter 3. Notions such as 'logics of practice' and 'moral economies' are useful for making sense of the sort of personal decisions made by, for example, the couples in Chapter 2, the sexually active or pregnant teenagers in Chapter 3 and the demands of people with disabilities for facilitated sex in Chapter 4, precisely because they recognize that we all make decisions which are informed by our local context and culture as well as wider social factors.

3.3   Personal biographies, welfare professionals and intersecting personal lives

While policy may have interventionist intentions it is never simply nor straightforwardly implemented. In practice, its 'success' (as well as the way in which it is experienced) is dependent on any number of contingent factors, including the sexual (and also the gender, racial and/or ethnic, cultural, religious, generational and physical) biographies of the individuals concerned with the implementation and practise of social policy. By this we mean that the values and attitudes towards sexuality held by, for example, welfare practitioners and bureaucrats, as well as their personal sexual biographies and experiences, are played out through policies and in practice. In this way, personal lives can be understood as relational. Each of our personal lives contributes to, shapes and affects the personal lives of the other, as, for example, when we come into contact with each other as welfare workers or welfare users. There is, of course, a range of factors which influence policy-making and implementation. The policy process is complex, mediated and shaped by factors such as economics, politics and ideology. Our purpose is not to dismiss these factors, nor to suggest that structures of inequality are absent from relations between welfare professionals and users, or groups of users, but rather to foreground the part sometimes played by one factor – personal biography – which tends to be ignored.

Personal biographies may affect, for example, carers' caring, teachers' pedagogic strategies and the bureaucratic interpretation and application of policy. Additionally, they may conflict or coincide with normative assumptions, thereby influencing eligibility and experiences of welfare as well as the allocation of resources. Conflicts can occur when individual and bureaucratic moralities and values and personal and policy rationalities differ, as illustrated in this book by the examples of lesbian and single women seeking fertility treatment, birth-controlling couples, sexually active young people, and personal assistants and people with disabilities; similar conflict can also be seen in decisions that are made about what counts as care (**Fink, 2004**) or need. How such conflicts are negotiated and resisted is embedded in socially structured relations of power, the effects of social differences and patterns of inequality. All these are in turn implicated in and impact upon the personal lives of the welfare subjects with whom they come into contact. For example, in Chapter 1, section 6.2 we saw how the attitudes of national assistance officers meant that all single women claiming supplementary benefit were under suspicion of adultery or of cohabitation. Policy-makers' and carers' views about disability, sexuality and facilitated sex (Chapter 4, section 6) can have serious implications for attempts by people with disabilities to live independently and autonomously.

Research (Brown, 1998; Langley, 2001) shows that many welfare professionals find issues of sexuality difficult to deal with in their practice because they feel awkward or embarrassed or lack sexual knowledge. Often in such circumstances professionals and welfare bureaucrats also believe that they have a right to protect their own 'personal' when at work. In doing so, they deploy discourses of the personal as being private and sacrosanct and outside of the realm of the office/surgery/school/prison/social. Conversely, each of us may also resist the attempts of welfare professionals and administrators to enter our own personal sphere. As Chapter 3 showed, young people are distrustful of teachers seeking to enter their personal worlds and will deploy strategies which undermine or resist such attempts in ways that 'sexualize and "other" the teacher in the process' (section 4.5). Or, as we saw in Chapter 1, section 4.3, prior experience of homophobic incidents may mean that lesbian and gay welfare clients 'pass' as heterosexual by allowing welfare professionals' assumptions of heterosexuality to go unchallenged.

For welfare professionals, whose sexual biographies are gay or lesbian, this may mean that they too have to hide their sexuality, because it is less 'protected' by notions of the private and more vulnerable to homophobic abuse and prejudice. They are particularly under pressure to hide their sexuality in intimate, caring situations or where they work with children and young people. For example, one professional asks 'How can I risk working openly with gay youth? I would be accused of recruiting and could lose my practice' (quoted in Logan, 2001, p.567). It can also mean being unable or unwilling to challenge normative assumptions and prejudices in the workplace and in welfare practice. Thus, even in the realm of social policy, our personal lives, as welfare users, professionals, administrators, or policy-makers, interact with and impact on the personal lives of others. An individual's personal is constructed relationally in negotiation with partners and friends, welfare professionals and administrators, as well as within the specific social policy and welfare contexts that are available to them.

The way in which a welfare intervention or strategy is received is likely to be influenced not only by the particular dynamics centred on sexuality, but also with the gender, 'race' and cultural dynamics of the intervention. This can mean, for example, that, where sexuality intersects with 'race', the personal lives of those individuals concerned are subjected to greater scrutiny, surveillance or regulation by welfare practitioners and bureaucrats – this might be the case for migrants, refugees and asylum seekers (Chapter 1; **Saraga, 2004**), 'mixed race' marriages (Chapter 1) or disabled people (Chapter 4), for instance.

Finally, and in a very different way, social policy aims can be frustrated by the 'personal' lives of politicians. In the early 1990s, UK Prime Minister John Major's 'Back to Basics' policy was undermined by a series of media revelations about the sexual personal lives of Members of Parliament.

The discussions and examples in the sections above illustrate some of the ways in which an individual's 'personal' travels across the boundaries of the so-called private realm into the public world of work, government, policy-making and practice. They also indicate some of the processes and channels through which personal lives and social policy are mutually constitutive. These mutual processes are neither even nor consistent and impact of one on the other is never certain. Social policy may fail in its intentions and individuals may accept or resist the subject positions constituted for them in social policy. We look at such resistances next.

3.4 Contesting social policy

We have considered how the choices we make about our sexuality can transform our personal lives. Implicit in the discussion has been an exploration of some of the ways in which social policy responds to the choices we make about our personal lives and sexualities. In the main, we have tended to look at the ways in which policy restricts and regulates, but policy can also provide opportunities to transform personal lives in ways that are affirming. Social policy is a site and focus of contestation, political action and social change. Activists and campaigners have used social policy as an instrument for positive change to challenge inequalities and discrimination, change social attitudes and welfare practices and redirect welfare resources, as well as to validate diverse personal lives.

This can take many forms and take place at individual, group or organizational level. In Chapter 1 we saw how transformations in social policy and wider society came about through the actions of individual heterosexual couples seeking to reduce the size of their families, which in turn resulted in demographic changes. In that same chapter we saw too how a feminist-led movement developed to campaign for the repeal of the Contagious Diseases Acts of the 1860s, which focused on challenging the sexual double standard that lay at the heart of the Acts. These Acts were eventually suspended in 1883. In Chapter 4 we saw how some sections of the disability community have begun to challenge normative representations of sexuality and disability and to make demands for a reconceptualizing of disabled people's sexualities, and for sexual rights. In some cases this has led to demands for a redirecting of welfare resources towards the provision of facilitated sex. In Chapter 3 we also saw how social policy texts and documents can be reinterpreted. For example, whereas one teacher may have been happy to interpret Section 28 to mean that she or he was not permitted to teach about homosexuality, another may actively challenge homophobia by using official guidance on bullying to legitimate their actions.

4 Conclusion

Sexual experience, relationships and identities are aspects of our personal lives which are interpreted and constituted through social meanings and interactions. The sexual is not, as an essentialist paradigm would have us believe, something we possess independently of the social. Rather, it is produced through and in our interactions with the meanings, discourses and representations of what counts as sexual knowledge at any one time and in specific contexts and locations.

This is not to suggest that the social determines the sexual. As the chapters in this book have shown, this is a mutually constitutive relationship and we, all of us, play a part in constituting our own sexuality albeit within the confines of existing knowledges and the meanings of sexuality available to us. In the context of social policy the choices we make about how to live our sexual/personal lives also contribute, in diverse and important ways, to the forms that social policy takes, its concerns and effects.

We are all involved in shaping policy formations. Sometimes we do this by conforming to normative conventions, thereby reinforcing definitions of what are acceptable and normal sexualities, practices and relationships. At other times, we may do this by subverting or directly challenging existing policy parameters and assumptions. The relationship between social policy and personal lives, as we have seen, is a complex and mutually constitutive one.

References

Bourdieu, P. (1977) *Outline of a Theory of Practice*, Cambridge, Cambridge University Press.

Brown, H. (1998) *Social Work and Sexuality*, London, Macmillan/British Association of Social Work.

Carabine, J. (2001) 'Constituting sexuality through social policy: the case of lone motherhood 1834 and today', *Social and Legal Studies*, vol.10, no.3, pp.291–314.

Fink J. (ed.) (2004) *Care: Personal Lives and Social Policy*, Bristol, The Policy Press in association with The Open University.

Foucault, M. (1991) *Discipline and Punish: The Birth of the Prison* (trans. A. Sheridan), London, Penguin. (First published in 1977.)

Home Office (2002) *Protecting the Public: Strengthening Protection Against Sex Offenders and Reforming the Law on Sexual Offences*, Cmnd 5668, London, Home Office.

Langley, J. (2001) 'Developing anti-oppressive empowering social work practice with older lesbian and gay women and men', *British Journal of Social Work*, vol.31, pp.917–32.

Logan, J. (2001) 'Sexuality, child care and social work education', *Social Work Education*, vol.20, no.5, pp.563–75.

Mort, F. (1987) *Dangerous Sexualities: Medico-Moral Politics in England Since 1830*, London, Routledge and Kegan Paul.

Saraga, E. (2004) Chapter 4 in Lewis, G. (ed.) *Citizenship: Personal Lives and Social Policy*, Bristol, The Policy Press in association with The Open University.

Social Exclusion Unit (1999) *Teenage Pregnancy*, Cmnd 4342, London, The Stationery Office.

Weeks, J. (2000) *Making Sexual History*, Cambridge, Polity Press.

Wolfenden, J. (1957) *Report of the Committee on Homosexual Offences and Prostitution* (The Wolfenden Report), Cmnd 247, London, HMSO.

Acknowledgements

Grateful acknowledgement is made to the following sources for permission to reproduce material within this book:

Text

Chapter 1: *Extract 1.8:* Keep, G. and Hamilton, C. (2001) *Is It Legal? A Parents' Guide to the Law.* With permission from National Family & Parenting Institute; **Chapter 3:** *p.97:* © The Cole Porter Musical and Literary Property Trusts; **Chapter 4:** *Extract 4.5:* Hermeston, R. (2002) 'Tender love – and care', *Disability Now*, February 2002.

Figures/Illustrations

Figure 1.1: front cover – Carer's Allowance Claim Pack, DS700, April 2003. Crown copyright material is reproduced under Class Licence Number C01W0000065 with the permission of the controller of HMSO and the Queen's Printer for Scotland; *Figure 1.2:* front cover from Keep, G. and Hamilton, C. (2001) *Is It Legal? A Parents' Guide to the Law.* With permission from National Family & Parenting Institute; *Figure 1.3:* photo Marc Garanger © Gallimard; *Figure 1.4:* Simmons, P. (2002) *The Guardian/G2*, 18 October 2002. Reprinted by permission of Peters Fraser & Dunlop Group Ltd on behalf of Posy Simmons. Copyright © Posy Simmons; *Figure 2.1:* © The Women's Library; *Figure 2.4:* from *Punch*, 25 December 1880; *Figure 2.5:* © The British Library; *Figure 2.6:* woodcut by George Cattermole from Charles Dickens, *The Old Curiosity Shop*, Chapman & Hall, London, 1841; *Figure 2.7:* © Museum of London; *Figure 2.8:* from *The Popular Herbal*, London Hygienic Stores, c.1910; *Figure 3.2:* © Barnardo's; *Figure 3.3:* © Councils and Education Press Ltd; *Figure 3.4:* © Committee for a Free Britain. Newspaper advertisement placed 8 June 1987; *Figure 3.5:* © Fran Orford; *Figure 3.6: Sex Education Matters*, Issue 26, Autumn 2001. With permission of the National Children's Bureau; *Figure 4.1:* © Alexa Wright; *Figure 4.2:* front cover from *The Burden of Proof...*, Annual Review 1992–1993, The ME (Myalgic Encephalopathy) Association; *Figure 4.3:* Disability Living Allowance (DLA1 – Section 2). Crown copyright material is reproduced under Class Licence Number C01W0000065 with the permission of the controller of HMSO and the Queen's Printer for Scotland; *Figure 4.4:* © Sunrise Medical Ltd.

Table

Table 3.2: Wellings, K. et al. (2001) 'Sexual behaviour in Britain: early heterosexual experience'. Reprinted with permission from Elsevier (*The Lancet*, 2001, vol.358, p.1847).

Every effort has been made to contact copyright holders. If any have been inadvertently overlooked, the publishers will be pleased to make the necessary arrangements at the first opportunity.

Index